The Power and Passion of Freemasonry

By
George Peter

With the assistance for publication:
William J. Edwards
Lawrence J. Hammel

The Power and Passion of Freemasonry

A Cornerstone Book
Published by Cornerstone Book Publishers
An Imprint of Michael Poll Publishing

Copyright © 2012 by Paula Peter
All rights reserved under International and Pan-American Copyright Conventions. No part of this book may be reproduced in any manner without permission in writing from the copyright holder, except by a reviewer, who may quote brief passages in a review.

Cornerstone Book Publishers
New Orleans, LA
www.cornerstonepublishers.com

First Cornerstone Edition - 2012

ISBN: 1613420447
ISBN 13: 978-1-61342-044-7

MADE IN THE USA

Notes to the Reader:

This book is a compendium of writings by George Peter, who was born in 1921 and grew up on a farm near Ithaca, New York. He joined Freemasonry at the age of twenty-seven and over a Masonic career that spanned fifty-nine years he wrote about and taught for Masons and non-Masons alike his conviction about the true meaning of Masonry. This teacher and philosopher insisted that the Masonic fraternity was the finest educational institution created by man.

The material included in this book was written over his distinguished Masonic career and is generally written in the context of the time when it was originally published. When possible, the material has been updated to reflect current usage.

You may ask, "What value does this book offer to the non-Mason?" Freemasons believe that the Masonic life should be an orderly life, and that it should be a public-spirited life. Furthermore, it should be an industrious life in pursuit of one's vocation and a physically sane life with due regard to bodily health. A sound body, orderly industry, public spirit, but primarily the building of character: these emerge as major laws of successful living. A life exemplifying these worthy and outstanding traits is important to all members of humankind. This book is intended for all to read and to participate in all that it has to offer.

That the non-Masonic reader might have a clearer understanding, the following terms are defined:

Freemasonry or Masonry or Craft - the world's oldest fraternity, it is believed to have evolved from the medieval guilds of operative stonemasons, whose skills made them builders in high demand. "Free" because they—alone of all the tradesmen—were free to travel across the European continent and construct castles, cathedrals and other monuments of antiquity.

Brother - the title conferred on every member of the Craft denotes that in Masonry, as it should be in life, each stands in a family relationship to each. It denotes equality, also. In Masonry a man may be elected or appointed to an office for a time, but there are otherwise no distinctions of class or rank or wealth or status. It is also a term of greeting.

Master Mason - the level attained upon consummating the three Degrees of Masonry; the culmination of the initiation process.

The Master Mason is entitled to all of the benefits of the Masonic Lodge and the fraternity.

Worshipful Master (W∴ or W) or Master - the chief executive officer of a Lodge, usually elected to a one-year term.

Most Worshipful (M∴W∴ or MW) - this term is reserved as a title or form of address for the Grand Master of Masons in the State of New York. In New York the Grand Master serves a two-year term but he retains the honorific for life.

Right Worshipful (R∴W∴ or RW) - this is a title of respect for elected or appointed officers and representatives of Grand Lodge, and having earned this recognition, a Brother will be so acknowledged for life.

Very Worshipful (V∴W∴ or VW) - this title is bestowed upon Assistant Grand Lecturers in each District of the State. Their function is to instruct and oversee the execution of Freemasonry's distinctive ritual to assure standardization of delivery across the State.

The Grand Lodge of Free and Accepted Masons of the State of New York (GLNY) - the full name of the governing body of all Masons in the State of New York. It was originally established as the Provincial Grand Lodge of New York, under a Charter issued in 1781 by what is today known as the United Grand Lodge of England. In this publication it is also referred to as the Grand Lodge of New York, Grand Lodge or the Grand Lodge of the State of New York.

The following is a list of publications referenced in the book:

The *Empire State Mason Magazine* is the official quarterly publication of The Grand Lodge of Free and Accepted Masons of the State of New York. Visit the magazine online at http://www.esmason.com. Our Brother George published regular columns in the magazine when he served as the Grand Historian.

Some of the material written by Right Worshipful Brother George has been incorporated into Masonic resources published by The Grand Lodge of Free and Accepted Masons of the State of New York. These include:

* *The Officer Training Guide (OTG) / Masonic Executive Manual* is now called The *24-Inch Gauge Masonic Resource Guide.*

* The previous Leadership Development Course (LDC-10) is now available online as the LDC-8. This is an eight-session online course available through the Masonic University of New York. Visit www.emuny.net for additional information.

* The Lodge Services Letters 8801, 8802 and 8803 written in 1988 have been incorporated into *The 24-Inch Gauge Masonic Resource Guide*. The resource guide is a comprehensive collection of useful Masonic information specific for the New York State Mason. The letters are also included here in the education section to allow easy access to this valuable reference material.

* Other educational resources available include the Masonic Development Course (MDC), Road to the East (RTTE), Lodge System of Masonic Education (LSOME), Individual Development Course (iDC) and "The Master's Chair."

Masons can obtain copies of the Masonic resources by contacting The Grand Lodge of Free and Accepted Masons of the State of New York's Lodge Services Department at 1-800-3-MASON-4 for more information on ordering these educational resources.

All readers of this book are welcome to visit The Chancellor Robert R Livingston Masonic Library of the Grand Lodge at its New York and Utica branches to experience one of the best collections of Masonic material in the United States. Locations, hours of operation and partial listing of materials available can be viewed by visiting the Library's website at www.nymasoniclibrary.org.

Foreward

The articles and talks included in this book are a compilation of material written and spoken over the past 30 years. As District Deputy Grand Master of the Grand Lodge of Free and Accepted Masons of the State of New York. and later as chairman of the Lodge Service Committee (changed to Leadership and Educational Services Committee). I began writing articles of Masonic interest as early as 1972. Some may be dated and are generally written in the context of that time, but the messages contained therein are still valid and will always be so. I collaborated with Bill Edwards on the project and he has helped organize and proof the material.

Most articles are aimed at changing the culture of the Fraternity to develop a greater awareness of the great power and passion that lies within the essence of the Craft. Too many Brothers get caught up in the ritual and in the structure of the Fraternity while losing sight of what we "came here to do." The ritual is what sets us apart from the rest of the world, but it should not stand in the way of making the Fraternity the educational institution that I claim it is intended to be. The ritual is an important part of the lessons that direct Freemasonry in its teaching.

Many of the articles were written to impress upon the votaries that which is so valuable and that which may need to be modified or strengthened to make us an even more effective institution.

Dedication

First and foremost this book is dedicated to my late wife, Gloria Ann Barnell Peter, who helped me so much and was my companion and supporter in all of my Masonic and other endeavors. Also I dedicate this book to my four children, Michael J. Peter, Patrice Helen Peter DiLorenzo, Denice Villa Peter Karamardian and Paula J. Peter. They, with their mother, have been the glue that has helped me connect the lessons of Freemasonry and to put them into practice.

I also dedicate this book to all of the thousands of Freemasons who have been an important part of my life and they are thanked and recognized for their individual support and Masonic love.

Acknowledgements

- Jennifer Cole - First editing
- Neal I. Bidnick, Past Grand Master of Masons in the State of New York, for his support with my Masonic writings
- Lawrence J. Hammel – Inspiration and assistance with preparing the material for printing
- Stephen King – Assistance with preparing the material for printing
- Madison R. Williams – Technical and secretarial assistance
- Stephen L. Zabriskie – Guidance and assistance with preparing the material for printing

George Peter
Summer 2008

Introduction

- What is the Ground plan of Masonry?
  - *Instruction*
- Why?
  - *Because no man living is too wise to learn*
- Who are entitled to knowledge?
  - *All men that have a desire to gain it, and abilities to improve.*

Illustrations of Masonry
Lectures in the First Degree
William Preston, 1787

On August 10, 2008, Right Worshipful George Peter laid to rest his working tools. Before his untimely passing to the *Celestial Lodge*, he asked that I help finalize this book project for publication — an honor indeed! For the thoughtful Mason, there will be much to study and reflect upon within the following pages. After my own personal study and contemplation of George's writings, I have found the essence of his approach to Freemasonry to encompass the principles of Brotherhood, Education and Service. Like George, I believe that by being committed to creating a culture that nurtures brotherhood, education and service, this will allow the Power and Passion of Freemasonry to flourish.

Brotherhood is the foundation stone of Freemasonry. We are human brothers united under the fatherhood of God. Throughout history there are many examples of Masonic Brothers, in times of peace and war, extending outstretched hands of greeting and support. In our conversations, George commented that it was this special bond that he noticed amongst friends that first attracted him to Freemasonry. In today's world of television, motion pictures and make believe, we can quickly forget that many emotions are fleeting reactions to cinematic choreographed moments, which are not real. Freemasonry is real and its presence can be genuinely experienced. In a world full of personal isolation, hatred, angst and self absorption the power of Freemasonry can shatter these shackles of despair and can really relieve the distressed soul. The ability to unite men who might otherwise remain distant was experienced in

George's own life. In 1915, George's grandfather and uncle were killed during the Armenian Genocide conducted by the Ottoman Turks. This horrific event implanted anger deep within George. Later in his life, this anger was going to be quelled and transformed by the working tools of Freemasonry. A visiting scientist at Cornell university of Turkish descent, (and a Freemason), sought admittance to George's Lodge. Over time, George let go of his hereditary anger against this man and accepted him as a Brother. George was proud to tell me that before the visiting scientist returned to Turkey, they had become good friends, even sharing dinner together with their spouses. Now that is the Power of Freemasonry.

Freemasonry is an educational institution! George was passionate about education and the learning process. Many of the essays in this book are about the need for education. Education includes Leadership Education, Masonic Education and Personal Education through self knowledge. The charge of the ancients was to *Know Thyself*. It is important that we learn and perform the ritual in a quality manner. However, this is not enough. We need to be active students of Freemasonry. The ritual is the outer form of our teachings. We must peel back the ceremonies of the degrees and dig for a deeper understanding of the symbolism. This understanding will allow us the opportunity for personal improvement and transformation. Freemasonry is built upon a fundamental human truth. If a person decides to, they can change their personal situation in life. The masterpiece is found within the rough stone. However, it is easily demonstrated that knowledge alone does not produce change. One must take actions and tools can be provided to aid in the process. George was active in this cause. One example is the creation of the Leadership Development Course. Initially offered as a correspondence course, it is now available online through the Masonic University of New York (MUNY). This course allows participants to develop their leadership skills and their knowledge of Freemasonry.

Service – ich dien – I Serve! This is the call of Freemasonry! Service is a way of being and encompasses our relationship to God and our fellow man. Freemasons want to make the world a better place and out of this desire to serve comes the Freemason's passion for charity. Nobel Laureate, Albert Schweitzer, said it best, "*Seek always to do some good, somewhere. Every man has to seek in his own way to realize his true worth. You must give some time to your fellow man. For remember, you don't live in a world all your own. Your brothers are here too."*

Bernard of Chartres, a twelfth century teacher, is known for the phrase, "dwarves sitting on the shoulders of giants." A teacher of classical philosophy, de Chartres was referring to building upon the work of those scholarly giants who had come before him. George Peter is one of those giants. His lifelong commitment to Freemasonry was impressive. As you experience his writings, and what he came to call the "Power and Passion" of Freemasonry, I hope that it will gently agitate your own passions and encourage you to live the Power of Freemasonry in your daily life. George's vision is our call to action and the task at hand is to make it so!

V∴W∴ William Edwards
Fall 2011

Table of Contents

Section I – Power of Freemasonry

Part I
Reflections on Freemasonry
Page 1
Part II
A History of Freemasonry
Page 43

Section II – Passion of Freemasonry

Part I
Leadership
Page 121
Part II
Education
Page 167

Section III – PostScript

Swan Song— Adios
Page 208
In Memoriam
Page 210
George Peter Medal
Page 214
Mini-biography
Page 215

The Power and Passion of Freemasonry

Section I
The Power of Freemasonry

Part I
Reflections on Freemasonry

George Peter

What is Freemasonry?

This question is asked time and again. Very few Freemasons can give an easily understood, simple answer. Why? Most of what is written on the subject is in such lofty words that the average Freemason is uncomfortable trying to translate the same into everyday language. A second problem occurs because Freemasonry means different things to different people. Perhaps the main problem lies in that the question cannot be answered in a few words.

A concise answer may be found in an edited version of a statement by Brother Michel Brodsky, Senior Warden of the Quatuor Coronati Lodge No. 2076, printed in the *Lodge Transactions* October 1995:

Freemasonry is a structured association of men, grouped in primary associations called Lodges federated in a Grand Lodge from which they obtain their authority to meet. The Lodges are self-governing bodies composed of men of diverse origin who are not bound together by trade or profession. The Lodges have only the power to admit new members whose essential qualification is a belief in a Supreme Being. The degrees conferred by the Lodges consist in the transmission of traditional ritual communicated according to specific fashion whose absence (of such fashion) would invalidate the whole procedure.

But Freemasonry is much more than this and deserves a more comprehensive description:

Freemasonry, first and foremost, is the oldest, largest, most prestigious fraternal organization in the world. All others have copied one or more aspects of the essence of Freemasonry. It is the root from which all others have sprouted. The first Grand Lodge structure from whence Freemasonry sprung was in England in 1717. There is strong evidence that it existed long before that time.

It is a place where a sense of belonging, a sense of family, is developed and promoted. No Freemason is a stranger in any Masonic Lodge.

Freemasonry is a brotherhood where any of us can turn to another for help and guidance. And we can depend on the same kind of caring for our families.

It has been said that Freemasonry is the last bastion of trust. Each brother is taught to trust a brother, to be trustworthy and to be able to trust himself.

Freemasonry is a philosophy– a way of life. It is made up of men who are taught to make a difference toward the advancement of civilization.

Freemasonry is a group of men determined to make a better world by helping to make each individual a better man.

Freemasonry is a supplement to religion but is not a religion. It is religious by nature in that no one is accepted who does not profess a belief in a Supreme Being.

Freemasonry is the philosophy of charity put into action. Freemasons give over $2 million dollars a day to charities in the United States.

Freemasonry is an educational institution with the command to each of its members to be aware that life is a process of learning.

Freemasonry teaches honor, integrity, honesty, upright living and it encourages each to have the impulse to do right.

Freemasonry expects each member to think for himself.

Freemasonry is a place for "the high, the low, the rich, the poor to meet together with one common purpose, the perpetuation of each other's friendship and each other's love."

A Masonic Lodge is a place to be transformed from the mundane world into a setting where brotherly love prevails. It is a break from worldly concerns into spiritual refreshment. It is a statement that says, "There is more to life than just the next dollar to earn or the next career to advance."

Freemasonry is made up of three Masonic degrees in which, through a series of beautiful rituals, moral lessons are taught. Symbolism and allegory are used as teaching tools.

Freemasonry is not a secret organization but it does have modes of recognition which have been handed down from the beginning. These signs and passwords are not promoted to the general public.

For further study we commend studying the following essay, "Twelve Reasons for Being Loyal to Freemasonry" or "The Power of Freemasonry," found in Chapter one of *The 24-Inch Gauge*.

George Peter

Twelve Reasons for Being Loyal To Freemasonry
(There are more)
Or
The Power of Freemasonry

To Educate, Inspire, Excite, Interest and turn On the brothers:

    1. Freemasonry is the oldest and most prestigious fraternal organization known to recorded history.

    2. Fraternalism is needed more in our present society than perhaps ever before.

        a) Members of a family learn to love, respect, appreciate, have compassion for and to live harmoniously with each other.

        b) Freemasonry is an expansion of the family circle. Masons learn to be better brothers within the Masonic family and thence to the world at large.

    3. A genius of Freemasonry is the emphasis it places on the need to support a set of moral values which have been honed by the test of time. It is a privilege to be loyal to that Fraternity which continues to stabilize a moral code- a code which is being eroded by indecision, experimentation and indifference by others.

    4. A second genius of Freemasonry is its proposition which states that one cannot build a better society without first building better ingredients for that society- men. Freemasons can be proud to perfect the ritual which is filled with lessons on how to be a better and more "upright" person.

    5. Freemasons played a noble and impressive role in the formation of the United States government. Much of the insights, concerns and brilliance of Masonic stalwarts such as George Washington, Ben Franklin, Peyton Randolph, Robert Livingston and scores of others helped to develop that profound document we call our Constitution. Every Freemason can be proud of American and Masonic heritages which are so closely related. The concepts of liberty, freedom, and fraternity are important Masonic concepts.

    6. The Masonic Home at Utica is an example of Masonic principle put into action. It is a sense of satisfaction to know that, at the Home, over 450 older people are guests of New York State Freemasons.

    7. The Masonic Medical Research Laboratory, also at Utica, and operated by the Grand Lodge of Free & Accepted Masons of the State of New York, continues to make regular and important

contributions in medical research. This work ultimately will lengthen and enhance the quality of life of every human being.

8. Fraternities can help to break down the greatest of all barriers to a healthy society- the caste system which grows out of uncontrolled egos. Freemasonry is unique in this effort by teaching that it is a place "for the high, the low, the rich, the poor to meet together- on the level." This one important contribution alone is worth all the support that can be given to Freemasonry.

9. Freemasonry is an international Fraternity. It exists in nearly every country except where totalitarian governments and others have outlawed it by decree. Freemasonry is perhaps the strongest tie that binds the world into a universal brotherhood. It certainly has the potential to be an even stronger cord for that noble purpose.

10. Freemasonry is an educational institution. It teaches that part of being a Freemason is to learn to improve ones' self. It offers and promotes many opportunities for its members to grow as individuals.

11. Freemasonry is probably the first, and certainly continues to be the strongest, force to promote tolerance for the religion of others.

12. An outgrowth of the messages contained in the Masonic experience is the charities supported by the Craft. Over $2 million dollars a day are contributed, in one form or another, by Freemasonry in the United States alone.

DEFINITION OF A FREEMASON

The real Freemason is distinguished from the rest of mankind by the uniform unrestrained rectitude of his conduct. Other men are honest in fear of punishment which the law might inflict; they are religious in expectation of being rewarded, or in dread of the devil in the next world. A Freemason would be just, even if there were no laws, human or divine, except those written in his heart by the finger of the Creator. In every climate, under every system of religion, he is the same. He kneels before the universal throne of God in gratitude for the blessings he has received and in humble solicitation for his future protection. He venerates the good men of all religions. He disturbs not the religion of others. He restrains his passions because they cannot be indulged without injuring his neighbor or himself. He gives no offense because he does not choose to be offended. He contracts no debts which he is not certain he can discharge, because he is honest upon principle.

–Bruce D. Hunt,
Past Grand Master, Missouri

The Philosophy of Freemasonry
By: Russell D. Martin

In preparing for these brief comments on the Philosophy of Freemasonry, I asked myself, "Just how does a person go about telling someone else what Masonry is and is not?" I came to the conclusion that perhaps a starting point would be with a definition of Freemasonry. Actually, there were two that I ran across recently. The first said: "Masonry is more than social good fellowship, more than ritual, more than organized charity. It is a way of living; a philosophy of life." Another definition said: "Freemasonry is a charitable, benevolent, educational, and religious society." For the next few minutes, let's take these definitions apart and see what they really mean.

First of all, many will say that Freemasonry is a secret organization. Actually, its only secrets are in its methods of recognition and of symbolic instruction. We maintain secrecy but purely as a means of mutual identification. We take an oath but only after assurance that it "will not improperly affect any duty we owe to God, our country, our neighbor, or ourselves." We have forms and ceremonies and symbols but these are all external.

Actually, the entire ritual is a symbolic representation of the course of a man through his life, leading him step by step from birth, through manhood, to old age, and leaving him with the hope of immortality. The first Degree, called the Entered Apprentice, represents man as he comes into life; helpless, ignorant and dependent, and carries his education through the period of his youth. The second, or Fellow Craft Degree, represents man in his middle age; and the third or Master Mason Degree takes him through old age and ends with a beautiful lesson in the unconquerable hope of immortality. Through the three Degrees, the candidate is taught increasing wisdom in the art of upright living.

Now let's look at that part of our definition dealing with religion. Although in remote antiquity Freemasonry was affiliated with various religions, it has long since ceased to be a religion. It is the friend of every religious faith but is not itself a religion. Essentially, it is the practical application of a philosophy of life or way of living.

Not being the product of any one race, or system of government, or economics, or philosophy, or religion, Freemasonry welcomes men of every race and creed if they have sufficient integrity of character to become good Masons and if they believe in a Deity.

Instead of trying to be a religion, Freemasonry deliberately seeks to provide a common meeting place where men of every religion can remain true to their own religions and yet, submerging their differences, can work together in harmony to manifest the finest fruits of all religions.

While the emphasis of religion is often on intercession for forgiveness of shortcomings, the Masonic emphasis is essentially on the more positive side of seeking to measure up to one's obligations rather than on any theological doctrines of forgiveness. Similarly, Masonry stresses one's duties rather than his rights. Just as Freemasonry exhorts its members to be true and loyal citizens of whatever country is entitled to their allegiance, so, likewise, Freemasonry expects each of its members to be a true and loyal supporter of his chosen religion and of the church, synagogue, or other unit of its organizational worship.

Now, let's look at other parts of our definition, first that of being a social organization. Freemasonry is a social organization only so far as it furnishes additional inducement that men may forgather in numbers, thereby providing more material for its primary work of education, of worship, and of charity.

Through the improvement and strengthening of the character of the individual man, Freemasonry seeks to improve the community. Thus, it impresses upon its members the principles of personal righteousness and personal responsibility, enlightens them as to those things which make for human welfare, and inspires them with that feeling of charity, or goodwill, toward all mankind which will move them to translate principle and conviction into action.

We believe that the Masonic life should be an orderly life, and that it should be a public spirited life. Furthermore, we believe it should be an industrious life in the pursuit of one's vocation and a physically sane life with due regard to bodily health. A sound body, orderly industry, public spirit, but primarily the building of character — to us these emerge as major laws of successful living.

Just what, then, does Freemasonry say about man's relationship with his God and with his fellowman?

1. In a world of greed and force, it teaches self restraint and reason.

2. In a world permeated with the spirit of selfish rivalry, it teaches Universal Brotherhood.

3. In a world of intolerance and bigotry it teaches tolerance and kindness.

4. In a world of cynical disbelief it teaches reverence for Deity.

5. In a world floundering in the depths of a great moral and spiritual depression it teaches industry and self-reliance and temperance and integrity.

6. It aids and comforts and reassures and inspires individuals.

7. It leaps the barriers of race and space to draw together the finest aspirations of all men and unites them in a Universal Brotherhood.

And finally, we can say that purity of heart, sincerity, truthfulness, fidelity to duty, and similar qualities are emphasized over and over as necessary internal qualifications. The attainment of wisdom, prudence, temperance, justice, reason, self reliance, strength and beauty are practical objectives. Self-restraint, upright conduct, and morality are worthy means toward the accomplishment of these objectives. These are typical of the Masonic Philosophy.

Yes, Masonry is more than social good fellowship, more than ritual, more than organized charity. It is a way of living; a Philosophy of Life.

Note: This paper was written about 1985 and was used as a part of the original 10-lesson, Leadership Development Course. Brother Martin was a Past Master of Hobasco Lodge #716. He is now deceased.

The Mission of Freemasonry

At the most recent publications committee meeting in Utica, the Grand Historian delivered parts of the following remarks:

In Freemasonry we are taught that "before entering upon any great or important undertaking we ought always to invoke the aid of Deity." At the same time we ought to remember the story of the Vermont farmer. His preacher came by and said, "My, what a lovely garden you and the Lord have going here." The farmer said "Ah yeh, but you should have seen it when God was taking care of it all by himself." The lesson here is that we can't depend on God to do the work for us.

We must prepare our own field, select and plant thoughtful seeds and ideas, weed out the superfluous, and cultivate the lessons indicated in the rituals and in our traditions. And then we need to collect them into useful messages to be consumed by our Brothers and everyone else.

A charge to publication people is (or ought to be) to design and produce publications that have an impact. I have always argued that every Lodge communication should be EIEIO. That is Educational, Interesting, Exciting, Inspiring, and designed to turn On the Brothers and others. Likewise every publication should be the same. If you have trouble remembering the letters EIEIO, think of the story of the two football players. They were a little bit less than astute. The Professor was about to flunk them, but the coach implored him to pass them one way or another. So after being cajoled by the coach and by the Dean, the Prof. put the kids in a room and turned on a tape player that went on for an hour playing, "Old MacDonald Had A Farm, EIEIO", over and over again. The Prof. then wrote on the black board: "Old MacDonald Had A ___." He told the kids to fill in the blank and they would pass. He left the room for an hour and the guys tried to solve the problem. One asked, "What do you suppose it is? "I think that it is FARM," said the other lad. "How do you suppose it's spelled?" "I don't know; maybe it is EIEIO."

For our purpose, EIEIO spells Educational, Interesting, Exciting, Inspiring, and designed to turn On the Brothers. Let's include this in all that we say and write!

The first step in planting a garden is to decide what you want the harvest to be. That means that the first step is to define the mission. What is the mission of Freemasonry? We seldom talk about the mission, but we darn well ought to do so before attempting to write or speak on the subject.

Mission of Freemasonry

1. To help Freemasons develop the proper attitudes to have toward their fellow human beings and towards their God.

2. To educate Freemasons to become better citizens, parents, men, husbands, and fathers.

3. To promote the ideas and principles of morality, truth, honesty, integrity and respect for others and their religion. (Morality is defined by a set of values honed by the test of time.)

4. To help, aid and assist Brothers and others- charity.

How to Carry Out the Mission

1. Promote an atmosphere to keep Brothers and others inspired, involved and active.

2. Provide EDUCATIONAL programs, which involve everyone in the development and presentations of the same.

3. Communicate the MISSION of the craft in effective ways to all.

4. Communicate The MESSAGE that Freemasonry is an EDUCATIONAL INSTITUTION and that every Lodge program and every Masonic publication should be Educational, Interesting, Exciting, Inspiring and designed to turn On the audience about the Power of Freemasonry.

5. Involve as many as possible in the programs and or publications.

What do Freemasons do that contradicts the lofty ideals and concepts that lead to a more vigorous Fraternity? Well, it seems to me that we tend to spend more time on pomp and ceremony than on substance. This is not to be critical of any publication or any editor or any Lodge, but it seems to me that we have evolved over the years from the ideal to what tends to be more pomp and less power.

How has this evolution taken place? Well, some time ago I wrote a piece entitled, Cardinals, Aprons and Titles. In it I postulate that we spend too much time on the emphasis of Titles and Aprons and not enough time promoting the basic title of "My Brother."

Perhaps we need to minimize the title stuff and talk about Brothers. There is no higher title than that of "My Brother."

My concern is that really thinking people don't want to take the time to be involved in a hierarchy that consumes the majority of their time, and the time and energy of others, expended in glorifying the leaders. Let me quote from an ancient Chinese philosopher, Lao Tse:

"As for the best leaders, the people do not notice their existence; the next the people honor and praise; the next the people fear; and the next, the people hate. When the best leader's work is done, the people say 'We did it ourselves'."

I confess that in Freemasonry, we spend more time talking and writing about leaders than we do about what we came here to do. We came here to serve as an educational institution. Let's try to remember that.

Again this is not critical of any individual or Lodge or publication. The *ESM*, for example, is a very professional piece. It and other Masonic publications do a great job of showing Freemasonry as an alive and vibrant entity. That is good. And at least it does not start each article with a comment about the weather or the season.

But on the subject of substance vs. pomp and ceremony, I submit to you some examples of the kind of thoughtful articles that appeared in Masonic publications when Freemasonry was more vibrant. *The Masonic Outlook,* Dec. 1925 and Mar. 1926 are just some examples of serious and meaningful articles.

Dec. 1925: Page 110 – an article about the meaning of the Golden Fleece
Page 112 – an article about the Masonic orphanage
Mar. 1926:
Page 199 – The Fifth Estate – about radio
Page 201 – The Meaning of Hiram Abiff
Page 204 – The Symbolic Colors

Well, these are some examples. The publication was not nearly as glitzy as our *ESM*, but there were some articles of substance. My contention is that we should try to provide material that is EIEIO. It will attract more thinking people and less of those interested only in Titles, Aprons and Pomp.

The **ESM** is a terrific publication. But there is nothing so terrific that cannot be improved. Nothing can be improved unless we examine it critically and begin by reviewing our mission statements. I've tried to inspire us to do so.

Let's keep up the good work and let's "look for more meat and less potatoes" in the substance of the articles. Let's meet on the level and promote the power of the Fraternity in all that we do, say and write.

Originally printed in The *Empire State Mason* Magazine, Summer 2002

MISSION OF FREEMASONRY

- To teach Freemasons the proper attitudes to have toward their fellow human beings and the proper attitudes to have toward God

- To educate Freemasons to become better citizens, parents, men, husbands, and fathers
- To promote the ideas & principles of morality, truth, honesty, integrity and respect for others (morals as defined by a set of values honed by the test of time)
- To help, aid & assist brothers, and others– charity
- To serve as an educational institution
- To promote ecumenism

HOW TO CARRY OUT THE MISSION

- Promote atmosphere to keep brothers inspired, involved & active
- Provide educational and developmental programs and involve everyone in the process
- Communicate the MISSION of the Craft in effective ways to brothers and to the rest of the world
- Communicate the message that Freemasonry is an EDUCATIONAL INSTITUTION and that every lodge program should consist of a short presentation by a different brother. Programs need to be Educational, Inspiring, Exciting, Interesting and designed to turn On the brothers about the power of Freemasonry (EIEIO).

PROPOSED IMPROVEMENTS and/or CHANGES

- Shorter forms for ritual opening and closing
- Officers meetings prior to the regular meeting
- Better & more concise reading of minutes by the secretary
- Better education of the officers and of their duties
- Educational programs by all– consider EIEIO programs
- Establish a lodge one-year and five-year plan
- Establish a few community service projects that are in keeping with the aim of Freemasonry
- Keep business meeting short (10 mins. max)
- Main part of the communication should be a talk by a brother (15 minutes ideal time; 20 minutes max.) Involve as many brothers as are willing to present programs. Involvement is the key to membership activity and lodge vitality

Note: This is a summary review of discussion from a program held on 4/25/1998

The Masonic Mystique

There was this storekeeper in Burke, Vermont who was out of a certain popular item and was asked if he'd have it in stock before long. "Nope," he replied. "Why not?" the customer wanted to know. "Moves too damn fast," came the answer.

Masons in the Cayuga-Tompkins District should **not** be that kind of storekeeper. We have the most popular item in the world and we should be promoting it more than ever before. Our product is called "Brotherhood" and everybody in the whole wide world needs more and more of it.

If it hasn't been going well these days maybe it's because our price has been too high. We shouldn't be like the Vermont farmer who was accosted by a city slicker looking to buy land at a cheap price. The city fellow asked to buy $500 worth of the farmer's land. "Good," said the farmer, "very good! Go fetch your wheelbarrow and I'll fill it up for you."

Sometimes we have even loaded the customer's wheelbarrow full of that well-known barn-yard commodity instead of real down to earth friendship, brotherly love and affection. That happens when we don't know our product well enough to promote what we really have.

This leads us to the essence of one of the Grand Masters' message. The gist of it is that Masons ought to know their product, be convinced of its value and then be prepared to promote it so that others may be exposed to its good effects.

1. In order to know our product better we need to present ourselves at Masonic activities. The programs of the District Deputy Grand Master and Committees are planned to enrich our knowledge and interest in the Masonic mystique. We invite all Masons to join us at the visitations throughout the district. Programs will be varied, informative and interesting, but not too long. Fellowship is always thrown in for good measure.

2. The Masonic mystique is no more and no less than brotherhood, fellowship, and the Masonic principles which bind us together in support of a morality that encourages society to be civil. We ought to be zealous now, because, more than ever, that is what society needs. It isn't so much that Masonry needs society but more that society needs Masonry and its influence.

3. We can best promote Freemasonry by so living and so acting that we always display to others the image of a true Mason. And there is work to be done. I'd like to see us challenged to sponsor more civic projects. There are Explorer Posts, Masonic Youth organizations, local essay contests and scholarships to sponsor. There are such projects as the Masonic Research Center at Utica, the Brotherhood Fund, relief projects and many others to support. We can be proud of past performance; we can boast of a Masonic Home, Health Center and Research facility second to none; and we can be thrilled that we are a part of the overall Masonic benevolence that gives millions of dollars annually for a variety of humane causes. But that is not enough. We must act out the creed that says human values are Masonic values and we must act it out daily. Then people of the highest caliber will be clamoring to buy our product.

The Masonic mystique is the same mystique which causes all contemplative people to search for honor, knowledge, justice, purity and truth.

The Rites of Passage

"The Rites of Passage" originally meant the formal ritual to celebrate a child's coming into adulthood. It also has come to mean different things to different people. Webster defines, "passage," "as change or progress from one condition to another." It is transition. "Rite" is defined as "related to ritual- formal or ceremonial observance or procedure."

From this, we may define the rites of passage as the process of change that takes place in human life. Life is a constant transformation from one phase to another. This continual change is what makes life fascinating and exciting. Without change life would be very dull and meaningless.

A review of electrical theory reminds us that transformer action cannot occur in direct current (DC) circuits. Alternating current (AC) is necessary for transformer action. This implies that transformation cannot occur without the ability and willingness of the subject matter to change. In humans transformation occurs more in those who are receptive to change- to being transformed.

Some changes are physical and we have less control over them than others. We can't change coming into puberty, growth, and the aging process. Even so, recent scientific evidence indicates that we may have more influence on these changes than was once thought.

Freemasonry, in its many forms, stresses the change in the life of man. This is the *Rites of Passage*. Each of the three degrees represents a different period in human life.

In every period of that life there is a place for philosophical contemplation. Freemasonry puts emphasis on the need for humans to reflect. "it leads the contemplative to view with reverence and admiration the glorious works of creation and inspires them with the most exalted ideas of the perfection of their divine creator."[1]

Contemplation leads us to an awareness of who we are, what we are and what we are here to do. To reflect on these important questions on a regular basis can only help to make us more effective Freemasons, brothers, human beings, and citizens of this great republic. "Freemasonry is a discipline concerned with spiritual and humanistic qualities or values the intrinsic worth of the individual."[2]

Ritual helps us to be contemplative. We survey ritual in nature every day. It is a natural part of life. Someone has said that a sunset or a sunrise is a ritual. The opening of a Masonic Lodge certainly is a ritual. We should take time to reflect on what effect each of these forms of ritual can have on the human spirit. "Take time to smell the roses!" "Since man's earliest history, he has passed on the basic truths of the universe to subsequent generations via the use of elaborate and meaningful ritual. To see that these ancient truths are sustained in their purity and power, Freemasonry has developed a symbolic liturgy that keeps the eternal message fresh and clear."[3]

The opening ceremony of a Masonic Lodge is designed to take us from the mundane world and to transform us into an atmosphere where brotherly love can prevail and all can meet on the level. It is important to understand the purpose of the ritual in order to perform it with precision and meaning so that brothers in attendance will be inspired. Brothers at a Masonic communication need to be prepared to be transformed. It won't happen if we are rigid and in a steady state. We need to be like AC not DC.

All of us need the discipline which is inherent in formal or ceremonial reminders of the transitional nature of life. Such discipline can elevate us to a higher level of effective service.

A simple analogy of how a maser works is to liken the electrons to ping pong balls stimulated to a higher step. This makes them more readily movable (sensitive) to external signals. Ritual can stimulate us in the same way– to make us more sensitive to forces about us.

At a conference on Indian affairs at Cornell University, we were reminded of the strong attraction to ritual by the Iroquois Indians and other tribes. This may be why many of them were attracted to Freemasonry (e.g. Ely Parker, Joseph Brant, *et al*).[4]

A paper by Arthur C. Parker tells of the Iroquois ritual which is similar in many ways to our own Masonic ritual.[5] The fascinating point is that here are two different cultures from two different continents who have formulated a ritual to express man's most noble contemplations. These rituals are so similar that it is striking. But this is not unusual. Ritual is found in every social order.

The process of moving up the chairs in Freemasonry is a form of ritual. It is a perfect example of the Rites of Passage. Every new experience adds maturity to the individual and transforms him. If we allow ourselves to be attuned to what is happening during that process, we will gain more from the experience. It is an apprenticeship program as ancient and effective as any system devised.

Has Freemasonry been effective in transforming us from the "rough ashlar" to the "perfect ashlar?" Has Freemasonry taken good men and made them better? Can it do so by its teachings and ritual alone? Perhaps it could do much better than it has, but it can only do so to the extent that we allow ourselves to be transformed. The rites of passage that will take us from ordinary men to new levels of moral and meaningful service will come about when we become attuned to the real power in the Masonic message and the Masonic experience.

The mission of Freemasonry is, "to seek that which is the most worth; to exalt the dignity of every person, the human side of our daily activities and the maximum service to humanity; to aid the search in God's universe for identity, for development, and for destiny; and thereby to make better men in a better world..."[6] When we consider this mission, we cannot help but agree that Freemasonry can be a positive force in any society.

If there is a limitation to the power of Freemasonry, it is set by how well we educate the new brother to a full awareness of the power, nature and purpose of the Institution. If we can do a better job of educating new members, and old ones alike, this will result in a greater awareness of what is happening at a Masonic communication. Brothers will be better attuned to receive the beauty and message of the ritual. The rites of passage will have more significance.

Originally printed in *The Empire State Mason Magazine*, Winter 2001

References:

1. Masonic ritual– Middle Chamber Lecture
2. Mervin B. Hogan. "What of Mormonism and Freemasonry." *Miscellanea*. Vol. XII, part 4 & 5. 1985, 1986.
3. ibid
4. *American Lodge of Research*, vol. VII– Number 2. Jan. 30, '61 - Dec. 27, '61
5. Arthur C. Parker. *American Indian Freemasonry*. Buffalo Consistory. 1919
6. Grand Commander Henry C. Clausen. *Clausen's Commentaries on Morals and Dogma*. 1974

The New Meaning of Masonry
Grand Historian Report

In 1922 W.L. Wilmshurst published a book, *The Meaning of Masonry*. (We today like to be specific and call our Craft, "Freemasonry," but for this report we will follow the style of the British author, Wilmshurst.) His book was reprinted in 1999 by Barnes and Noble. It is available in those stores and others. The book is a must reading by any Masonic scholar. It is a compilation of a series of papers written for the Masonic Fraternity of the Grand Lodge of England.

Wilmshurst contends that we falsely expect reception into Masonry to automatically provide all understanding necessary to appreciate the intricacies and depth of the Craft. Such is not the case. Ritual is not enough. Initiation is but a formality, and if not accompanied by study and practice, will result in a member's eventual boredom. That's why some brothers become tired of the convention and drop out.

Masonic study will provide an understanding that there exists a higher and more noble path of life than we have followed hither-to. Masonry offers direction and charts the way. It "indicates the qualifications and conditions of progress."

But energies and efforts by the Craft have been diverted to less than the original design of Masonry. Social and charitable purposes are important in their own right, but carried to an extreme, they detract from the real mission of the Craft. That mission is to be an educational institution. Instead, we have allowed our secondary activities to leave us as "an initiating instrument of low efficiency."

The future value of Masonry depends on the view we have of the system. Masonry suffers from lack of instruction and not lack of desire by the brothers. It behooves us to return to the educational aspect intended for Masonry. We came here to seek light-knowledge.

First we need to examine what is Masonry. The most often quoted definition is that it is "a system of morality, veiled in allegory and illustrated by symbols." That description is only a fraction of the full definition. More information is needed to differentiate Masonry from any ordinary club or benefit society.

Seldom or never do we use the Lodge meeting for more than to perform the ritual and assume it is the "be-all and the end-all" of Masonic work. There is little effort to detail the "mysteries" of the Craft. (I would note that we have stayed clear of the term "mysteries" for fear of providing fodder to the anti-Masons who claim that we are a sinister, secret society.)

Wilmshurst contends that we avoid probing the mysteries of Masonry because we have never been exposed to or been introduced to that which Masonry was formed to study. He states that it is absurd to think that Masonry was formed only to teach grown men the symbolic meaning of the building tools or to impress upon us basic virtues. All of such education is available in schools, churches, synagogues, and elsewhere. (It was in his time.)

The Craft we refer to as a "science" or "royal art" has a far greater end. So what is Masonry?

From the beginning of history, secret societies have existed outside the limits of organized religious institutions. They existed in the East, Chaldea, Assyria, Egypt, Greece, Italy, among the Hebrews, Mohammedans, Christians and elsewhere.

The great teachers of humanity, Socrates, Plato, Pythagoras, Moses, Aristotle, Virgil, St. John, St. Paul, and many others were exposed to the mysteries. St. Paul referred to these great teachers of humanity as the "stewards of the mysteries." All religious systems, including Christianity and the school of Cabalism, were outgrowths of these great humanitarian mysteries.

Fraternities and orders such as the great order of Chivalry, the Rosicrucians, Spiritual Alchemy, and many others, were also out-growths of these mysteries. And of course, we now have Masonry.

Wilmshurst claims that he is acquainted with a 5000 year old Egyptian ceremonial system which taught the same things as does the Masonic Fraternity. It is taught in terms of the ship builder's tools rather than those of the architect.

This is not to claim that there is a direct connection between the ancients and Masonry. The connection is the spiritual doctrine contained in all these groups throughout the ages. The connection is the search by man, since time immemorial, for an understanding of our spiritual power.

Our charge is to view Masonry more than just a pleasant social order. We are to view it as a "sacred and serious method of instruction into the profoundest truths of life." Masonry offers via dramatic form and ceremony, "a philosophy of the spiritual life of man and a diagram of the process of regeneration." It offers answers to the questions: What am I? Whence come I? Wither go I?

Note: This is only the introduction to Wilmshurst's book. We are still in Chapter one. It is a valuable source of education sitting on library shelves since 1922. There is much more.

Originally printed in The *Empire State Mason* Magazine, Summer 2001

Freemasonry International

Have you wondered why the Freemasons are so into promoting the idea of liberty, the idea of freedom? Have you wondered why we consider it so important to recognize the very valuable contributions of each culture which makes up the America we know today?

Well, we have come by it naturally. Even the operative masons (who were actually more than masons but in fact, were the architects as well) were free to travel in foreign lands to ply their trade. Most others were not. The name "Freemason" goes back at least to the time of Sir Frances Bacon, who was writing about the advancement of knowledge and the freedom to think. Free and Accepted Masons were free to read and to discuss philosophy. Remember that in those days only the clergy and a few special people were allowed to do so. Freemasons met in secret in order to pursue this important privilege.

No wonder that the Freemasons in France were the first to promote the Statue of Liberty gift idea. They sponsored a drive and raised 200,000 Francs for the project. The sculptor, Frederick Auguste Bartholdi, was a Freemason. It is quite certain that his good friend, Prof. Edourd Rene LeFebune de Laboulaye was also a Freemason. He was the backbone of the drive to build and send the gift to

America. The cornerstone for the pedestal was laid on Aug. 5, 1884 in a Masonic ceremony. One hundred years later, again in the rain, on Aug. 5, 1984, that ceremony was reenacted by the Freemasons.

Very closely related to liberty and freedom is an even more important concept that Freemasonry has espoused these many years. Freemasonry is the oldest, and still the strongest, force in the world to support ecumenicalism. Rudyard Kipling sat in a Masonic Lodge room in India and said, "Where else but in Freemasonry can I sit in a room with a Hindu, a Muslim, a Christian, and a Jew and know that I am among brothers?"

In this very room, a few years ago, the Grand Master of Masons in Lebanon was our guest. He said, "Where else can you travel halfway round the world and know that you are among brothers and friends?" My good Jewish friend, Emanuel Dick from NYC, tells of being a guest in the home of this same Lebanese Freemason during the height of one of those too many Arab-Israeli wars. We can't help but wonder whether, if Freemasonry were more widespread, it could be the only power strong enough to break down those bitter animosities which threaten to destroy all of the Middle East.

But we are not here to detract from honoring the heritages represented by the speakers here this evening. Their cultures are now a part of the America we know and love. Let each of us be reminded to appreciate each individual and each culture. We can best do so by being reminded that the poem on your program, which is the same poem affixed to the pedestal of the Statue of Liberty, was written by a young Jewish woman, Emma Lazurus. Frederick Auguste Bartholdi was a Frenchman but more likely of Italian descent. He studied the great Greek sculptures, among others, to help him envision what the "Lady" should look like. And the monies used to pay for your dinner this evening, the proceeds of which will go to the Statue of Liberty restoration fund, are defined in Arabic numbers. Yes we are all Americans, but we are also a great part of all the cultures in the world.

We thank the speakers who helped us appreciate each culture even more so than before. Thank each of you for your kind attention and for sharing this program with us.

Empire State Mason: Grand Historian Report
Philosophy (from the Greek: "Love of Wisdom")

In a recent letter seen on the *New York State Mason* web site, the author laments how sad it is that we cannot return to the "good old days" when people were clamoring to join Freemasonry. He contends that it was the thing to do for personal gain. Anyone who was anyone was a Freemason. The Fraternity conferred status, prestige, and influence to its members.

These are sad reasons for being a Freemason. They are absolutely the wrong reasons. In previous columns we have talked about the power of Freemasonry and what it can and should do. Brothers will have the right reasons for being a Freemason if and when we understand the philosophy of Freemasonry and what its real power is. A good source for the real philosophy of Freemasonry is found in the 1964 Proceedings of the American Lodge of Research. A paper by Brother Herman Sarachan, a great Masonic scholar from the Rochester area, is entitled, "The Philosophy of Freemasonry." Brother Sarachan leans on material from the writings of Roscoe Pound who we have written about at length in previous columns. Both writers referred to the basic philosophy as defined by the four great early scholars of Freemasonry.

William Preston, 1742-1818, believed that knowledge, love of knowledge, the seeking of truth, and education were the purposes of Freemasonry. Karl Krause, German professor, 1781-1832, held that Freemasonry was MORALITY. Freemasonry's purpose was to help foster and develop morality in law and government. Dr. George Oliver, 1782-1866, was an English clergyman. For him Freemasonry was to serve as the one best approach to God. Albert Pike, 1809-1891, an American, defined the purpose of the Fraternity as a system, through its symbols and allegories, to help each brother in his search for the highest good. Brother Sarachan then outlined his views of Freemasonry as being composed of four pillars:

1. Spirituality
2. Universality
3. Brotherhood
4. Service - the practical manifestation of brotherhood

He summed it up by saying "the purpose is to join together men of good character of all faiths into a brotherhood dedicated to the service of its members and all mankind."

George Peter

From the Masonic Service Association *Short Talk Bulletin*, Mar. 1999: "Freemasonry has ever been the patron of learning. Its votaries long ago discovered that ignorance was the cause of nearly all of the evils that afflict humanity; that education dispelled that evil and set free the victims of its influence." That sums it up very well. We join a Lodge because in some small way (it could be a much larger way) the Fraternity is here to help dispel ignorance, bigotry, prejudice, injustice and all the other evils that surround us. No other reason is more noble and no other reasons deserve the loyalty that Freemasonry attracts.

The writer of the letter in the *New York State Mason* web site went on to explain that we lack the leadership to turn Freemasonry around. I tend to agree and that is why we have, in New York State, implemented the Leadership Development program. We have a long way to go, but we are on our way. New leadership will help to divert us from the boring, long business meetings and transform Lodge communications into stimulating programs designed to turn on the brothers about the Power of Freemasonry. This is Freemasonry acting as an educational institution.

To that end, the *24 Inch Gauge Masonic Resource Guide* lists "12 Reasons for Being Loyal to Freemasonry." It is fitting that they be more widely distributed; hence they are listed here in condensed form.

Twelve Reasons for Being Loyal to Freemasonry

1. Freemasonry is the oldest and most prestigious fraternal organization in the world.
2. Fraternalism is desperately needed in our present society.
   a) Family members learn to love, respect and love each other.
   b) Freemasonry is an expansion of the family circle.
3. Freemasonry supports a set of moral values tested by time.
4. Freemasons are taught that we cannot build a better society without first perfecting the individual building blocks.
5. The concepts of Freemasonry and its leaders played a noble role in the formation of our government– concepts such as liberty, freedom, and justice.
6. Our Masonic Home at Utica is an example of Masonic principle put into action.

7. The Masonic Medical Research Laboratory and the exciting breakthroughs in Science and health give us a great sense of pride and satisfaction.
8. Freemasonry breaks down the barriers to the greatest of all obstacles to a healthy society–the caste system. "The high, the low, the rich the poor" meet on the level.
9. Freemasonry is an international fraternity which helps to forge stronger bonds between nations.
10. Freemasonry is an educational institution teaching all of us to improve ourselves.
11. Freemasonry is the first and strongest force to promote desperately needed ecumenism.
12. Freemasons put their values to work by contributing over two million dollars per day to charity in the USA alone.

It is recorded that from the mid-seventeen hundreds until today, the philosophy of the Fraternity and the rationale for its existence are solid and valuable. When more of its votaries understand this power, we will attract the caliber of leader who can make a greater impact.

The Power of Brotherhood – A personal testimonial

At a leadership seminar conducted by Free & Accepted Masons of the State of New York, we referred to the list of twelve reasons why we should support Freemasonry. Perhaps the most powerful reason of all is its emphasis on respecting the right of each individual to practice his or her own religion. Rudyard Kipling said it best, "Where else can I sit in a room with a Muslim, a Hindu, a Christian and a Jew and know that I am among brothers!"

That prompted me to tell this story: As a person of Armenian descent, it has been difficult for me to warm up to a Muslim Turk. They took my gandfather and oldest uncle outside of their homes and shot them. My two aunts were taken as slaves. My ancestors were a part of the 1.5 million Armenians who were slaughtered by the Turks during the genocide of 1915. I grew up hearing stories of horrible atrocities reported by the few eye-witness survivors. I heard about how my father and two of his brothers wisely fled the country before the genocide. After the war they were able, through the Missionaries, to discover the whereabouts of their two sisters and to buy them back from the Turks. They also arranged to pay their passage to America where my two aunts married and raised families.

We now fast forward to about five years ago. My Masonic Lodge in Aurora was holding an open house. A young man and his wife and son came into the building. He introduced himself as a Freemason from Turkey. I gave him a tour of our very unique and historic building. He asked if there was a Lodge in Ithaca where he could attend while he and his wife were doing research at Cornell. I told him about my Lodge in Ithaca which he attended regularly while he and his wife were at Cornell.

They invited Gloria (my late wife) and me to dinner at their home. We had them at our house for dinner and our friendship grew. When they left to return to Turkey, his wife made a special trip to Aurora to give us a going-away gift.

We never talked about the past history – his Country's version or mine. The Brotherhood of Freemasonry with the principles for which it stands, had the power to remove prejudice. I was able to treat these Turkish people as members of the human family. Such power is desperately needed in the troubled world of today. It could help erase anger, hatred and resentment. It is the kind of force to help us be respectful of our fellow human beings.

The world desperately needs such a force. Freemasonry is the strongest such force.

Originally printed in The *Empire State Mason* Magazine, Winter 2006

Why Temples, Altars and "G" in the East

In reviewing the histories of Lodges it is noted that reference is made to Temples. Pictures of Lodge rooms often show an altar and the letter "G" in the East. It may be in order to explain to the non-Mason the significance of these elements in order to minimize any misinterpretation of the nature of Freemasonry.

First, many Lodge buildings, especially in the early days, were referred to as Temples because, historically, much of the ritual is based on the building of King Solomon's Temple. A Lodge room is symbolically a representation of the inner room of that Temple. This does not mean that Freemasonry is based on any specific religion, ethnicity or bias. It does mean that Freemasonry is an outgrowth of tradition and history.

Likewise, the altar in the center of a Lodge room does not mean that the Fraternity is a religion or that it promotes a specific religious belief. It does mean that Freemasonry is spiritual in nature and that it encourages each of "its votaries to be steadfast in the faith of his acceptance."

The letter "G" located in the East of every New York State Lodge room is there because it is "The initial of the Great and sacred name of God." This perhaps expresses the only dogma, per se, that is connected to Freemasonry. A person cannot be accepted into the Fraternity without an expressed belief in some form of a Supreme Being. Without that belief we could not claim for ourselves a Fraternity of Brothers. There cannot be a brotherhood without a fatherhood.

It may also be in order to explain from whence the terms Mason and Masonic are derived. The history of the Fraternity is ancient and somewhat lost in antiquity. The most direct root from whence present Freemasonry is believed to have evolved is from the stonemasons and architects who built the cathedrals throughout Europe in the Middle Ages. When such construction was coming to an end, it is believed that the masons' guilds began to take into their numbers some of the gentlemen of the day as (what we would call today) honorary members. Those guilds not only taught the mason's trade, but they also instilled moral lessons that had been handed down from "time immemorial." That made it natural for the Fraternity to develop into the system of education that it is today.

This leads to an explanation of the universal symbol of Freemasonry– the square and compasses. In Freemasonry we are taught to use the operative mason's tools as symbols for teaching moral lessons. The square is an emblem used to teach us to "act upon the square in all our actions before God and Man." The compasses remind us "to keep our passions in due bounds."

The term Freemasonry is a more exact title for our present Fraternity. The terms Mason, Masonry, Masonic Temple, or Masonic Hall are misnomers. The correct terms are Freemason, Freemasonry and Freemason's Hall.

Hope and Love

This is the season of hope. Spring has always been considered a symbol of hope, even before the resurrection of Jesus Christ, for which we will celebrate Easter Sunday a week from today. The rebirth of plant life and the beginnings of new life all around us are evidences enough that life goes on and on and hope is in the air. Hope is eternal, as they say. But the life and death and rebirth of Jesus Christ is certainly the most beautiful message of hope that can ever be understood.

This service we have witnessed this morning is sponsored by the Freemasons of the Trumansburg area because Freemasons not only have hope, but we have a strong conviction of the immortality of the soul. This is our landmark. It defines what a person must believe before being accepted as a brother Freemason. We probably don't emphasize this point strongly enough. Without a belief in a supreme being and the immortality of the soul, the title of brother would have no significance and it would ring hollow.

Hope won't work the miracles we expect without its counterpart: LOVE. Without love there is nothing. Love is the other ingredient of the life of Christ that makes hope a reality. Jesus said, "Greater love hath no man than this, that he lay down his life for a friend."

Let me quote from a recent article in a local newspaper by a woman who is my former administrative aide. She started her article by quoting another author. It goes like this: "…we could each write the answer and the answer was always the same: love each other, love each other, love each other." My friend then went on to say, " … my own inner answer has always boiled down to an attempt to be honest and fair, to be kind in my face-to-face dealings, one on one, with the humans around me. This approach, admittedly weak and corny at best, imperfect and passive at its worst, is founded upon some faith that SMALL ACTIONS HAVE AN EFFECT UPON LARGER ONES." She goes on to say, "We must move more actively toward understanding that, on this earth, we are all each other's family, and we must move more toward that understanding. We must continue to believe in the power of the answer, even if it is always the same: love each other, love each other, love each other." We are all each other's family. Those of us who are Freemasons know about the importance of the extended family. We need to be reminded often of the importance of living a life of love.

My favorite story is from the great Middle Eastern prophet, Kahlil Gibran. He asked his friend, Barbara, if she could think of the five most important words. She said, "life, God, love, beauty, and nature." She gave them in that order: life, God, love, beauty, nature. He said, "yes, but you left out the two most important words:

YOU & ME. What is life, God, love, beauty, or nature without YOU & ME?" Even though we understand that God comes first, without you and me, what difference would it make to us? We would not exist to experience God, Life, Love, Beauty, or Nature.

We must never reduce our respect for the role of the individual. Each one is vital. To the extent that each of us understands this point, to that extent will we help to make this a better place for each of us to live. We must maintain our own dignity and help give dignity to everyone else.

It matters not how famous one has been or how many great accomplishments are recorded. The impact that an individual makes in his or her small or large circle of friends is what counts. In our Lodge we recently lost a brother who some would refer to as not very highly exalted. He never became a line officer of the Lodge except to serve as tiler for many years. He was a perfect gentleman and a wonderful brother at all times. It was always a pleasure to be in his company. We honored him with the Dedicated Mason Award some years ago. We do miss him and remember him as fondly as we do the brother who became Dean of Engineering at Cornell University.

As you can imagine, the Dean seldom had time to attend Lodge. He lived a busy life filled with service. We presented him with the Distinguished Mason Award a few years before he died. Our former tiler also lived a life full of service. He was the first to volunteer to help whenever there was a need either in the Lodge or for a neighbor. How can you beat that? Each brother made an impact in a different and important way.

How best can we define our role in life? Jesus said, "Greater love hath no man than this, that he lay down his life for a friend." The first reaction is that Jesus was asking for a pretty big order, at least from the average run of the mill individual like you and me. Not really! At least it is more palatable if we first define life. On a corner stone of the Statler Hotel, on the Cornell University Campus, are these words: "Life is Service." Now we have: "Greater love hath no man than this, that he lay down a life of service for a friend." And in Freemasonry everyone is our friend and everyone is our brother. This is what makes for a purposeful and meaningful life. Love each other. Serve each other. Lay down a life of service to each other. In one way or another, each individual provides service to someone else.

George Peter

True happiness comes from doing just that: helping others. Some of you know that I conduct a leadership development course. You must have known that I would throw in a commercial for it sooner or later. In lesson #10 of that course, one of the questions asked is: The officer of a Masonic Lodge should consider himself a servant?_____, a leader?_____, a teacher?_____ Too many of the people who take the course do not check "a servant." True happiness and true success come from serving our fellow human beings.

That is much better than fretting over others who do not treat us justly. Pythagoras said, "Don't complain so much about being treated unjustly. Real unhappiness lies in acting unjustly." Pythagoras might have been talking about the newcomer who moved up to Vermont. He asked one of the natives, "how are the neighbors around here?" "How were they where you came from?" was the response. The newcomer allowed that they were absolutely terrible where he came from. "You will find them to be absolutely terrible here, too," was the Vermonter's reply.

By contrast, we have the option to love and to serve and to lose ourselves in being concerned for others. I am the first to realize that these thoughts are much easier to put on paper or to recite from a podium than they are to put into practice. The reality of individual behaviors always seems to muddle things up. The real challenge is to live these ideas at home with family, in our social encounters, and especially in the work place. If each of us could be better at loving each other, the work day would be so much more pleasant that productivity would escalate and the improvement in products and service would be overwhelming.

But the best part is that life would be so much more fun and so much more exciting. Love each other, love each other, love each other, and the hope for a better tomorrow will spring up all around us. Love will work the miracles that fulfill your hope and mine. Hope is as strong a part of the human experience as is the warmth of the sun that brings forth spring plants. Plants can't grow without the warmth of the sun. Hope cannot exist without love. Love one another.

Note: This talk was given during a church service. Freemasonry accepts men of all religions and encourages them to practice their faith. Brother George was a Christian and an active member of his church.

The Secret is Out

You've heard the question, "How many Freemasons does it take to change a light bulb?" And the answer is, "Sshh, I can't tell you. It's a secret." Well, that's our problem. There are all these misconceptions about the supposed secrecy of the Fraternity. And it's our own fault. For too long we have gloated and bloated about the so called secrecy of Freemasonry. Members somehow gained the impression that being secretive was some sort of special feature. It has come back to haunt us and may be the main factor which has prevented the Craft from growing more vigorously.

Most of our critics use this perceived secrecy as a reason for distrusting the Fraternity. An email message came to me about a piece written from Canada. Some quotes from that article are disturbing and some are very accurate. The writer says, "The Freemasons are old and their ancient traditions are threatening to keep them that way. Leaders of the 'secret society' say it's time to lift the veil on closely guarded rituals and start luring young recruits."

What to do to dispel the notions that "Freemasonry has more to do with religious cults, world domination, and sacrificial goats?" The answer is simple. Stop feeding the rumors that we are a secret society. Anyone can search the web sites to find out just about anything they want to know about the Craft. Our so called secret ritual is no secret.

Visitors come to our Lodge and I point to the many Masonic symbols on the walls, in the ceiling and all around the room. I explain what those symbols are and how they are used in the ritual to teach moral lessons. Why do we want to keep this information from the public? It's valuable information that we should be proud to share.

Recently, Brother Poltenson from Syracuse brought a young lady who is a high school Junior to our Lodge. He wanted her to see the historic room and for me to tell her something about Freemasonry. She was writing a paper about the Freemasons. All she had heard were the negative falsehoods and something about the Morgan affair. By the time she had spent less than an hour in the Scipio "Living Museum," she had an entirely different view of the Craft and she went away awed by the Power of the Fraternity. Here is what she wrote me after she had made her class presentation:

The paper I wrote was an informal response to my initial questions going into the project and how they were answered through research. I believe that the presentation was helpful to the class. It shed light on a topic that they knew little or nothing about. I initially asked what everybody knew about Masonry. The response was a smattering of replies concerning the 'Morgan Affair' and 'a crazy secret club.' But mostly I received blank stares. This also sums up my initial knowledge of the Fraternity, so I understood the response and did my best to correct the misconceptions. Several of my other teachers asked me about my knowledge of Masonry. The public, if they know anything at all about Masonry, is curious about the organization. There is a perceived secrecy surrounding Masonry. I enjoyed learning the truth about it. –Rachel

There are many ways to dispel the falsehoods about our Craft. We should be working at it with vigor. Back in 1974 we held a program to promote knowledge about Freemasonry. (It is now called, "Brother Bring a Friend Night.") We invited the local Catholic Priest. His thank you letter said, "Nothing dispels distrust more than the truth." So let's stop keeping secrets and start telling the truth to more people and in more venues.

Ancient, Earnest and Fraternal – Not Secret
December 1996

"It doesn't matter what they say about us as long as they are talking about us." – P.T. Barnum

Freemasonry seems to be under attack more and more these days. E-mail reports claim that Freemasonry is the organized conspiracy which assassinated John F. Kennedy. The report goes on to say that Masons then covered up the deed in the form of another conspiracy. Another E-mail message states that Jack Kemp is a 33rd degree Mason, and therefore is privy to the highest secrets of Satan and Satan-worshippers.[1]

That's just the tip of the iceberg. A main agenda item of the Southern Baptist Convention (Houston, Texas, 1993) was the question: Should all Freemasons be expelled from the Church unless they renounce membership in the Fraternity? That proposal failed, but a resolution did pass which made it clear, in no uncertain terms, that the Church held Freemasonry in ill repute. John Ankerberg makes a small fortune selling a video tape which exposes all the secrets of Freemasonry– and it's only $29.95. Pat Robertson's new book, *New World Order*, offers more alleged proof that Freemasonry is evil. Louis Farrakhan has done

Freemasonry a favor by telling his followers how bad we are. And the list goes on.

Interestingly enough, at the same time, academic scholars are beginning to write about Freemasonry. And they are presenting the Fraternity in a favorable light. Dr. Kathleen Smith Kutolowski, Professor in the Department of History at SUNY Brockport, has researched the effects of Freemasonry on American history.[2] Her favorable assessment of the role played by Freemasonry is a breath of fresh air.

The fall 1996 issue of the *Empire State Mason* magazine featured a book review by the editor, Scott D. Harris.[3] The book by Steven C. Bullock, *Revolutionary Brotherhood: Freemasonry and the Transformation of the American Social Order, 1730-1840*, was published in 1994. The book is complimentary to Freemasonry and to the role played by the Fraternity in the making of America. Bullock says, "...The fraternalism expressed in Masonry offered a set of resources that could be used for a wide range of purposes. Although the order cannot be seen as a master key to all early American history, it opens up that mysterious ground where pragmatic action (behaving in ways that 'work') intersects with attempts to create moral and intellectual coherence out of experience."[4]

In the August/September 1996 issue of *Civilization* magazine an article by Richard Brookhiser is entitled, "Ancient, Earnest, Secret, And Fraternal" – "Since the founding of the first American lodges in the 1730s, Freemasons have attracted prominent members, done good deeds– and sometimes sparked open hostility."[5]

(Brookhiser got three out of the four correct in his title. **We are not a secret society**.) He does present Freemasonry in a favorable light, as have other recent scholarly writers. He nevertheless, still leaves out two important elements of a complete discussion on the subject of Freemasonry and its detractors. Refer to an article by me called, "Whys and Wherefores." It was published in the October 1994 issue of *Philalethes* Magazine.[7]

References:

1. Acacia Press Online: http://www.crocker.com/~acacia/antim.html.
2. Paper presented by Dr. Kutolowski to Philalethes, Finger Lakes Chapter.
3. The *Empire State Mason* Magazine, fall 1996 issue
4. "Ancient Earnest, Secret And Fraternal," *Civilization Magazine*, August/Sept. 1996 issue
5. ibid
6. "Whys and Wherefores," by George Peter, Oct. 1994, *Philalethes* Magazine, addendum added - 1994

George Peter

False Witness
July 2, 1989

This essay was prepared by request of the deacons of a church in Scipio Center. They had asked me to come and respond to a film shown by their pastor to an adult Sunday School class. Most of the deacons were members of Cayuga Lodge #221 in Scipio Center. The Masonic building is adjacent to the church and is used by the church for their summer Bible school program.

Prov. 6:16: These six things doth the Lord hate; yea, seven are an abomination unto him: 17. A proud look, a lying tongue, and hands that shed innocent blood, 18. A heart that deviseth wicked imaginations, feet that be swift in running to mischief, 19. A **false witness** that speaketh lies, and he that soweth discord among brethren.

Perhaps the greatest human attribute given to humans by the Lord is this thing we call ego. No progress is possible without it. And yet uncontrolled ego is the most dangerous human weakness and is the most anti-Christ aspect of human behavior. Uncontrolled ego causes people to believe that "my race, my color, my religion, my church, my way of life, etc. is the only one that is right."

It causes people to bear false witness against their neighbors. It leads people to make the film that was shown in this church. It causes people to be combative. It makes it very difficult to help bring about peace in the world. It is contrary to everything that Jesus Christ tried to teach. He taught by example how to be selfless instead of selfish. He did not coin the phrase, "you cannot drag others through the mud without getting more on yourself," but He certainly left us with a similar message. His example was to minister to the woman at the well. The message of the film seems to be, "stay away from any and all who do not interpret God's word exactly as I do– don't even fraternize with them."

A Response to the Film

First we must clarify what Freemasonry is and is not. It is not a religion (regardless of whether we quote one Masonic scholar of 200 years ago). It teaches and urges each of its members to support the religion of his choice. The fact is that perhaps 95% of its members are the strongest supporters of their respective churches. It is not in competition with the church but, on the contrary, is the greatest supporter of the church.

Freemasonry is the oldest fraternal organization in the world. It grew out of the stone masons and architects who designed and built the cathedrals throughout Europe. It teaches that we cannot build a better society without first perfecting each individual who makes up the building blocks of society. It therefore promotes a set of moral values which have withstood the test of time. All of these moral values are the same ones that the churches, through the ages, have promoted.

Freemasonry gets in trouble with the Catholic Church and with dogmatic religions because it is the first, the oldest and the strongest force in the world for ecumenism. And regardless of the message of the film, ecumenism is a teaching of Christ. It is not Christ, but the ego of humans, which leads to preaching against fraternization.

Now let us discharge the false accusations against Freemasonry:

1. Blacks ARE NOT barred from Freemasonry. It is true that for too long Masonic Lodges did not have many blacks as members. That has been changing at a pace that is too slow, but it is changing. We could make the same accusation about this church. How many blacks are members? There is a Lodge in New York City that is made up of mostly blacks. We have black members in neighboring Lodges and blacks are on an equal as they should be. Every aspect of our society has discriminated against blacks and all of us are making every effort to correct for this. "He who is without sin, cast the first stone."

Note: Since the writing of this essay, Mutual recognition with the Most Worshipful Prince Hall Grand Lodges of the State of New York, Connecticut, Massachusetts and Colorado has been established. Relations with other Most Worshipful Prince Hall Grand Lodges have continued to grow stronger. PROGRESS!

2. No place in Freemasonry has it ever been said that Freemasonry is all that a brother needs. Each brother is led to the open Bible and is instructed "to direct his steps through life by the light he shall find therein." And he is instructed to support the church of his faith. An atheist is not considered for membership.

3. It is another lie to claim that Freemasonry denies Christ. Because Freemasonry does not claim to do so, nor does it want to replace a person's religion. Religion and politics are forbidden to be discussed in the Lodge room. This gives the bearers of false witness the chance to distort the truth and to claim that Jesus Christ is denied by Freemasons.

4. The next false claim is that Freemasonry has more than one God. We accept members who proclaim that they believe in one ever-living and true God. They may call Him "Allah" or whatever name is given to Him in their faith. Rudyard Kipling said, "Where else can I sit in a room with a Christian, a Jew, a Hindu, a Moslem, and know that I am among brothers?" Remember that the term, "Brother" connotes children of One God. If we heed the message of the film, it seems to me that it would be just as evil to play a game of ball, or any other sport, with anyone except a Christian. Isn't that attitude the one that has gotten the world in the trouble we are in now? My ancestors came from the Middle East, and if people there would stop being suspicious of each other's religion, there could be some hope of finding peace.

5. The next accusation is the most absurd of all. The film claims that the Bible says that we should not swear. By taking a statement out of context we can have the Bible say anything we want it to in order to bear false witness. Freemasons are not forced to swear but, yes, we do take an obligation (which is our word for oath). We obligate ourselves to uphold the Constitution and laws of the country in which we live; we vow to uphold the Constitution and by-laws of the Fraternity, to support each other as well as widows and orphans. These are some of the things we vow to do. But if this is against the Bible, it must also be against the Bible to stand in a Court of law and to swear "to tell the truth, the whole truth and nothing but the truth."

These should be enough examples of how easy it is to bear false witness. It is done by not controlling one's ego and thus believing that "only I have found the truth."

Luke 3:14 ...Do violence to no man, neither accuse any falsely.

How sad that people who confess to be followers of the teachings of Jesus Christ, spend all of their effort teaching and preaching hate. The message of Jesus Christ is **love**.

Let Them Talk -- The Truth

Even before suggesting that the Grand Lodge of the State of New York should be involved in a public program to teach Leadership Development via the internet, the enemies of Freemasonry have been attacking what we do. Other Grand jurisdictions have various sorts of programs to promote Freemasonry via the internet. A friend told me about a radio program which castigated Freemasonry because of such programs. There is concern that we will incur the ire of more anti-Freemasonry groups.

Hey, it has been happening since the beginning of the Fraternity. Even before the Papacy issued a decree in the early 1700s which forbade its members from joining the Fraternity, there have been anti-Masonic movements.

The news media and various other groups tend to say inaccurate and, sometimes, offensive things about Freemasonry. To a great extent it is our fault. We keep the truth from them. Most Grand Lodges preserve and promote our heritage fairly well. But that is not always the case on the district or lodge level. We need to do a better job at every level.

What is the public saying about us? The natural tendency is for the news media to refer to Freemasonry as a secret society. e.g.: *The New York Times*, in an otherwise favorable report about the Grand Lodge dedication of its building, in its Dec. 14, 1997 issue, referred to the Fraternity as a secret society. Why does this happen?

Inaccurate and nasty things are said about Freemasonry because we are so quiet, and yes, so secretive, about who and what we are. The reality is that we are quiet and secretive because the average brother knows so little about Freemasonry. And so we continue to act like black holes instead of spreading enlightenment about ourselves and the Fraternity. The public can only conjecture about us and listen to our detractors.

It behooves each of us to be alert as to what the public can learn about Freemasonry. That means that we should be vigilant to preserve our history, to know our history and to share our history with the rest of the world. We need to be telling the world the truth about Freemasonry. We must do so for the following reasons:
1. To deflect the false image which our detractors spread.
2. To give accurate accounts of the real power of Freemasonry.
3. To discover that the more we know about our history and philosophy the more excited we become about the Craft.

4. To realize that the more we know about the Craft the more will be our potential to spread its beneficent influence on all mankind.

How shall we proceed?

1. Provide programs at the district level which are designed to educate the officers of Masonic lodges.
2. Provide a lodge or district newspaper to disseminate Masonic news and information.
3. Provide material in the publications and education programs which are designed to educate, inspire, excite, interest and turn on the membership- and any one else who is exposed to the material.
4. Don't stop there. Submit articles of historical and philosophical nature to the local press, radio and TV networks.
5. Offer to provide a regular column in local newspapers. Most everyone is interested in history. Such a column could prove to be a real plus for the Craft. But it must be done very professionally and with tact. Use material already available. Create new material and ideas.
6. In all endeavors, emphasize the role played by Freemasonry in the shaping of America and the role it plays in making a civilized society.
7. Encourage Grand Lodges to provide educational, interesting, exciting and inspiring material in their memos and publications. Most material should be designed to turn on the brotherhood. We need more substance and less pomp and circumstance.
8. Each lodge should establish Masonic study groups from within itself. We are an educational institution and should carry out that role more effectively.[1]
9. Be proud. Be humble. Be aggressive. Be innovative. Be industrious and active.
10. Be a Brother Freemason

That is our charge.

References:

1. Peter, George, "Back to Basics" and *24-Inch Gauge Masonic Resource Guide*

Who and What to Love, What to Hate

JOHN 15: 12, 13

12. This is my commandment: that ye love one another, as I have loved you.

13. Greater love hath no man than this: that a man lay down his life for his friends.

We are **who** and **what** we love. We are also **what** we hate. It is very appropriate to talk about love on this, or any, Palm Sunday. In fact it is very appropriate to talk about, to feel, to experience and to give love every day and every moment of our lives.

It may not be as appropriate on Palm Sunday to talk about hate. On the other hand, perhaps we have become so politically correct that we are taught not to hate anything. Jesus said, "Love your enemies." But he didn't say to love what your enemies do, when what they do is wrong. We need to know right from wrong, and we need to love the right and to hate the wrong. We have been told otherwise lately. Just possibly that is why we have so many social ills.

Let's not dismiss our discussion of hate, but first, let's talk about love. It's what makes the world go round. It is what makes life so wonderful. We are **what** and **who** we love. So **who** should we love? **What** should we love?

In Freemasonry we talk about being true first to God, second to our neighbor and lastly, to ourselves. In Palm Sunday terms, we can say that first is to love God, second is to love our neighbors and finally is to love self.

It may not be theologically correct, but a pretty good argument can be made for loving self first. It's pretty hard to love God or anyone else if one first doesn't love one's self. I like myself, but mostly I like myself because I was so clever and so lucky to select such a wonderful wife named, Gloria. I like who and what I love and I also am satisfied with what I hate. We'll talk about that later.

We've all seen people who obviously don't like themselves. It shows all over and it shows in how they mistreat others. I can't imagine it is very easy to love God if you first don't like yourself. We come from God.

So we've pretty much defined **who** we should love. The answer is everybody. Yes, Jesus did say, "love your enemies." In the Army Air Corp we had a saying, "the difficult we do immediately; the impossible takes a little longer." To love our enemies certainly is difficult. Some would say it's impossible. So maybe it will take a little longer– but we're not to give up.

With hard work and commitment we can learn to love everybody. But again, this doesn't mean that we have to love what everybody does. This is where we get into trouble– not understanding the difference between people and what they do. We have been indoctrinated to think that we can't love the evil doer unless we treat him or her the same way as we treat good people. We need to separate the sin from the sinner. It's okay to hate the sin, love the sinner, and treat said person in a firm way to help correct the sinning. Sounds very much easier said than done.

We all know that family is synonymous with love. Family is perhaps the most powerful force for love. It certainly is an excellent laboratory to practice and demonstrate love. In Freemasonry, we know that the Fraternity is the extended family. We are taught to use it to promote love. Our next charge is to extend that family to limitless bounds.

Now that we have defined who we should love, let's talk about what we should love. That is easy! First is to love life. Love and enjoy life to its fullest. The Vermont Farmer was asked if he had lived here all his life. His immediate reply was, "not yet!" He had a lot of living yet to do. That's how we ought to think about life. Every day is an experience and a challenge and a celebration. My brother - Jake, just died and the funeral was Thursday. We didn't spend time mourning his death. We couldn't do that because the suffering was too great to want him to hang on. We celebrated **his life** and how much he enjoyed his family.

If we truly love life, we've covered the waterfront. Life encompasses everything. But let's enumerate some of the specifics. My brothers in Freemasonry love the Fraternity. We love what it stands for and what it teaches. We love what it can do to help bring society back to its senses– to promote a set of moral values which have been tested by time and experience.

We love the Constitution of the United States of America. We love it because it guarantees some of the same principles that are embodied in the teachings of Freemasonry. We know these to be of importance to grow the human spirit. We love it so much that some have given their lives in its support. Most of my generation was willing to do so by serving our country when the need arose to defend these principles.

"Greater love hath no man than this: that a man lay down his life for his friends." On a plaque at the Statler Hotel is a quotation from Mr. Statler. It reads, "Life is Service." Couple this with the Biblical quotation and we have, "Greater love hath no person than this: that he or she lay down a life of service for others." To me that is what life is all about and to truly love life is to love to provide service to others.

Service comes in many forms. Few people have heard of the service of Joe and Helen Peter (except their family) but I can tell you of service of the highest calling. They both as immigrants met in Myers, raised 8 children, worked day and night to provide for those children and to educate them the best they could. Six of those children served their country in time of need. All have worked hard and have contributed in positive ways to the welfare of the nation.

What else should we love? We are taught to be builders of a temple of honor, of justice, of purity, of knowledge and of truth. To me this is translated to mean that we are to love honor, justice, purity, knowledge, and truth. These are indeed values we should love and promote. Wouldn't it be great if we elected only politicians who understood the importance of these virtues?

It's hard not to comment on the fact that we have an administration that has 3 or 4 top leaders who have had to resign because there is evidence that they did not guard their own honor, they were confused about justice, they could not reveal the truth, and/or purity was not a part of their vocabulary. They may have great knowledge but certainly not knowledge about how to live a life of service.

Lest you think I am becoming political in this talk, be aware that these conditions have existed in other administrations as well as the present one. It's we who are to blame for not demanding that our elected officials love and protect their own honor, justice, purity, knowledge, and truth.

In summary of who to love: It's God, neighbor, and self. All of this is manifested in **family**. Extend it as far as possible. What to love? Love life, love Freemasonry, love the Constitution of the United States of America, and love service to others. Love the cardinal virtues and especially love your own honor, love justice, love purity, love knowledge, and love truth.

At this stage it is almost sacrilegious to talk about hate. But you note that we did not say **who** to hate. The answer to that is: nobody. Hate nobody. But hate what some people do. Hate it with a passion so strong that you will want to fight for the elimination of what we know to be harmful to society.

Specifically, it's time we stood up and were counted for hating the violence, drug abuse, and deviant behavior that seems to permeate society today. We need to say, in no uncertain terms, that we will fight to correct these ills. And if the fighting involves treating the perpetrators in less than loving ways, so be it. It's just possible that true love is to do what has to be done to defend society from the ills which have befallen it. We don't do anybody any favor by turning our backs on that which is evil.

Our challenge is to love the good, to love the right, to love what makes for a harmonious and happy society. In so doing, justice, peace, and happiness will ride triumphantly into Jerusalem and into all the cities and country sides of America. Peace will reign.

Theology of Crime – Revisited

In the fall 2000 issue of *ESM* I wrote about Dr. E. S. Ryan's new book, *The Theology of Crime and the Paradox of Freedom*. The second edition of this book was published by Anchor Communications in early 2001. In March of 2001 Dr. Ryan and I conducted at Cornell University a "Theology of Crime Seminar" in which we used the Armenian genocide as a first case study of the message in Ryan's book. This was six months before the 9/11 attacks on the World Trade Center and the Pentagon. It's easy to have afterthoughts, but the book and the seminar were testimony to prophetic insight as to what can happen when theological fanaticism goes out of control.

A third edition of the book has been published this year by the same publisher with the addition of two chapters entitled, "Chosinness and the Theology of Terror" and "Theology of Crime and the World Trade Center." Obviously these additions to the book are designed to explain how the warnings of the original book are translated into the reality of what happens, as Ryan puts it, when "Live is reversed and becomes Evil."

Dr. Ryan has a penchant for playing with words to make his points. He has created a new word "chosinness" to explain what happens when one chooses one God as his God and his God only at the detriment of all others. He points out that one is no longer practicing chosenness, but instead is involved in sin, hence "chosinness."

Dr. Ryan's analysis of how theologians have excluded, rather than included, the theologies of others is a much needed awakening to the reality of crimes committed by entrenched systems. His writings address example after example of crimes committed in the name of, and with the power of, organized groups – often religious.

The book is a must read especially by Freemasons because the world so desperately needs an understanding of how none of us can solve human discord and anger by looking outward to expect others to change. Dr. Ryan admonishes us to look inward and correct our own behavior and biases. Freemasons need to understand that such is our charge and our mission- to accept all people as brothers and sisters and to act accordingly with them.

Lest we think that our intellect alone can save us from the theology of terror, Prof. Ryan reminds us that at the World Trade Center was a highly educated engineer. He points out that Goebbels and Mengele, PhDs were perpetrators of the German murder machine. "This terrorist inversion of life (into evil) can best be understood as a criminal metaphysic or belief system."

An example of how Ryan plays with words to make a powerful point is his statement: As Freemasons we must "choose the proper spiritual SYNTAX, so as not to tax others with the SINTAX of the sinful choice of Chosinness."

Ryan further admonishes us not to assume that being good at charity is all that we need to do lest we be "defined as a growing charity and a declining spirituality." Spirituality and charity are not mutually exclusive, but to accentuate one without remembering from whence charity is derived is to lose our way.

Our way is to grow in understanding of the role of Freemasons to promote universal chosenness and to wage war against invidious chosinness.

Ryan's words are not just lofty ideals, but in fact, are scholarly approaches to the problem of what has gone wrong, and what has to happen to right that wrong. His message in this book is to lead us to become a greater force for the ecumenism we espouse.

All of us would be better qualified to serve in that role if we read and digest the contents of Dr. Ryan's book, *The Theology of Crime*.

An equally interesting development is a plan to offer a series of other "Theology of Crime" Seminars. These will be a part of the newly formed MUNY (Masonic University of New York) system of education and leadership development. Stay tuned.

Originally printed in The *Empire State Mason* Magazine, Fall 2004

Part II

A History of Freemasonry

George Peter

A History of Freemasonry

You've heard the story of the Vermont preacher who had convinced his congregation to redecorate the church sanctuary. When the work was completed and dedicated he then asked the Deacons to consider the installation of a new chandelier. The Deacons met and returned with the decision not to buy the chandelier. "Why not?" The minister wanted to know. "For three reasons," was the reply from the chairman: "We can't spell it, no one knows how to play it, and what we really need is better lighting."

With that introduction let us try to chandelier, or rather throw some light, on the history of Freemasonry:

The oldest RECORDED evidence that something like Freemasonry existed is the Regius Poem which was transcribed by a priest in 1390. It is in Chaucerian English verse, hence it is referred to as a poem. It is called the Regius Poem because it was part of the Royal Library of England which commenced with Henry VII. It was presented to the British Museum by George II. There is evidence, but not proof, that it is a copy of an earlier manuscript. The poem contains 15 articles and 15 points dealing with the morals of a Mason which are similar to the philosophy of Freemasonry as we know it today.

The other interesting aspect of the poem is that it seems to be written about Masons instead of to Masons, who were at that time, the operative Masons engaged in the building of cathedrals throughout Europe. This leads to the conjecture that it may have been written to the gentlemen of that day. If that is correct then speculative Masons were accepted as early as, or even earlier than 1390. The common belief has been that speculative members (sort of honorary members) were not taken into Masonry until the time when cathedral building was coming to a close in the late 17th and early 18th century. That is our heritage and, in part, explains why we are called "Free and Accepted Masons" today.

The earliest recorded Grand Lodge system, whereby Masonic Lodges were bound to a Grand Lodge hierarchy, was formed in England in 1717.

How far back do the guilds of the operative masons go? Who knows? Obviously masons were building pyramids in Egypt, and the building of King Solomon's Temple employed craftsmen with skills in masonry. The builders of the pyramids most likely possessed knowledge of the Pythagorean Theorem long before

Pythagoras. But again, on these matters, we can only conjecture. And yet when King Tut's tomb was opened, Dr. Kinamon commented, "Evidently there was something akin to Freemasonry when the boy King was entombed." It is said that some of the artifacts found were an apron and other emblems related to the Craft.

Freemasonry came to America with the earliest settlers. The history of Freemasonry in America is almost synonymous with the history of our country. It is claimed that the first Masonic Lodge in the new world was in Providence, R.I. One of the most famous Lodges was St. Johns Lodge in Boston. John Adams, Paul Revere and many other famous early patriots belonged to that Lodge. Many of the participants in the Boston Tea Party were members of St. Johns Lodge in Boston.

Peyton Randolph, first president of the Continental Congress was Grand Master of Masons in the Virginia Colony. He died during the time of the second Continental Congress in 1775. At about the same time, General and Dr. Joseph Waren (or Warren), Grand Master of Masons in Massachusetts was killed at the Battle of Bunker Hill. Ben Franklin was Grand Master of Masons in Pennsylvania. It is believed that his influence and strong Masonic ties in France (he was an honorary member) and the rest of Europe may have attracted Masonic stalwarts such as Lafayette and Baron Von Steuben to come to the aid of the colonies.

George Washington was the only President (of 14 Presidents who are known to have been Masons) to have served as President of the U.S. and Master of his Lodge at the same time. Harry Truman was President and Grand Master of Masons in the State of Missouri.

Some of the early leaders who were Grand Masters of Masons in New York were Robert Livingston, Daniel Tompkins, DeWitt Clinton, Stephen Van Rensselaer and many others.

It may or may not be a coincidence that the concepts of the freedoms that are embodied in our Constitution are of the same philosophy taught as lessons in Freemasonry. There can be no doubt though that the men who were Freemasons and who also were involved in the formation of our government were influenced by the precepts of the Fraternity which they supported and honored.

As with any history, it does not end by reciting the past. It goes on and is being made every moment. The future of Freemasonry is in our hands and tomorrow it will be Masonic history. How we act out our role of being a brother to our fellow human beings determines whether the history of Freemasonry will continue to be as glorious as that which I have related to you.

George Washington

On Dec. 17th, 1999 CSPAN aired a program which was the reenactment of the funeral of General, President, and Brother George Washington. The ceremony was reenacted 200 years to the day from his funeral. Remember that he had died Dec. 14, just three days earlier.

The Women's Assoc. of Mount Vernon sponsored the program. The Masonic funeral service was done exactly to a tee as to the way it was done 200 years earlier. Someone played the part of Dr. Elijah Cullen Dick, who was Washington's attending physician and Master of Alexandria Lodge #22 in 1799. The laying of the apron on the coffin and the laying of the sprig of acacia on the coffin by each brother (as it was done in those days) was done impressively.

We forget how greatly Washington was admired and respected by his countrymen. He was revered by all. At the original funeral there was genuine grief, weeping and affection for this giant of a man.

We hear modern historians make stupid statements like, "he wouldn't be so great if he lived in today's society." They don't get it that he did not live in 1999. He lived in his time and his place. Modern historians remind me of the cartoon strip, "Peanuts." Snoopy is fantasizing that he is a soldier at Valley Forge. He salutes and says, "Yes sir, General." He goes to Woodstock, the bird, and says that the general wants us to chop up some firewood. Woodstock talks to Snoopy and they agree that they will go tell the General just to turn up the thermostat.

Brother George Washington rose to great heights, at least in part, because he was exposed to the principles of Freemasonry. Again historians remind us that he did not attend many Masonic meetings. Hey, when did he have time?

Washington was raised a Master Mason on Aug. 4, 1753 in Fredericksburg, VA. He was charter member of Lodge #22 and elected Worshipful Master in 1788. He was offered Grand Mastership of a Grand Lodge of the USA. He turned it down as he did turn down the Grand Mastership of VA. He was a member of American Union Lodge (a military Lodge which traveled with the troops.)

He laid the cornerstone of the Capitol building in full Masonic regalia wearing the Masonic apron given him by General LaFayette. It was made by Madame LaFayette.

We should have no doubt that he was raised to a higher level of leadership and service by his association with Freemasonry. In his correspondence, he never failed to express his love for and respect for the Craft. See: *American Lodge of Research*, Vol. 5, #3, page 353.

Closer to home, just last month, on Jan. 22, we participated in a ceremony where a brother donated a Revolutionary War powder horn to the George Washington Masonic Historic Site at Tappan. Three years ago the district went by bus to visit that site. The original DeWint house was constructed in the year 1700 (300 years ago.) George Washington used the home as his headquarters four times during the Revolution. DeWint was a friend of the General. Interestingly enough, the powder horn was in the DuBois family since the revolution and they lived within one mile of the DeWint house.

In a way this makes us feel a little closer to Brother George Washington, first in war, first in peace, and first in the hearts of his countrymen– and most assuredly, first in the hearts of all his brother Freemasons.

Originally printed in The *Empire State Mason* Magazine, Winter 2000

Benjamin Franklin

The History Channel recently featured a two-hour documentary on the life of our Brother Benjamin Franklin. It was extremely well done and covered much of the exciting attributes and successes of Ben Franklin. But no biography can do justice to the breadth and magnitude of this unusual human being. Even so, the documentary was fairly well inclusive of his many contributions and interests. Unfortunately however, no mention was made of his Masonic affiliation and influence in, (and by) our Fraternity.

Among other sources, a "Google" search on Ben Franklin and Freemasonry contained over 50 pages of a condensed biography of Ben Franklin. The article starts out by stating that, "Research demonstrates the importance of Lodges from the time of the Revolution. The Committees of Public Safety and Correspondence were critical in the organization of the Revolution. These committees carried out their activities in Masonic code...The secret private loans made by the French to George Washington were underwritten by the Masonic connection."

Quoting from the *American Heritage*, the article goes on to say, "Important parts of American history cannot be understood without knowledge of the Freemasons. The link with France, which many say saved the revolutionary cause, the Committees of Public Safety and Correspondence, who organized the psychological war against England were Freemasons to the core...The influence of Freemasons has shaped American Political thought more than any other element...The postal connection to Masons is via the publishing business- information, newspapers depended on the post- the internet of its time- the Dutch printers and Franklin's media empire were Masonic in their desire to spread the word of the enlightenment..."

Brother Franklin was steeped in Freemasonry. He was Grand Master of Masons in Pennsylvania. While in France he was active in the Lodge of Seven Sisters. "As a dignitary of one of the most distinguished Masonic Lodges in France, he had the opportunity of meeting and speaking with a number of philosophers and leading figures of the French Revolution." Voltaire contacted Franklin because he wanted to meet this famous philosopher. Franklin helped in the initiation of Voltaire and later he led the Masonic funeral service for Voltaire.

His Masonic connection in France and England opened many doors and helped him to serve the Colonies in a multitude of capacities before, during, and after the war. Congress appointed Franklin, Silas Deane, and Arthur Lee to "transact the business of the United States at the court of France." It was fitting that Franklin, John Jay, and John Adams were the committee to conclude a treaty of peace with Great Britain in Sept. 1783. It was fitting that Franklin was an active member of the Constitutional Convention which drafted the United States Constitution.

It would take many pages to describe the genius and list the unbelievable number of inventions and contributions of this Freemason. Franklin was acclaimed on both sides of the Atlantic Ocean and crowds gathered time and again to honor his arrival or presence.

He died on April 17, 1790 at his home on Market Street in Philadelphia. His funeral was held on April 21. "More than twenty thousand people were assembled." The flags on the vessels in the harbor were at half mast and discharges of artillery were heard to honor the life of this American "self-made," self-educated, genius, and humanitarian Freemason.

His Masonic connection cannot be omitted from any biography of this great man. He was a Freemason through and through.

Originally printed in The *Empire State Mason* Magazine, Spring 2005

Miracle or Masterpiece

A definition of the purpose and function of the U. S. Constitution perhaps was stated best nearly 50 years after its making. Senator John C. Calhoun said, "Governments exist to restrain people; the Constitution exists to restrain government."[1] In 1972 Justice William O. Douglas commented that, "the Supreme Court is the keeper of the conscience and the conscience is the Constitution."[2]

The essence of the Constitution is found in these very basic but profound ideas. And the ideas are very much greater than the Constitution itself. Where did the concepts now embodied in the Constitution originate? Certainly none of the governments of Europe could be used as models for it. Some great minds such as John Locke, Brother Montesquieu and others had proposed thoughts on the subject, but none had ever been tested in a system.

This paper is to propose that the essence of the Constitution came from two major but very different sources– the teachings of Freemasonry and the government of the Iroquois Indians. It is not important nor is it possible to determine which source had the greatest influence. Ideas from both sources fed on each other to crystallize in the minds of the framers.

The Iroquois Confederacy came closer as a model for our present government than did any system before it. The concepts of freedom, of family expanding into the ever larger family, of the dignity and sacredness of the individual all are concepts of Freemasonry and also of the Iroquois Indians. Freemasons talk about "meeting on the level." The Iroquois form of government was to govern by consensus. Freemasonry teaches us to live responsibly in society, to promote virtue, to seek knowledge. The Iroquois Indians select leaders who exemplify these same virtues. Their word, "chief" means he who is of the good. The word, "Iroquois" means family.[3] In Freemasonry we emphasize the concept of brotherhood of all mankind– family. These concepts all are essential ingredients of a successful democratic form of government. Even in its earliest form (and although it had been referred to as merely a bunch of compromises), the "conscience" embodied in the Constitution came closer to safeguarding the ideas of brotherhood, family, responsibility as citizens and rule by consensus than had any previous system except for the Iroquois Confederacy.

Few historians have suggested the slightest possibility that the Iroquois Indian form of government had any influence in the development of the Constitution, leave (or let) alone that there was any influence by Freemasonry. To make this claim and to prove it 200 years after the fact may be a formidable challenge. Several Freemasons have written in support of a Masonic influence. Except for Lewis Henry Morgan, only recently have modern anthropologist historians proposed an Indian connection. We shall use material from these sources, as well as from conventional writers, to support our proposition. Also we shall demonstrate that the nature of Freemasonry and the nature of the Iroquois ideology are similar in such ways as to make it natural for a democratic form of government to be bred from these perspectives.

One danger we see in making this proposition is that women will complain that we act like male chauvinists by leaving them out of the picture. After all, Freemasons were and are all men. Well, so were all the makers of the Constitution. But the Indian society was a matriarchy and the influence of women was great. Furthermore, none of this is to deny that we might have had an even better system if women had been involved. After all, a good example of their involvement resulted in the 19th amendment which radically improved the document.

The bicentennial celebration of the Constitution has generated much reflection on the document itself, as well as on its derivation. The Sept. 1987 issue of *National Geographic* appropriately has a two-part article dealing with James Madison and the Iroquois Confederacy. James Madison is said to be the author of the Constitution. He prepared the Virginia plan, which was used as a basis for the final compromise and refinements.

"While out on a 'ramble' with the Marquis de Lafayette in 1784, James Madison attended the preliminaries for a treaty ceremony at Fort Stanwix, NY. The treaty was between the fledgling U. S. and the Six Nations Iroquois Confederacy." There he witnessed the Iroquois 'forest diplomats,' whose own oral constitution, the Great Law of Peace, preceded ours by centuries. It is based upon strength through union and embodies Iroquois notions of free expression and representative government with checks and balances.

Could it be that the U.S. Constitution owes a debt to the Iroquois? Benjamin Franklin cited their powerful confederacy as an example for a successful union of sovereign states, and contemporary accounts of the American 'noble savage' living in 'natural freedom' inspired European theorists such as John Locke and Jean-Jacques Rousseau to expound the philosophical principles that helped ignite the Revolution and shape the Constitution." [4]

At a Conference on Indian Affairs held at Cornell University, Sept. 11 & 12 '87, we heard papers presented by these distinguished professors who are some of the leading experts on Indian history and anthropology:

Dr. Dan Usner	Cornell University
Dr. Donald Grinde	California Polytechnic Institute
Mr. Bruce Burton	Castleton College
Dr. Bruce Johansen	University of Nebraska
Dr. Robert Venables	Dir., American Indian Community House Gallery
Dr. Greg Schaaf	DQ University, California

The overriding theme of all the speakers was the connection between the Iroquois Great Law of Peace and the United States Constitution. Some main points from those talks are listed:

Although mention of Indians only appears twice in the Constitution, their tradition of making treaties set the stage for the formation of U. S. Indian Affairs. It was an obsession with George Washington, Jefferson and others. An early encounter with Indian negotiations was the treaty at Albany in 1775. Ben Franklin, Thomas Payne and John Rutledge were among those present. John Rutledge wrote the first draft of the Constitution. Referring to the Albany meeting, John Hancock relates the Iroquois history and writes, "They are wise– one arrow is easily broken, 12 united can't be broken."

Franklin, in his many speeches in Europe, often quoted the Indian philosophy of government. He used their terminology; "I give you a chain of friendship." "Let us brighten up the covenant chain." Franklin wrote many letters to Indians during the Continental Congress. He designed the coin with 13 links to a chain. He talked about the Indian government to many people in Europe and in this country. Franklin pushed for the Iroquois plan of government. The concept of representation and self-rule was a part of their vocabulary. Franklin used the Indian term, "Grand Council," when he presented the Albany plan to Congress.

The Articles of Confederation used the term, "enter into a firm league of friendship." This term is borrowed from the Great Law of the Iroquois which was the "league of friendship." Dr. Bruce Johanson put it this way, "Indian confederations were all along the American seaboard. Americans were swimming in a sea of Indian people and influence. When you swim, you get wet."[5] The lack of credit given to the Iroquois is rooted in the fact that they were the enemy. Most of the Iroquois fought on the side of the British. Also, ego tends to get in the way of giving credit to another race of people who were referred to, more often than not, as savages. As early as 1751, Franklin said, "why can't the English get together if the Iroquois can? Who are the real savages?"

George Morgan was an Indian agent for the early U. S. government. He met with Franklin in Philadelphia and shared his knowledge of Indian culture and philosophy. Franklin formed a social club the purpose of which was to share Indian culture. Before the Declaration of Independence, Iroquois ambassadors came to Philadelphia to meet with Colonial leaders. Hancock referred to their League as the "Great tree of liberty." Theirs is probably the oldest document in the world of participatory democracy. A major difference between the Iroquois system and our Constitution is that the rights and the role of women are defined in the League of the Haudenausaunee, or Iroquois. Their role was more like that of our Supreme Court. (We finally have one woman on ours).

"Lewis Henry Morgan, 'father of American anthropology', noted checks and balances in the Iroquoian system that acted to prevent concentration of power. 'Their whole civil policy was adverse to the concentration of power in the hands of any single individual, but inclined to the opposite principle of division among a number of equals.' The Iroquois, according to Morgan, maximized individual freedom while seeking to minimize excess governmental interference in peoples' lives. The government sat lightly upon the people, who in effect were governed but little." [6]

In 1930, Arthur Pound wrote, "...in this constitution of Five Nations are found practically all of the safeguards which have been raised in historic parliaments to protect home affairs from centralized authority."[7] In 1940, Clark Wissler mentioned the advice given by the Iroquois chief, Canassatego at the Lancaster, Pa. treaty of 1744 to the effect that the colonists could benefit by forming a union along Iroquoian lines.[8]

Evidence to support Iroquois influence goes on and on. Dr. Bruce Johansen's book, *Forgotten Founders*, is an excellent reference for further study. Dr. Gregory Schaaf has produced a pamphlet, "The Great Law of Peace & the Constitution of the United States of America." In it he compares our Constitution, article by article, to the Great Law of Peace (Kaianerekowa) of the Haudenausaunee, Iroquois Confederacy which was founded sometime between the 10th and 15th centuries. Even the preamble has a striking resemblance to the opening oration (wampums 1, 2, & 3) of the Kaianerekowa.[9]

Both Drs. Schaaf and Johansen were excited by the information I shared with them for the case for a Masonic connection to the Constitution. Especially intriguing is an article by Arthur C. Parker, 32^0 (great-nephew of Ely S. Parker) *American Indian Freemasonry*, by Dr. A. Parker describes the similarity in ideology and message of Iroquois ritual to that of Freemasonry.[10] Again, this leads to a logical conclusion that both the Iroquois and the Freemasons were of a similar persuasion to produce democratic societies. It makes it easier to understand why certain influential Iroquois leaders were receptive to join the white man's Freemasonry– Joseph Brant, and later, Ely Parker being two of the more notable.

In 1987 the Freemasons of Cayuga-Tompkins district commissioned my wife, Gloria, to write a play about the making of the Constitution. She researched the subject thoroughly and produced a three-act play which was presented, in Colonial costume, in 7 areas of central NYS. Her bibliography included a book, *A Machine That Would Go of Itself*, by Pulitzer Prize-winning, Prof. Michael Kammen. He is considered one of the foremost experts on American history.

I invited him to critique the play. He was impressed with Acts 1 and 2 and how well Gloria had captured the essence of the issues and how those issues were resolved. But he could not accept Act 3. The third act is presented as a hypothetical meeting of Freemasons discussing the role that Freemasons played in the formation of the Constitution. He questioned whether Freemasons had any more influence than did any other group. He said to me, "George, my uncle was a Mason and I am not anti-Mason, but the Presbyterians, Anglicans, Methodists and every other religion or group could make the same claim as do the Freemasons." My first reaction was to accept his critique and to ask Gloria to change Act 3. Gloria's response was, "my research is accurate and authentic for Act 3 as well as it is for the first two."

So I did some research of my own. Fortunately, nearly every American publication has been providing researched articles on the making of the Constitution. Perhaps the best is the *Masonic Philatelist* magazine, Dec. 1985 issue. See the bibliography for others.

My conclusions are that Prof. Kammen is wrong. His contention is that the Presbyterians, Anglicans, Methodists and every other religious group could claim their influence. Anyone who understands the nature of Freemasonry and how it differs from religions could not make that statement. It was the very first, and still is today, the strongest force in the world for ecumenicalism. It teaches unity. Rudyard Kipling said, "Where else can I sit with a Moslem, a Jew, a Christian, a Hindu and still be among brothers?" On the other hand, even level-headed George Washington refused to send his step-son to New Jersey College (now Princeton) because he was suspicious of that "nest of Presbyterians."[11]

Freemasonry was an important force which helped to bind the colonies into one common cause and to minimize distrust and suspicions of each other's political agendas. The slave states distrusted the non-slave states and vice-versa. The large states had different interests than did the small states. And so it went. Freemasonry was the cement of brotherly love and trust– the strongest binding agent known to man. George Washington, the Freemason, used the Masonic expression, "cement" often in his correspondence about the Constitution. By contrast, there was little unity within the various religious communities. There was not a unified education system nor was there a national unity or a unity of the press.

At the same time, a less than honorable characteristic of humans is that we allow our egos to lead us to believe that our religion, our color, our position in life, our style of haircut, etc. is the best. The nature of Freemasonry and its POWER is that it helps to minimize elitism. It is a mechanism to help us be less suspicious of our neighbor.

It is reasonable to assume that this power of Freemasonry helped break down the barriers of suspicion between the various interests represented at the convention. It was Franklin's reputation as a Freemason that allowed him to meet and discuss the need for French support to the American cause. How much more effective was his and Washington's Masonic connection to sway opinions those summer evenings of 1787!

Beyond the nature and power of Freemasonry to develop a bond of trust, there were these many framers of the Constitution and civic leaders who were exposed to Freemasonry and its teachings.

George Washington, LaFayette, Von Steuben, Past Grand Masters Franklin, Livingston, Blair, Bedford, Randolph, Brearly, Dr. Joseph Warren are just a few of those of influence who had Masonic credentials. Brother John Hancock was involved in writing the Bill Of Rights. Grand Master Randolph would not sign the Constitution because it did not contain the guarantees of such a Bill. When he was assured that it would be added later, he fought for ratification of the document. The Bill of Rights reads like a Masonic lecture.[12]

The preamble is filled with Masonic vocabulary and thought.

It's, "We the people". It is not we the rulers, not we the wealthy, the strong, the ruling class. It's we the people meeting upon the level and parting upon the square. Freemasonry had taught the blessings of a "perfect Union." Likewise to "establish justice for all"– the low, the high the rich, the poor (not just the high and mighty); this was a new idea for government, but not a new idea for Freemasonry. And to "insure domestic tranquility" is to promote the doctrine of unity– "how pleasant it is for brethren to dwell together in unity". Freemasonry has always taught unity and exhorts its members that, "harmony being the strength and support of all institutions."[13]

"Freemasonry's goal of universal brotherhood leads naturally to the ideals of the inherent political equality of all people and their right to personal liberty within a harmonious social context."[14]

Freemasonry has always stood for freedom of religion– "seek light (in the Holy scriptures) as ye there shall find it."

Equality before the law– "all on the level."

Equality of opportunity– "a place for the high, the low, the rich, the poor."

The need for universal education– "to improve myself," "to seek light."

And so it goes; every lecture of the three degrees defines principles which we find in the Constitution.

It can be said that Freemasonry was the only institution born in Europe which embodied in its nature the freedoms of the American Constitution. Even today, Europeans are still somewhat awed by royalty and the concept of inherited authority. The thought that allowed for a break-away from this inherited ideology was born of contemplative minds.

Freemasonry teaches that we should reflect regularly on matters to help us be better citizens and better disciplined to be just and upright individuals. Our ritual, like the ritual of the Iroquois, is designed to help us be contemplative. This leads to the awareness of who and what we are and what we are here to do.[15]

Having been exposed to Iroquois Indian culture and having experienced the tyranny of unrepresentative government, the framers of the Constitution were primed to be receptive to concepts of Freedom. Furthermore, at least 31 of the 55 delegates had been exposed to the concepts taught in Freemasonry.

Yes it was a miracle wrought at Philadelphia that hot summer of 1787. But it was much more than that. It was a masterpiece put together by many master craftsmen and by mostly very learned people. Most of them were well versed in the propositions of other systems of government. They had seen the model made by the Iroquois. They saw that it worked to guarantee the freedoms which heretofore had only been discussed as being ideal. Freemasons especially were receptive to concepts of freedom and equality. Though the delegates came from different parts of the country and with different agendas, the Masonic connection served as a cement to bind them into a common cause.

Written: 1987 – for the Bicentennial of the U.S. Constitution
Presented to the American Lodge of Research, June 10, 1988
Published in the *Transactions of the American Lodge of Research*, Volume XX. 1991.

References:

1. Dr. Frank Annunziata, Prof. of American History, Rochester Institute of Technology– talk to NY College, S.C.R.I.F. Aug. 23, 1986 (recording provided by Dr.S. Sturges)
2. Michael Kammen. *A Machine That Would go of Itself*. Alfred A. Knopf. 1986
3. American Indian Program, Cornell University Sept 11 & 12 1987
4. "The Iroquois: Keeper of the Fire." *National Geographic*. Sept. 1987
5. American Indian Program. Cornell University. Sept. 1987
6. Bruce E. Johansen. *Forgotten Founders*. Gambit Inc. 1982
7. ibid
8. ibid
9. Dr. Gregory Schaaf. *The Great Law of Peace & the Constitution of the United States of America*.
10. Arthur C. Parker. *American Indian Freemasonry*. 1919
11. "Signers of the Constitution of the United States." *Masonic Book Club*. Vol. 7. 1976
12. "Freemasonry and the Constitution." *Masonic Philatelist*. Dec. 1985
13. "We the People– The U.S. Constitution & Freemasonry." *Masonic Service Association*. Mar. 1985

14. Sion Honea. *Freemasonry*. 1988
15. George Peter. "Rites of Passage." 1987

Bibliography

Annals of American History, Volumes 2, 3 & 4
Milton R. Benson. "Masonic Presidents and the Constitution." *Miscellanea*. Vol.12 part six 1987
Alphonse Cerza. "Masonic Parallels with History." *Masonic Service Association*
Henry C. Clausen. "Why Paint the Lily." May 1984
Conference on Indian Affairs. Cornell University. Sept. 1987
"Countdown to a Miracle." *Readers Digest*. Sept. 1987
Marcus Cunliffe. *George Washington, Man & Monument*. 1960
"Freemasonry & The Constitution." *Masonic Philatelist*. Vol. 41 #4 Dec. 1985
Wm. T. Hagan. *Longhouse Diplomacy & Frontier Warfare*
"The Iroquois, Keepers of the Fire." *National Geographic*. Vol. 172, #3 Sept. 1987
"James Madison, Architect of the Constitution." *National Geographic*. Vol. 172, #3 Sept. 1987
Bruce E. Johansen. *Forgotten Founders*. Gambit Inc. 1982
Michael Kammen. *A Machine That Would go of Itself*. Alfred A. Knopf. 1986
"The Miracle at Philadelphia." *U. S. News & World Report*. April 27, 1987
Edmund S. Morgan. *The Genius of George Washington*. 1980
Arthur C. Parker. Ely S. Parker- Man and Mason. *Transactions of the American Lodge of Research*. Vol. 7 #2 (Notes on E.S. Parker- Man & Mason by Temple Holcroft)
Arthur C. Parker. *American Indian Freemasonry*. Buffalo Consistory. 1919
George Peter. "The Rites of Passage." 1987
George Peter. "We The People." 1986
Thomas E. Rigas. "Celebrating Our Constitution." *Knight Templar Magazine*. Sept. 1987
Allen E. Roberts. Articles on the making of the Constitution. *Philalathes Magazine*. June, August, & Oct. 1987
Dr. Gregory Schaaf. *The Great Law of Peace & The Constitution of the United States of America*.
"Signers of the Constitution of the United States." fwd. by Wendell K. Walker. *Masonic Book Club*. Vol. 7. 1976
"We The People- The U.S. Constitution and Freemasonry." *Masonic Service Association*. Mar. 1985
Esmond Wright. *Franklin of Philadelphia*. Belknap Press, Harvard. 1986

New Roof: Corning Press Release
May 21, 1989

"NEW ROOF," a play about the making of the U. S. Constitution, is to be presented Sunday, May 21, 1989. This date is set for area residents to celebrate the 200th Anniversary of the inauguration of the first president of the United States of America. The play will be preceded by the re-enactment of the first inauguration. The program will commence at 3:00 PM in the Scottish Rite Cathedral in Corning, N.Y.

The actual first inauguration took place 200 years ago on April 30, 1789. New York State Freemasons celebrated this event in New York City where Former Chief Justice Warren E. Burger participated in the ceremony on April 30, 1989. New York's 124,000 Freemasons, members of the world's oldest and largest fraternal order, have a special reason for commemorating the Bicentennial of George Washington's first inauguration, according to Roswell T. Swits of Schenectady, Grand Master of Masons in New York. "It was virtually an all Masonic ceremony," he said "and it took place at Federal Hall in New York City, then the fledgling nation's capital." What was unique, according to Swits, was not that Washington was a Freemason (many of the Founding Fathers, including 13 signers of the Constitution, belonged to the ancient order). It was that the oath of office was administered by Chancellor Robert R Livingston, then Grand Master of Masons in New York. The oath was given on a Bible borrowed by Major Jacob Morton, a Washington aide and the Master (presiding officer) of St. John's Lodge No. 1, located then around the corner from the scene.

In this Bicentennial year, President George Bush took his oath of office as our 41st President on that same Bible, still in possession of the Lodge, on January 20th, in Washington, D.C. Three other American Presidents, Warren G. Harding, Dwight D. Eisenhower, and Jimmy Carter, have done likewise, although only Harding was a Freemason. All told, 14 Presidents have been Freemasons, the latest was Gerald Ford. Two of these, Andrew Jackson and Harry Truman, served as Grand Masters in their States.

During April and May, New York Masonic Lodges will pay special tribute to their renowned brother by holding special observances and taking note of this historic date and event. "All will recall Washington's service as Master of his Lodge in Alexandria when he was President and his 46 years as a Freemason," said Swits.

This play was presented in eight different venues in the Finger Lakes region. The cast was in colonial costume and made up of Masons from the Cayuga Tompkins District. Copies of the U.S. Constitution were distributed to the audience after the play. Copies were provided by Congressman Frank Horton.

New Roof
A three-act Play by Gloria Peter

ACT I – The Blueprint

(Scene shows a large picture frame in center stage. Curtains allow only picture frame to be seen. Washington enters stage left, in front of curtains, speaks, exits same as entry)

<u>GEORGE WASHINGTON</u>: You will permit me to say, that a greater drama is now acting on this theater than has heretofore been brought on the American stage, or any other in the world. We exhibit at present the novel and astonishing spectacle of a whole people deliberating calmly on what form of government will be most conducive to their happiness; and deciding, with an unexpected degree of unanimity, in favor of a system which they conceive calculated to answer the purpose.[1]

<u>NICHOLAS GILMAN</u>: (Enter stage rt. Stands at rt. of frame.) Good evening. I'm sure you recognized the gentleman who just spoke to you. You probably don't know me that well. My name is Nicholas Gilman and I am one of the youngest signers of the Constitution, representing New Hampshire. Ben Franklin is the oldest delegate at the Federal Convention. But I'm here to try to help you understand how and why this great government of ours is coming into existence.

      We have the Continental Congress so why do we need something else? That congress was just what we needed during war time. And we have a union of States, each of which has a constitution of its own. But something is wrong and many figure they know just what it is. As Noah Webster has written–

<u>NOAH WEBSTER</u>: (Appears behind frame, speaks, leaves) The American states, as to their general internal police, are not united: there is no supreme power at their head; they are in a perfect state of nature and independence as to each other; each is at liberty to fight its neighbor and there is no sovereign to call forth the power of the continent to

quell the dispute or punish the aggressor. It is not in the power of the Congress. They have no command over the militia of the states– each state commands its own, and should any one be disposed for civil war, the sword must settle the contest and the weakest be sacrificed to the strongest.

BENJAMIN RUSH: (Appears behind frame, speaks, leaves.) Most of the present difficulties of this country arise from the weakness and other defects of our governments. These consist first, in the deficiency of coercive power;[2] second, in a defect of exclusive power to issue paper money and regulate commerce, third, in vesting the sovereign power of the United states in a single legislature; and fourth, in the too frequent rotation of its members. The custom of turning men out of power or office as soon as they are qualified for it has been found to be absurd in practice.

OLIVER ELLSWORTH: (from behind frame.) The territory, later known as Vermont, is claimed by its neighbors, New York, Mass., and New Hampshire. Neither State is willing to give up its rights and Congress can do nothing about it.

FRONTIERSMAN: (From behind frame.) Foreign attitude toward the United States is causing us loss of trade. England refuses to sign a treaty with us, France is unwilling to sign a trade treaty, and Spain refuses to grant the U.S. free navigation on the Mississippi River and the "right of deposit" at New Orleans.

CONGRESSMAN: (From behind frame.) When Congress asked the states for $11,000,000 to run the government they came up with less than $1,500,000. There is nothing we can do about the situation.

GILMAN: So you see, we have a National deficit even before we have a president to blame it on. But the constitutional Convention came about as sort of an accident. Another dispute arose between Virginia and Maryland over navigation rights on the Potomac. Washington called a meeting of the two states at his home. The next year a conference was to be held in Annapolis. Only five states sent representatives to this meeting, and it was decided to ask Congress to call a Convention to revise the Articles of Confederation. It was evident, however, that a revision was not enough– A new type of stronger government would have to be created to meet the needs of the times.

(Scene changes to convention. While Gilman is speaking, the Scene of Convention floor is opened behind him and the frame is removed. Washington's podium is to the left. A few delegates sit to left and back of him.)

GEORGE WASHINGTON: "It is too probable that no plan we propose will be adopted. If to please the people, we offer what we ourselves disapprove, how can we afterwards defend our work? Let us raise a standard to which the wise and honest can repair. The event is in the hand of God."[3]

GILMAN: Fifty-five delegates from twelve states are to be in attendance. Rhode Island is not represented. The members are relatively young but their experience is high. Almost three quarters of them have served in Congress. Most of them have worked in state government as well. Over half are lawyers and quite a few of them have lived abroad or in states other than those they represent here. Those who have already arrived have selected George Washington to preside. Some of our well known leaders are not here. Thomas Jefferson and John Adams are representing our country abroad. Thomas Paine and Sam Adams were not elected delegates. Patrick Henry, who is an elected delegate, is not here because he mistrusts the convention. Today, we are listening to some of those who will take part in the debates.

(More delegates arrive– one or two at a time.)

After an all day delay while waiting for most of the delegates to arrive, the convention finally opens. Though it will be kept secret, James Madison will keep notes so future readers can see what actually happened behind the closed doors.

G. WASHINGTON: Will the Secretary please call the roll.

(background of roll-calling while Gilman continues)

GILMAN: With twelve separate state governments represented there is agreement, believe it or not, on a few essential parts of what a new government should contain if there were to be a national government at all. The secretary is listing these points.

WM. JACKSON: (as secretary) The new Congress should have the powers to levy and collect taxes and regulate foreign and interstate commerce.
    2.) There should be a national executive to enforce the laws.
    3.) A national judiciary should be created.
    4.) Property rights should be safeguarded.
    5.) The powers of the common people should be limited.

GILMAN: Although there will be more debate to follow on some of these items, it is a start. Some delegates from larger states were here on the designated date and spent their time formulating their plan of government. This "bundle of compromises," as the future document may well be called, receives the first push when Gov. Randolph presents the plan on which the early arrivers have worked.[4]

Gov. RANDOLPH: Mr. Madison's plan, submitted by Virginia, is this: The national legislature ought to consist of two branches. Members of the first should be elected by the people, the second elected by those of the first. A national executive should be instituted, elected by the Legislature (who with a council) have the authority to examine every act of the national legislature and every act of a particular legislature before it becomes final. A national judiciary should be established and inferior tribunals to be chosen by the national legislature. Provision should be made for the admission of new states and these states should be guaranteed a republican government. Provision should be made for the revision and amendments for the Articles of Union for the continuation of Congress.

WM. PATTERSON: On behalf of the smaller states I would like to propose the New Jersey Plan, which goes back to the modification of the Articles of Confederation, but will strengthen the federal government, giving them limited powers. The United States would remain a confederation of limited powers representing not people but strong state governments, each with an equal voice.

(Much dissention among the delegates)

GILMAN: Madison and Wilson lead the attack against this plan. Alexander Hamilton uses the occasion to voice his strong nationalist views. It seems now that it is well under-stood that the conflict of equality is not only large states against small ones. The real difference is between North and South. Slavery is the subject that really divides the five southern states against the eight northern ones.

COL. MASON: The delegation from Delaware is obliged by their instructions to withdraw if the matter of representation is even discussed.

MADISON: The equality of suffrage established by the Articles of Confederation ought not to prevail in the national legislature– An equitable ratio of representation ought to be substituted.

WASHINGTON: In view of the circumstances, we will postpone the vote to a later date.

PATTERSON: Most of the delegates are ordered by their instructions not to alter the established rule of suffrage.[5]

BREARLY: I second that. Unless each state had had an equal vote under the Articles, the smaller states would have been destroyed before this.

PATTERSON: We have no power to go beyond the federal scheme; and if we had such, the people are not ripe for any other. We must follow the people; the people will not follow us. There is no more reason for a rich state to have more votes than a poor one.

WILSON: If the smaller states do not unite, the larger states might be reduced to "confederation" among themselves. If such a partial union has to be formed, it would leave the door open for the others to come in when they see the wisdom in it.

PATERSON: Let them unite if they please, but they have no authority to compel the others to unite. New Jersey would never confederate. She would be swallowed up.

WILSON: The majority, or even a minority of states, have a right to form a union and the rest of you can do as you please. The equality can not be retained when a state has been made a member of a civil government. Shall New Jersey have the same influence on government as Pennsylvania? I say "no." I will never confederate on the plan!

BUTLER: Money is power and ought to have weight in government in proportion to the wealth. South Carolina has perhaps 11,000 more inhabitants than Connecticut. But in South Carolina 100,000 of the inhabitants are slaves. This would give the few inhabitants of Connecticut, with few slaves, greater voting power than South Carolina.

KING: Let's try a trial vote to the effect that suffrage in the first branch be according to some equitable ratio.

GILMAN: So the battle goes on from June 10 to July 18, almost a month and a half. At last Connecticut proposes an acceptable, if not pleasing plan. The Connecticut Compromise is presented by Roger Sherman and backed by Wm. Johnson.

SHERMAN: A large part of the Virginia plan is agreeable to all the delegates, but knowing that neither the large states or small states will give up to the other in the area of representation, let there be two houses in the Legislature; Representation by population in the lower house and each state would have an equal vote in the upper house.

GILMAN: With the "great compromise" achieved, the others come about more quickly.[6]

MADISON: We have come to an agreement to follow the Ruling of the Confederate Congress of four years past: count three-fifths of the slaves for purposes of both representation and taxation.

JACOB BROOM: Who has the authority to tax? We feel that measures of taxation should originate in the House, to which we elect members directly. Amendments could be made by the Senate representing state governments. Taxes should be uniform throughout the United States. Export taxes should be abolished.

DAN CARROLL: The Separation of powers among the three branches of the national government, along with a system of checks and balances, is one of the neatest compromise solutions imaginable. For example, the President has veto power over Congress but Congress, by a 2/3 vote in each house, override that veto. And while the judicial branch might denounce laws as unconstitutional, the president through his appointing powers, and Congress, through its power to change the number of judges, could indirectly change the Supreme Court's mind.

RUFUS KING: And what about commerce? The Northern states would hope that federal navigation acts would favor American ships over foreign both in coastal or overseas trade. The South who are the major exporters, but are not ship owners, would like foreign ships to be admitted to ports without discrimination so they could benefit from the competition among the ship owners.

COL. MASON: The South is willing to forgo a total ban on navigation acts in favor of the requirement of a two/thirds vote in each house of Congress to enact such measures. Further, we will give up effort to restrict navigation acts in exchange for a Northern agreement not to ban the importation of slaves prior to 1808 or to tax imported slaves more than $10 each.

GUNNING BEDFORD: The most difficult of solutions involves the presidency. To effect a compromise between those who fear a single executive is no different than a king and those who fear direct election by the people who may not be qualified voters; and between those who fear popular vote would give the larger states the advantage and those who feel that selection by the Congress destroys separation of powers, we have agreed upon the following: whereby a single executive would be elected for a four year term by electors in each state appointed as "the Legislature thereof may direct...equal to the whole Number of Senators and Representatives to which each State may be entitled to in Congress."[7]

GILMAN: And so after a long summer and with many, many little details ironed out, the delegates feel the secrecy can be lifted and their work be put to the test. We are not all that happy with the results. Some of us have departed earlier. Two of New York's delegation of three, Robert Yates and John Lansing, have returned home in protest over abandoning the Articles of Confederation. Rhode Island did not even send a delegate. Mr. Randolph will not sign the document because he feels the object of the Convention would be frustrated by the alternative which it presents to the people, and he predicts nine states "might fail to ratify." This does not mean however, that he opposes the Constitution. Mr. Blount of N.C. and Mr. Gerry decline to sign. Only 39 of the 55 working delegates will sign this document and some will do so reluctantly. Alexander Hamilton, Chairman of the Revision Committee, will give the instrument its final touches– including the Preamble. Half of the battle won, the Constitution written, our Mr. Franklin watches his fellow signers. Pointing to the picture of the sun, half up, carved on the back of the President's chair, he says–

(During the above speech by Gilman, the delegates file one at a time to the secretary's desk and sign the document.)

MR. FRANKLIN: I've been full of hope and fears during this Convention that whenever I looked at that sun behind the President, I could not say whether it was rising or setting. Now I do know; it is a rising and not a setting sun."

END of Act I.

NEW ROOF ACT II – Building

(This act opens with the map in place. Speakers #6 through 11 speak through map windows.)

GILMAN: Now that the Constitution is written, ahead of us lies the rest of the battle for a new government. In some way, or somehow, we must put the Constitution into effect. The federalists among the delegates found ratification by the state legislators to be unacceptable. They felt it would give the document the aspect of a treaty. Only endorsement by popular conventions would make it a real Constitution. At last the Confederate Congress got around to considering the document and after bitter debate over its merits, decided to send the proposed Constitution to the states. Even here Congress has not indicated their approval. So now we are in the thick of the battle. Among the State leaders there is no lack of indication– of approval or disapproval.

#6 SAM ADAMS: "I confess as I enter the building, I stumble at the threshold. I meet with a national government, instead of a federal union of sovereign states…If the several states in the union are to become one entire nation, under one legislature, the powers of which shall extend to every subject of legislation, and its laws be supreme and control the whole, the idea of sovereignty in these states must be lost." Above all, we must have a bill of rights.

#7 JAMES MADISON: "The second object, the due partition of power between the general and local governments was, perhaps of all, the most nice and the most difficult accomplishment of the Convention. As I formerly intimated to you my opinion in favor of this ingredient, I will take this occasion of explaining myself on the subject. Such a check on the states appears to me necessary (1) to prevent encroachments on the general authority; (2) to prevent instability and injustice in the legislation of the states."

#8 RICHARD H. LEE: "Our object has been all along to reform our federal system, and to strengthen our government...but a new object now presents. The plan of government now proposed is evidently calculated totally to change, in time, our condition as a people." "When power is once transferred from the many to the few, all changes become extremely difficult; the government, in this case, being beneficial to the few, they will be exceedingly artful and adroit in preventing any measures which may lead to change; and nothing will produce it, but great exertions and severe struggles on the part of the common people."

#9 ALEXANDER HAMILTON: "The great source of all the evils which afflict republics is that the people are too apt to make choices of rulers who are either politicians without being patriots, or patriots without being politicians…Whether the new Constitution, if adopted will prove adequate–time, the mother of events, will show. For my own part, I sincerely esteem it a system which, without the finger of God, never could have been suggested and agreed upon by such a diversity of interests. I will not presume to say that a more perfect system might not have been fabricated; but who expects perfection at once?"

#10 PATRICK HENRY: "What right had they to say, 'we, the people'? My political curiosity, exclusive of my anxious solicitude for the public welfare, leads me to ask, who authorized them to speak the language of, we, the people, instead of we, the states? States are the characteristics and the soul of a confederation. If the states be not the agents of the compact, it must be one great consolidated, national government of the people of all the states."

#11 THOMAS JEFFERSON: "I like much the general idea of framing a government which should go on of itself peaceably, without needing continual recurrence to the state legislatures…I will now tell you what I do not like. First the omission of a bill of rights, providing clearly and without the aid of sophism for freedom of religion, freedom of the press, protection against standing armies, restriction of monopolies, the eternal and unremitting force of the habeas corpus laws, and trials by jury in all matters of fact triable by the laws of the land and not by the laws of nations...Let me add that a bill of rights is what the people are entitled to against every government on earth, general or particular, and what no just government should refuse or rest on inference."

GILMAN: Mr. Madison, Hamilton and John Jay have applied their writing talents and have been publishing their arguments in various newspapers under the penname 'Publius.' These letters have all been gathered into a paper called *The Federalist*. Regardless of the merits of the arguments on both sides, the supporters, by now known as Federalists, have the advantage. They are more organized, more united and are better politicians. They hold strategic positions in most of the states. Those against are widely scattered and though greater in numbers, no single issue could unite them all. So while the words have been flying back and forth, the state conventions are taking action on the Constitution.

BEDFORD: (from behind state window in map) December 7, 1787, Delaware unanimously endorses the Constitution. (All states remain at their windows until all have reported.)

GILMAN: Pennsylvania, one of the large states, had a bit more trouble. The opposition to the Constitution deliberately stayed away from the legislative chamber to prevent a ratifying convention from being summoned.

(This scene takes place in front of the map. Use the same background used for the Convention scene in first act. Penn State Legislature is in session.)

LEGISLATIVE SECRETARY: (calling roll) George Clymer, Wm. Findley, Thomas Fitzsimmons, Benjamin Franklin, Jared Ingersoll, Thomas Lloyd, Thomas Mifflen, Gouverneur Morris, Robert Morris, Thomas McKean, Benjamin Rush, John Smilie, Robert Whitehill, and James Wilson.

(When the name "Ingersoll" is called, there is a burst of loud voices and scuffling from outside. BEN RUSH and JAMES WILSON enter the room forcing WHITEHILL AND SMILIE ahead of them. They force

The Power and Passion of Freemasonry

them to be seated and hold them in their places while the roll is finished and all have answered).

PRESIDING OFFICER: A quorum having been reached, the legislature will proceed to set a date for the vote. We will convene on December 12 for the purpose of voting on the proposed Constitution. All in favor respond with the usual sign. (Ayes are loud and firm. The two nays are defeated.) Motion carried. This session is dismissed.

FORCED DELEGATES: (sputtering) But that's too soon. No time to prepare- much too soon.

GILMAN: So on December 12th-

BEN FRANKLIN: (pointing to the map) By a vote of 46 to 23 Pennsylvania endorses the Constitution.

DAVID BREARLEY: On December 18, the Constitution gets unanimous approval of the New Jersey legislature.

ABE BALDWIN: Without dissent, Georgia approves the Constitution on January 2nd, 1788.

ROGER SHERMAN: Connecticut, by a margin of 128-40 (3 to 1) endorses the Constitution on this January 9th.

GILMAN: Massachusetts finds the going a bit rougher. Sam Adams and John Hancock, as well as many other delegates to the state convention were skeptical. Hints of a high federal office for John Hancock seemed to help convince the "hold outs," including both of these gentlemen, to change their decisions. So we find-

RUFUS KING: February 6, 1788, Massachusetts ratifies the constitution.
JAMES MCHENRY: Today, April 26, Maryland defeats the opponents of the constitution by a 63 to 11 vote.

PIERCE BUTLER: South Carolina, despite misgivings about limited protection to both civil liberties and the slave trade, approves the Constitution by a vote of 149 to 73 on this date of May 23, 1788.

GILMAN: Many towns in New Hampshire had sent their delegates to the state legislature in February with instructions to vote against the Constitution. Those in favor of ratification managed to get an adjournment until June. By that time the proponents with persuasion and a promise to recommend 12 amendments, John Langdon was able to announce–

JOHN LANGDON: Acceptance of the Constitution by New Hampshire was achieved by a vote of 57 to 47 on this 21st day of June.

GILMAN: Under the Constitution, New Hampshire's acceptance could have triggered the beginning of the new government. But several other states, essential to the success of the endeavor, are deemed worth waiting for.

JOHN BLAIR: Virginia has much at stake. Patrick Henry, George Mason and Richard Henry Lee have spent a great effort to bring out the opposition. They are very persuasive. But Washington, James Madison, Edmund Randolph (the same Randolph who would not sign the document), and John Marshall are just as able supporters. To answer Patrick's demand for a bill of rights before ratification, James Madison pledged to work for such amendments after ratification. Approval for the Constitution is won on June 26 by an 89 to 79 majority.

HAMILTON: Prospects have looked dim in New York. New York City is favorable, but the up-staters, followers of Gov. Clinton, are suspicious of the Constitution and of those who are backing it. A vote to approve it only if it were amended to protect civil liberties lost 29 to 31. Ratification has finally been achieved on this 26th day of July by a 30 to 27 vote.

GILMAN: Only two states, North Carolina and Rhode Island rejected the proposed Constitution. But when the new congress proposed amendments which became the Bill of Rights, North Carolina held another convention and voted to join the Union. Rhode Island still opposed it. They had sent no delegates to the convention and refused to call a ratifying convention preferring to use a popular referendum. Advocates of a ratification refused to participate in the referendum. But by 1790 they at last join the Union by a narrow 34 to 32 vote. Vermont is admitted to the Union on January 10, 1791.

(George Washington walks out in front of the map. All at the state windows remain through his comments)

GEORGE WASHINGTON: "The reflection on the days of difficulty and danger which are past is rendered more sweet from a consciousness that they are succeeded by days of uncommon prosperity and security. If we have wisdom to make the best use of the advantages with which we are now favored, we cannot fail under the just administration of a good government, to become a great and happy people. The citizens of the United States of America have a right to applaud themselves for having given to mankind examples of an enlarged and liberal policy, a policy worthy of imitation. All possess alike liberty of conscience and immunities of citizenship. It is now no more that toleration is spoken of as if it was by the indulgence of one class of people that another enjoyed the exercise of their inherent natural rights. For happily the government of the United States, which gives to bigotry no sanction, to persecution no assistance, requires only that they who live under its protection should demean themselves as good citizens, in giving it on all occasions their effectual support."

END Act II

ACT III – Celebration

GILMAN: It is 1789, a few months after the inauguration of President Washington. Past Grand Master Ben Franklin has summoned several well known Freemasons to a special communication at the Blue-Ox tavern in Philadelphia. Although the meeting and place are fictitious, the people and facts presented are authentic.

(Scene opens on a Colonial Table Lodge. MW Benjamin Franklin is presiding.)

FRANKLIN: Thank you for your presence here in our great city of Philadelphia. A special thanks to those of you who have returned so soon after a previous sojourn. But I feel that your effort has been worth while. This has been a most productive meeting. Now may I present the Grand Officers among us? It is my honor to present to you Past Grand Master of Virginia, Most Worshipful John Blair. He is a signer of the Constitution and was third in seniority at the Convention. Another signer of the Constitution, the First Grand Master of New Jersey, MW

David Brearly. He is a member of the legal profession. I present MW Robert R Livingston, Grand Master of Masons in the State of New York. And now MW Gunning Bedford, Grand Master of Delaware and presently District Court Judge. Assist me in affording Grand Honors to these esteemed Brothers. (All do so)

Now, will the rest of the brothers please introduce yourselves, giving your state, occupation and position? We will commence on my left.

(The following introduce themselves)

DANIEL CARROL: I am Dr. Daniel Carroll from Maryland.

JACOB BROOM: also of Delaware. Founder and treasurer of the Wilmington library, and soon to be the first Postmaster of Wilmington.

JONATHAN DAYTON: I come from New Jersey where I am a member of the state Legislature.

JOHN DICKENSON: A member of Pennsylvania Lodge #18 located in Dover, Delaware.

RUFUS KING: of Massachusetts, which I represented at the Constitutional Convention. I am now a member of the New York Legislature and a United States Senator from New York.

JOHN HANCOCK: Governor of Massachusetts.

JAMES MCHENRY: of Maryland and member of the Maryland Legislature.

WILLIAM PATERSON: United States Senator from New Jersey.

GEORGE WALTON: presently, the governor of Georgia.

BEVERLY RANDOLPH: current Governor of Virginia.

NICHOLAS GILMAN: U.S. Representative in Congress from New Hampshire.

SAMUEL JOHNSON: from North Carolina and present Governor.

GEORGE WASHINGTON: Master, Alexandria Lodge #39, Virginia and President of the United States.

JACOB MORTON: Master of St. John's Lodge #1 of New York City- We are proud to state our bible was borrowed for the Presidential Oath.

MAJOR MORGAN LEWIS: of New York, who with Major Morton here, was a parade Marshal for the presidential inauguration.

FRANKLIN: Thank you, Brethren. Will all of you who signed the Constitution please rise.

(The 12 who signed stand– Washington, Blair, Brearly, Paterson, Dayton, Bedford, Dickenson, Broom, King, McHenry, Carroll and Gillman)

SAM JOHNSON: Everyone should be aware that Grand Master Franklin also signed it. Brother Franklin also printed the first Masonic Book in America, in 1734.

FRANKLIN: While we are standing, please join me in honoring the memory of Past Grand Master of Virginia, Peyton Randolph, who was first president of the Continental Congress and died during the second Continental Congress. Also we honor the memory of Past Grand Master of Mass., Doctor and General Joseph Warren. He gave his life at the Battle of Bunker Hill. We will observe a moment of silence in memory of these esteemed brothers and to all those who gave their lives on both sides of the revolution. Now as first native Grand Master, I declare this communication closed. We will go to refreshment. Brother Joseph, we are ready for our repast. You may serve now.

(Brother Joseph turns to his staff and gives them instructions. They come and go attending their duties through out the rest of the act.)

FRANKLIN: Again, greetings to all our brothers. Since so many of us contributed efforts to the Constitution, either by helping to form it or to ratify it, I wonder if you have any notion of how Freemasons became so involved in the national government.

JOHN BLAIR: When one considers the diversity of the states, it seems to me that a singular fact stands out. A major force all of the states had in common was Freemasonry. All Freemasons adhere to a set of principles that have served us well everywhere in the colonies. We forged a chain of common beliefs across our country.

WASHINGTON: That is very true. Those beliefs and attitudes helped us during our fight for Independence- they were shared by a number of my generals and their men, including the great Marquis de Lafayette himself. But these principles apply themselves to peace and government as well as on the battlefield. I offer a toast to unity which comes from tolerance: (raises glass)

Here's to Unity and Tolerance
Our country needs so much.
We have given the example
Of this all-important touch.
As we strive to make men happy,
Let's try bigotry to crush
As truth goes marching on.

(All the others raise their glasses while singing this verse and then the chorus to the "Battle Hymn of the Republic.")

GILMAN: But are these Attitudes the attributes of Masons only? It seems to me that all parents strive to give their children a sense of responsibility, honesty, etc. What's so different about Freemasonry?

W. PATERSON: Well, everyone must admit that equality- every man at the same level- is a different concept. Most governments are based on divine right, rights of the few, or some other selection method. Even the thinking of many of our fellow countrymen today, find it hard to allow the uneducated to share the same basic rights as themselves.

SAM JOHNSON: That's true. Think of how hard it was to convince our legislatures to ratify the Constitution because of this stumbling block. I think we should drink a toast to equality:

To equality of mankind no matter what his lot.
Be he laborer or tradesman,
May the diff'rence be forgot.

As we strive to make life better
Let's include others in our plot
So truth goes marching on.

(All toast this verse)

But speaking of education, we Freemasons have promoted that since back in the middle ages.

JOHN BLAIR: I feel very strongly about that point. To seek light or knowledge was a firm idea in the minds of Free-masons back when education was proper for a very select few. Everyone's right to an education is a relatively new idea even today. I hope this concept can be strengthened so as to provide many opportunities for growth of light in future years.

JACOB MORTON: Also our feeling about knowledge has brought many of society's educated men into our fraternity. The encouragement to learn has proven to be an asset both to our craft and to the country. There's no denying that Masonic thinking has helped this country in many ways. So now I offer a toast to education:

To the light of education now to everyone extended.
May it lead our brand new nation to the greatness we intended.
As we strive to further knowledge let our efforts be un-ended
As truth goes marching on.

(All sing and toast as before)

BEVERLY RANDOLPH: Remember– we Masons are builders! When we have the right foundations, the will to work, the patience to do precise work, and the fortitude to see it through, we become ideal participants in any endeavor– be it following our vocations or building a new government. The daring and the effort that went into this Constitution is proof that we are more than capable of constructing a **NEW ROOF** for the edifice of State. So I offer a toast to the builders!

A toast to all the builders
Who have made our nation great.
They have proven it is wisdom
To contribute each man's weight

As they work to build our system
We'll not fail to appreciate
That truth is marching on.

(All sing)

WM. PATERSON: Have any of you ever– Sir, may I have a refill please (motions to one of serving staff)…Lets see– what was I saying? Have any of you ever thought about what part religion has played in all of this?

GEORGE WALTON: We know all Freemasons are encouraged to follow the religion of their choice, and that Freemasonry promotes no special creed. It asks only that we believe in a Supreme Being. But the fact is that our religious beliefs and moral codes have been a basic part of our country's development and well being.

WASHINGTON: Yes, I brought that out in my acceptance speech. If you will remember the words–"No people can be bound to acknowledge and adore the Invisible Hand which conducts the affairs of men more than those of the United States. Every step by which they have advanced to the character of an independent nation seems to have been distinguished by some token of providential agency–" I believe this with all my heart.

MAJOR LEWIS: We remember. Every facet of our past government and the new constitution– the very fiber of all of us has been illuminated by the Creator of the Universe. A toast to Divine Guidance whatever form it takes:

Here's to guidance and enlightenment of the great Creator's will.
May it strengthen our endeavors and our country's hopes fulfill.
As he strives to make men holy may we follow him until
Our truth goes marching on.

JOHN HANCOCK: Well, Brothers– We all have to agree that all of these attributes, Masonic or otherwise, will come to naught if we are ever denied the freedom to use them. Our potential is great; the country's potential is unlimited if freedom is foremost in the minds of leaders and followers alike. Freedom allowed us to become Freemasons. Masonry encourages us to become leaders. Leaders can and must ensure freedom.

LIVINGSTON: Exactly! Our Constitution guarantees more freedoms because it restrains government. As one man in the future will say, "Governments exist to restrain men; the Constitution exists to restrain government." So–

And most of all to freedom, which allows us to proceed
With the principles and virtues that we and our country need.
As we toil to make it stronger let us strive to keep men free
And truth will go marching on.

(All sing last two verses, including choruses.)

GILMAN: We have built a roof over the edifice of state. It is a **NEW ROOF**, but any roof must be maintained. New material may be needed from time to time, but the basic structure is sound and will survive. As our cast sings the last toast, we invite the audience to join us in the chorus. At close of singing copies of the constitution will be distributed to all present. Please study it. The rights and freedoms we Americans enjoy today are the results of what these men, by their conscientious efforts, have projected to us.

   (The cast and audience sing last verse with chorus and then, "God Bless America.")

George Peter

The Sullivan Expedition – The Masonic Connection
October 8, 1979

It is fitting to observe the Sullivan-Clinton Campaign on this 200th anniversary of that event. Some have argued that the expedition resulted in the abuse of the Indians of the Iroquois Confederacy and hence we ought not to so celebrate. The argument as to whether General George Washington was morally wrong to plan the campaign against the Indians, who were aiding the enemy, will be left to a companion paper to be presented by the Rev. Leonard Hackney.

We cannot escape history. Nor should we ignore the events that shaped so much the fate of the early foundation of our Republic.

This paper is concerned with the influence of Freemasonry in terms of the people involved who were Masons and with the influence of the expedition on the development of Freemasonry in the affected area.

Chief Joseph Brant was initiated into Masonry on April 26, 1776 in London, England. He was presented a Mason's apron by no less a person than King George III.[1] Sir William Johnson, Commissioner of Indian Affairs under British rule, was responsible for initiating into Freemasonry several Indian chiefs, including Chief Joseph Brant. Colonel John Butler and Captain Walter N. Butler, who led the attacks by the Tories and Indians at the Wyoming Valley and Cherry Valley "massacres," were both Freemasons.[1] Sir William Johnson took Brant's sister as his second wife. Joseph Brant was married to the daughter of George Croghan, who was a land trader for Sir William Johnson.

It seems logical to assume that Freemasonry was, at least in part, a factor in the early fraternization and intermarrying between the White settlers and the Indians. And it is evident that Freemasonry was introduced into the region affected by the Sullivan-Clinton Campaign, even before that expedition took place.

In early May, Thomas Proctor was commissioned a Colonel in the Army Artillery and was ordered to join the Sullivan-Clinton Campaign. On May 18th he received a warrant from the Grand Lodge of Pennsylvania for Military Lodge #19.[2] Two days later he left Philadelphia to join General Sullivan at Easton.

The old minute book is not available, but from the amount of money turned in to the Grand Lodge of Pennsylvania, it is calculated that more than 150 men were raised Master Masons during the expedition. A meeting of Military Lodge #19 was opened in due form on St. John's Day, June 24, 1779 at Wilkes-Barre Mountain in Col. Proctor's marquee. This was a few days after Sullivan's Army had come upon the graves of Freemasons Capt. Joseph Davis and Lt. William Jones, who had been ambushed and scalped by the Indians a few months earlier. The ambush had occurred while Davis and Jones were coming to the aid of the inhabitants of Wyoming, Pennsylvania.[1]

It is of interest to note that Military Lodge #19 opened almost every night during the campaign when the Army was encamped. Meetings were held either in Col. Proctor's marquee or General Sullivan's tent.

The delay in starting the expedition afforded General Sullivan the opportunity to assure that many of the officers selected for the Campaign were Freemasons. There were not sufficient Chaplains hence it was Sullivan's belief that the leaders who were Freemasons would be concerned about proper respect and treatment of those casualties of battle and "would administer solace and comfort to those wounded, sick and distressed men of his army." He wanted to be assured that those who died or were killed in battle would be given burial by men who believed in Almighty God.[3] This was demonstrated by the Army when a formal ceremony was held to re-inter the bodies of Capt. Davis and Lt. Jones. A Shrine to their memory stands to this day at Laurel Run on Wilkes-Barre Mountain.

Military Lodge #19 held its first Masonic Conclave in New York State in the valley of Catherine Creek at Millport, on what is now known as the "Pinnacle," under a large oak tree. The existing Lodge in Millport is Old Oak Lodge #253, named to commemorate that early meeting of Military Lodge #19.

The Sullivan Expedition moved North and West to carry out its assignment. The purpose of this paper is not to recall the military details of the mission. Sufficient material has been written and spoken on that subject elsewhere.

Because the record book of Military Lodge #19 is not available there is limited information of Masonic import that can be related. We do know that when Lt. Boyd and Sgt. Parker were on a scouting mission they and their company were ambushed and captured in the town of Groveland near Geneseo. Stories are attributed to the effect that Lt. Boyd was a Freemason and that he evidently knew Chief Joseph Brant was also. The story goes that he gave a Masonic appeal to the Chief who recognized it and spared his life. But later, when Brant was called away, the Indians under the leadership of Col. Walter Butler tortured Boyd and Parker in cruel and savage ways. There is no proof to this story, and in fact, Houghton claims that no such event took place nor is there proof that Boyd was a Freemason.[1, 3]

When Sullivan's Army came upon the savage deed, the remains of Boyd and Parker were interred with full Masonic rites.[1, 3] In later years Freemasons arranged to have their bodies removed to cemeteries in Rochester.

On the return trip Sullivan's Army, that had been divided to come down different shores of Seneca and Cayuga Lakes, met at a spot that is now Ithaca. A celebration was held and a Masonic conclave took place. A marker to commemorate that event was affixed to the North-east corner of the now-demolished Ithaca Hotel. It stood on the corner of Aurora and State Streets (now the Ithaca Commons). Hobasco Lodge #716 promoted a ceremony in 1954 to observe the 175th anniversary of the Sullivan Expedition and to rededicate the plaque. Grand Master Raymond C. Ellis was the featured speaker. The plaque is now in the possession of the DeWitt Historical Society. There seems to exist strong sentiment against relocating the plaque for fear of offending the Indians. As an editorial aside: This is the sign of our times. Everyone wants to be politically correct. We display paranoia, guilt and shame but have no sense of history. The event did take place. The Campaign played an important role in the shaping of our country.

The soldiers who served in Sullivan's Campaign returned with glowing accounts of the land, crops and orchards of the Finger Lakes region. When the land became available for settling these same soldiers and others who had served in the Army and had heard of this beautiful region, clamored to settle here. Because so many of these men were Freemasons, Freemasonry came and settled with them.

Union Lodge #30 in Newton, now Elmira, was warranted by Grand Master Robert R Livingston in 1793– just 14 years after Sullivan's battle there. The first Church was not formed until 1795.[3] (The Lodge is now #95 resulting from the surrender of its charter during the Morgan affair.)

The first Masonic Lodge in Cayuga County was Scipio #58 (now #110 for the same reason above assigned) in Aurora, New York. Thirteen settlers petitioned Grand Lodge for a charter in 1795– one year after the town of Scipio was formed. The Charter was signed by Grand Master Robert R Livingston in 1797. Seth Sherwood, a soldier, was the first Master. The Sr. Warden was Col. Comfort Tyler and the Jr. Warden was Gen. John Tillotson. He became the second Master because the Sr. Warden had moved to Syracuse.[4] It should come as no surprise to Freemasons that in the Fraternity rank is not a factor. Hence the General was third in command under the leadership of a soldier.

The second oldest building erected as a Masonic Temple in New York State still stands in Aurora, New York. It was completed in 1806 and is suitably recognized by a New York State Historical marker. Also the oldest building constructed for use by Royal Arch Masons is still in use as a Masonic Temple in Aurora. The Cornerstone was laid in 1819 by Governor and Grand Master DeWitt Clinton.[4] DeWitt Clinton was the son of General James Clinton of the Sullivan-Clinton Expedition.

The oldest Masonic Lodge in Ontario County was Ontario Lodge #23. The petition for it was submitted October 31, 1791. The Charter was granted in 1792 by Grand Master Robert R Livingston.[5] He had granted over 80 charters during his term as Grand Master.[6] The first Master of Ontario Lodge #23 was Doctor Timothy Hosner who had served in the Second Continental Artillery as a surgeon. The Lodge was closed during the Morgan affair and reorganized as Canandaigua Lodge #294 in 1853.[3]

The first Lodge to be organized in Monroe County was Morning Star #223 in Pittsford in 1810 but the first to receive a charter was Harmony #212 at Riga in 1811. The Charter was signed by Grand Master DeWitt Clinton. The petition was endorsed by Avon Lodge #130. The successor to Harmony Lodge is Churchville Lodge #667.[7] Ten new Lodges were formed in the Rochester area within the next decade.

Only a few of the earliest Lodges of the area have been mentioned. The purpose is to demonstrate how Freemasonry was born in this region along with the establishment of towns and settlements. From these early Lodges others were sponsored. For example, in Cayuga County all of the present twelve Lodges, and others who have since closed their doors, can trace their ancestry to the original Scipio Lodge #58 (now #110) of Aurora.[8] But more accurately, it can be said that Freemasonry in the Finger Lakes and surrounding regions can trace its ancestry to the soldier-Masons of the Revolutionary War and especially to those of the Sullivan-Clinton Expedition.

As for the non-Masons of the same region, they also owe a great debt of gratitude to the Sullivan-Clinton Campaign. Whether we can justify the campaign against the enemy or not, the fact is that the campaign against the Indians of the Iroquois Confederacy was a success. Crops were destroyed. Food supplies that otherwise could have been used by the British Army against the Colonial forces were cut off.[9] Even the best of historians are unable to calculate the important effect this

81

had on the course of events. But of even greater importance than the military aspects of the Campaign, it is a significant accomplishment that General Sullivan waged a major campaign against a formidable enemy in unknown territory with absolutely minimal casualties on either side. Prisoners were treated in a humane manner and with the kind of decency that could be expected from officers who were steeped in the teachings of the Craft called Freemasonry.

List of officers / Masonic Status [1, 2, 5, 10, 11, 12 & 13]
Sullivan Clinton Campaign

Officer	State	Known Freemason
General Sullivan	N.H.	Grand Master of NH - 1779
General Clinton	N.Y.	Warren #17
General Hand, Edward	PA	Military #19
General Poor		
Col. Proctor, Thomas	PA	PA #2, WM of Military #19
Col. Butler, William	PA	#29
Col. Bolton		
Col. Dearborn		
Col. Joseph Cilley	N.H.	St. Johns #1
Col. GanSeVoort, Peter	NY	Union #1
Col. Van Cortlandt		
Col. Hubley, Adam	PA	#29
Col. Dubois, Lewis	NY	Solomon #1
Gen. Dayton, Elias	NJ	Military #19
Maj. Fogg, Jerimiah	N.H.	Visited American Union Lodge
Gen. Schuyler, Philip		
Capt. Spaulding, Simon*	NY	Joined Union #30 in 1793
Col. Smith		
Col. Israel Shreve		
Col. Pawling		

* Note: Spaulding was later a General. It is not known if he was a Mason at the time of the Sullivan campaign.
Note 2: Those not listed as members of a Masonic Lodge may very well have been Freemasons. No proof has been verified by this author

References
1 "Sullivan," Harry S. Vorhis, *N.Y. Masonic Outlook*, 8, 79
2 "Early History of Union Lodge #95," William H. Arnold, *Elmira Masonic News*, 3-1929
3 "Masonry in Chemung County," Fred T. Westcott, *American Lodge of Research*, Vol. X, #2, 1967
4 *History of Scipio Lodge #110*, Temple Hollcroft
5 "History of Freemasonry in Ontario County," John H. Stelter, M.D., *American Lodge of Research*, Vol. VIII, #3, 1962
6 *History of Freemasonry in New York State*, Ossian Lang
7 "History of Freemasonry in Monroe County," Herman A. Sarachan, *American Lodge of Research*, Vol. VIII, #1, 1960
8 "Ancestry of Cayuga Lodge #221," Clyde Myers, Unpublished paper, c.a. 1969
9 New York History ... July 1979, NYS Historical Assoc., Cooperstown, New York
10 *Masonic Membership of the Founding Fathers*, Ronald E. Heaton, Masonic Service Association
11 "Tentative List of Revolutionary Soldier Masons," Richard Wright & George Arlock, *American Lodge of Research*, Vol. V, #1, 2, & 3; Vol. VI, #1 & 2
12 "Sullivan-Clinton Campaign– Bicentennial Commemorative," NYS Bicentennial Committee., Chemung County Historical Society & a group of 12 County Historians, 1979
13 "The Sullivan Expedition Centennial & its Relation to Masonic History in the State of New York," Raymond W. Houghton, American Lodge of Research, Vol. VIII #2

Moral Implications of the Sullivan Campaign
By Rev. Leonard P. Hackney – 1979

A consideration of the Sullivan campaign against the Iroquois Nation in 1779 presents all manner of difficulties. Violence, especially to the point of death and on the scale of war between nations, has been condemned by sensitive people as morally wrong for centuries. A campaign directed not only against combatants but also against the shelter and food supply of an enemy and inevitably against women, children and the helpless aged is difficult to justify on moral grounds.

The Sullivan expedition, as warfare directed against non-combatants, would have to be linked with similar efforts of many centuries. To be sure, additional instances do not absolve blame, but do put it in historical perspective. The devastation of the South in Sherman's march to the sea in the Civil War, saturation bombing of cities by both sides in World War II, the use of the atomic bomb against Japan and many others were all vastly larger and more destructive instances of effort to gain an advantage in conflict by deliberately subjecting the civilian population of the enemy to suffering and death. The effectiveness of such warfare is open to question; the moral implications are even more so. Nevertheless, it has been used and used widely over the centuries as a matter of policy or in desperation to attempt to save a losing cause or, as in the case of atomic bombing, to hasten the victory. It was probably used reluctantly but still used.

At the time of the conception of a war against the Six Nations, to ease the pressure of attacks on the American settlers and to divert the attention of the British and Tories from other areas, the war was in something of a stalemate. Any long prolongation of the stand-off was certain to work to the advantage of the British with their superior resources of men and materials. A negotiated peace would have left the revolutionists with a narrow strip of territory along the Atlantic seaboard and continued British presence and influence. This was a very real possibility. It would have come short of a defeat but would not have attained the aims of the revolution as conceived by its instigators.

The element of praise or blame for the Sullivan expedition cannot be ascribed to General Sullivan alone. Sullivan was more the agent than the initiator. Any kind of moral assessment must be laid at the door of Washington and his advisors. It was not a snap decision made in the heat of battle, but a carefully considered and well prepared campaign. Basically it was an effort to break the spirit of the Indian allies of the British and to convince all Indians of the area of the strength of the American effort and the likelihood, if not the certainty, of an ultimate American victory. Most of the Indians were simply hoping to be on the winning side. Their loyalties were shallow. Their fighting ability could be considerable when coupled with a winning effort. They had no stomach for hard fought campaigns where even occasional defeats were encountered. Convinced of defeat, the Indians might be neutralized or even become helpers of the revolutionary cause. The Sullivan campaign did result in exactly this condition. It accomplished Washington's hopes for it, probably more fully than he might have expected. In fact, this may have been the turning point of the entire war. As such, it may well have been justified in the mind of the revolutionary leaders and the unpalatable aspects of military advantage at the expense of non-combatants felt to be acceptable.

From the general point of view, warfare is accepted morally if kept within certain norms. Armed conflicts are seen as inevitable. It has always been a part of the life of nations and probably always will be. Wars and rumors of war are the norm. Limitations of warfare are also recognized. The enemy may be fought as long as he is fighting or continues as a threat. The attack may not be continued when he ceases to resist. To kill the wounded would be deemed savagery. To kill the surrendering soldier would not be acceptable. To wage war directly on women, children and the helpless aged would offend the moral standards of most nations. Most commanders, however, are willing to override these objections in the hope of victory. They are quite aware that excesses of force and even cruelty are often overlooked in victory and cynically unimportant to the longer verdict of history.

Masons tend to regard all principles of life and morality in terms of absolutes. A square is an angle of 90 degrees. A horizontal is a level. A vertical is an exact perpendicular. There are no hazy areas. Virtue lies not only in intent and direction but in implemented exactitude. Masons further affirm that there are corresponding absolutes in human character and human action. The undeviating perfection of the physical world, as seen in mathematics and in practice in the swing of the planets, etc., is matched by the inner quality of life that is set upon undeviating moral principles and expressed in absolutes of human behavior.

Unfortunately, absolutes cannot always be made the moral standard of practices and behavior. Our human imperfection and condition make this impossible. Imperfect people under the pressure of events have to make difficult compromises. Probably the nearest any group ever came to undeviating adherence to principles were the Scribes and Pharisees of the Christian era. These groups regularly sacrificed human values in rigid conformity to accepted absolutes. Far from being hailed as models of morality, they have merited universal condemnation and their names made synonymous with hypocrisy. Rather, absolutes of behavior must be regarded in terms of the ability of imperfect human beings to conform to them. Further, these same imperfect beings, often acting under stress, must balance out conflicting values on uncertain scales. Is there, perhaps, but one absolute in human relationships– the philosophical goal of the greatest good for the greatest number over the longest period of time? The hard choices that might attain this are what human life and its moralities are all about. That "the end justifies the means" is undeniably a morally dangerous doctrine, but that danger is modified when careful, prayerful men are seeking long-term good. The possible suffering that might come from their action to the enemy was, after all, no different than that which they had undertaken for themselves and their own families.

Addendum

Moral systems must necessarily be presented in terms of ideals and absolutes. The ideal always stands in judgment of the real of any given time. The dream of world peace is held in the midst of conflict. The abundant life is visualized in spite of poverty. Political freedom is seen under tyranny. The knowledge of ignorance points to the opportunity of all to learn. Peoples in anarchy dream of law and order. The list is endless. The common element in all is the partly-attained ideal. A practical morality, then, is seen in the individual honestly doing his best to measure up to a goal that is too far away for his attainment, but which lifts him to higher levels than he would have otherwise been able to reach.

Masonic morality tends to move in the area of ideals, but never loses sight of the real situation. The entered apprentice is not condemned because he cannot do the work of the fellowcraft. The fellowcraft is not censured because his standard falls below that of the master mason. The broad mantle of Masonic charity and understanding falls over all. The white leather apron of innocence does become stained in the stress and strain of life.

Let that same Masonic charity be extended to General Sullivan and through him to General Washington and his advisors. They dreamed of a free nation based on government of the people, by the people and for the people– as Lincoln would state it later. Their principles promised a good life for themselves and for all people over a long period of time. So desirable was this goal and so philosophically consistent with aspirations of free men over the centuries that even the excesses of war could be temporarily accepted in movement toward it.

References

1 "Sullivan," Harry S. Vorhis, *N.Y. Masonic Outlook*, 8, 79
2 "Early History of Union Lodge #95," William H. Arnold, *Elmira Masonic News*, 3, 1929
3 Masonry in Chemung County, Fred T. Westcott, *American Lodge of Research*, Vol. X, #2, 1967
4 *History of Scipio Lodge #110*, Temple Hollcroft
5 "History of Freemasonry in Ontario County," John H. Stelter, M.D., *American Lodge of Research*, Vol. VIII, #3, 1962
6 *History of Freemasonry in New York State*, Ossian Lang, Grand Lodge of the State of NY
7 "History of Freemasonry in Monroe County," Herman A. Sarachan, *American Lodge of Research*, Vol. VIII, #1, 1960
8 "Ancestry of Cayuga Lodge #221," Clyde Myers, unpublished paper, 1969
9 New York History ... July 1979, NYS Historical Assoc., Cooperstown, New York
10 "Masonic Membership of the Founding Fathers," Ronald E. Heaton, Masonic Service Assoc.
11 "Tentative list of Revolutionary Soldier Masons," Richard Wright & George Arlock, *American Lodge of Research*, Vol. V, nos. 1, 2 & 3, Vol. VI, nos. 1 & 2
12 "Sullivan-Clinton Campaign– Bicentennial Commemorative," NYS Bicentennial Committee., Chemung County Historical Society & a group of 12 County Historians, 1979
13 "The Sullivan Expedition Centennial & its Relation to Masonic History in the State of New York," Raymond W. Houghton, *American Lodge of Research*, Vol. VIII, #2

Dewitt Clinton: A Pillar of Power
Oct. 29, 1991

DeWitt Clinton was born Mar. 2, 1769, the son of James Clinton and Mary DeWitt. James Clinton was a Brigadeer General in the Patriot Army. Through his mother, DeWitt was first cousin to Simeon DeWitt, the early settler of Ithaca, N.Y.

DeWitt was raised in Holland Lodge in 1793. This was the same Lodge that Franklin D. Roosevelt later joined. In 1794, one year after being raised, DeWitt was Master of Holland Lodge. Another year later, he was elected Jr. Grand Warden of the Grand Lodge of the State of N. Y. He served as Jr. Warden through 1797 and was Sr. Grand Warden in 1798. In 1806 DeWitt Clinton was elected Grand Master in the State of N.Y. He served fourteen successive terms through 1819, when he was succeeded by Daniel Tompkins in 1820.

DeWitt Clinton graduated from Columbia College first in his class in 1786. He was admitted to the Bar in 1790 and almost immediately went to work as the secretary to his Uncle, Gov. George Clinton. He was 19 years old at the time.

In 1798 he was elected State Senator and in 1802 he was elected United States Senator from New York. Between 1803 and 1815 he served as Mayor of New York City, off and on, during which time he was serving as Senator or Lt. Governor. He was Lt. Governor between 1811 and 1813. In 1812 he was narrowly defeated for the Presidency by James Madison.

DeWitt Clinton was the sixth governor of New York State. He served from 1817 to 1822 and again from 1825 until his death on Feb. 11, 1828. Clinton declined to run for Governor in 1823. Joseph C. Yates, one of the founders of Union College succeeded Clinton for a two year term. He was aligned against Clinton in the political world.

Besides his dynamic activities in the Grand Lodge of the State of New York and in State and National politics, Clinton became active in York Rite Masonry. He served as Grand High Priest of New York from 1798 to 1801. He was the General Grand High Priest from 1816 until his death in 1828. He was Grand Master of the Grand Encampment of N.Y. from 1814 until his death and also Grand Master of Knights Templar in the United States from 1816 until his death.

For a time he was Grand Master of Masons in the State of New York while he was at the head of all the York Rite bodies. Coupled with his political positions, this must have allowed him to wield a considerable amount of power. It causes us today to conjecture if this sort of power may have led to the events related to the Morgan affair.

Although Clinton is best known for his efforts to build the Erie Canal and his work to promote the public school system, he was a progressive leader in many other activities. Clinton encouraged agriculture, he fought for an honest administration, he worked to improve public health programs and he promoted the arts and sciences. His efforts to promote public improvement and the development of resources were manifested in his interest to build the Erie Canal.

Clinton was popular with scientific men. He was well informed on ichthyology, ornithology, mineralogy, geology and botany. He was well read in history, theology, metaphysics and philosophy. He well could be labeled, "the education Governor".

In 1805 a Society for Establishing a Free School in the City of New York was established. In the same year the Legislature passed an act to incorporate the Society. The first school building was dedicated in 1809 at which time Clinton delivered the address.

In 1809 Grand Lodge established a fund to send 50 children to the school. Two from each Lodge were chosen. Cooperation of Grand Lodge with the Society continued until 1817 when public support was sufficient to handle the situation. During all of this time, Clinton was involved as Mayor and/or in Albany. At the same time he was in Grand Lodge as an officer or as Grand Master. There is no question as to the influence he and Freemasonry played in the promotion of the public school system.

The capstone of DeWitt Clinton's career may very well have been on Oct. 23, 1823. On that day Governor Clinton, while serving as General Grand High Priest, laid the capstone of the Erie Canal in a public ceremony attended by dignitaries from around the State.

While Governor of the State and Grand Master of Masons, he laid the corner stone for the Masonic Temple in Aurora, NY. This was in 1819. The building still stands and is one of the most unique Masonic buildings in the country. It was built by Aurora Chapter #64 Royal Arch Masons, which was chartered that same year.

While in the Aurora area, Clinton stayed at the home of his good friend. Clinton and his entourage made a Mason of their host, Humphrey Howland, a Quaker and early settler of the region. Howland received all three degrees and the Royal Arch degree, all in one evening.

During the Morgan affair, which happened just a year before Clinton's death, he had the moral courage to speak up. We wonder where were the other Masonic leaders while Clinton was saying,

> I know that Freemasonry, properly understood, and faithfully attended to, is friendly to religion, morality, liberty, and good government; and I shall never shrink under any state of excitement, or any extent of misapprehension, from bearing testimony in favor of the purity of an institution which can boast of a Washington, and a Franklin, and a Lafayette, as distinguished members, which inculcates no principles and authorizes no acts that are not in perfect accordance with good morals, civil liberty and entire obedience to the government and the laws.

Clinton indeed was a man who wielded much power in and out of government. That much power comes to very few men. His ambition, integrity and diligence earned him the privilege to control that power.

George Peter

Originally printed in The *Empire State Mason* Magazine, Spring 2006

Bibliography:
History of Royal Arch Masonry
Masonic Americana 1987
New York Freemasonry, Lang & Singer 1981
Governors of New York State
Encyclopedia Britannica
"Old Dartmouth Historical Sketches #12", Mary J. Howland Taber Dec. 8, 1905

The Morgan Affair

Every Masonic Lodge in operation before 1826 was severely affected by the Morgan Affair. Most of said Lodge histories allude to some of the problems created by the event. This brief report is to treat the matter on a Statewide, and even National, scale.

William Morgan was a Captain who had served in the War of 1812. He claimed to be a Freemason and was admitted into a Masonic Lodge. Later he was described as a worthless ne'er-do-well, a drunkard, a loafer and a chronic borrower. When he was denied admittance to Batavia Lodge #433, he became angry and vowed to reveal the secrets of Freemasonry in a book. Morgan teamed up with a Col. David Miller and cronies. Miller was owner of the *Batavia Advocate,* a local newspaper. Word got out that the book was to be published. Morgan was jailed for misdemeanor charges in a Canandaigua jail. He was spirited out of the jail and taken by coach to Fort Niagara where he was housed overnight in the blockhouse.

It seems that some overzealous Freemasons decided to take matters in their own hands to see that Morgan did not carry out his plan. Morgan was not seen since that time and the accusations were that he had been taken out to the Niagara River and drowned. Most accounts indicate that he was taken to Canada, given some money and a horse and told never to set foot in the United States again. Of course there are contradictory accounts indicating that the Freemasons murdered Morgan.

As happens even today, politicians, the news media and the clergy geared up to castigate the institution of Freemasonry. Hundreds of newspapers sprung up for the sole purpose of criticizing the Fraternity. Churches issued decrees forbidding any member of the Church to be a member until renouncing membership in the

Fraternity. A new political party emerged calling itself the Anti-Masonic Party. A national convention was held to nominate a candidate for President on that party line. The State of Vermont elected a Governor to office in 1832 on the Anti-Masonic Party line. In the meantime, a body was found in the Niagara River. It was claimed to be that of Morgan. His widow, who later remarried and then married Joseph Smith as one of his plural wives, claimed the body to be that of Morgan. It bore no resemblance to the man, but as political boss, Thurlow Weed said, "It's a good enough Morgan till after the election." Later an Indian woman identified the body as that of her husband.

The hysteria subsided by the mid 1830s, but was still strong enough by 1882 for some anti-Masons to erect a 40' monument in Batavia. It states, among other things, "Sacred to the memory of Wm. Morgan, a native of Virginia, a Capt. in the War of 1812, a respectable citizen of Batavia and a martyr to the freedom of writing, speaking and printing the truth. He was abducted from near this spot in the year 1826 by Free Masons and Murdered for revealing the secrets of their Order." On the West tablet are these words: "The bane of our civil institutions is to be found in Masonry, Already powerful, and daily becoming More so I owe to my Country an Exposure of its Dangers."

In spite of all this, Freemasonry began to reemerge by the early and mid 1840s.

For further study of this matter are listed the following documents:

American Lodge of Research, Vol. lll, no. 1; Vol.Xll, no 3; Vol. XIV, no. 3 and Vol. XV, no.1. Also: Transactions of Quatuor Coronati Lodge, Volumes 105 & 106

Whys & Wherefores
November 1993

The disappearance of William Morgan in September of 1826 set the stage for one of the greatest shams in American history. Many volumes have been written about the events which led to the alleged abduction of Morgan and the resulting turbulent era. And yet very little has been discussed concerning how and why the event became so blown out of proportion.

A brief review of the details is presented: Morgan somehow proved himself a Freemason to the point where he was accepted into local Masonic Lodges. His personal characteristics of heavy drinking, neglect of family, and non-payment of personal debts caused the Freemasons to shun him. He was denied membership in one of the concordant Masonic bodies.

Morgan became disgruntled and teamed up with a local printer by the name of David Miller. The two advertised their intention to print all of the supposed secrets of Freemasonry. This disturbing news upset some over-zealous Freemasons who allegedly abducted Morgan from jail. Morgan was not heard from since.

A body was found in the Niagara River. A claim was made that it was that of William Morgan. Although it proved not to be the body of Morgan, this did not quell the taste for blood by the non-Masons who used the event to campaign against Freemasonry.

The anti-Masonic political party was one manifestation of the fervor of the time. Churches expelled from their congregations any member who would not renounce Freemasonry. Most Masonic Lodges were dissolved. A few remained in operation by meeting in secret.[1]

How and why could such fervor develop and why could an organization founded on such noble and lofty principles be the target of so much vilification and hatred?

Freemasonry was founded on most of the same principles supported by the church– the same church which turned against it. Roscoe Pound, Dean of Harvard Law School, 1916 - 1936, said of Freemasonry: "Society is divided sharply into classes that understand each other none too well. What nobler Masonic lecture could there be than one which took up the fundamenta of social science and undertook to spread a sound knowledge of it among all Masons?"[2]

Dean Veranus Moore, former Dean, Cornell University School of Veterinary Medicine, said, "Brotherhood does not require us to like all people, but it does demand that we give exact justice in all our dealings. Masonry therefore is a great training school in which men learn brotherhood by practicing it toward fellow craftsmen and then, later, practicing it everywhere." Brother Moore also talked about the sins of ignorance. He said, "No man who holds truth lightly or chooses to remain in ignorance or is intolerant of others can be a true Mason."[3]

An address by Fred P. Corson, President of Dickinson College, Carlisle, Pa., was printed in the Congressional Record on the occasion of the 150th anniversary of the ratification of the United States Constitution. President Corson was talking about the stability of our government. He said: "America owes its governmental stability and her success as a democracy to her spiritual foundation. Prior to 1787 the work of laying this foundation was by the Church and by the Masonic Fraternity. It was no coincidence that of the six men who produced the Constitution, at least half were members of the Craft." He cited especially the work of Freemasons, Washington, Franklin, Hancock and Marshall. President Thomas Masaryk once said, "Its members...have always been ardent propagators of the ideals of humanity."[4]

Hundreds of writers of great renown have spoken eloquently about the value to society of Freemasonry. There are lists of untold numbers of great leaders "who never deemed it derogatory to level with the Fraternity" and to give it their loyalty.[5]

Having this knowledge about the good influence of Freemasonry, knowing that many of the great leaders of the time were Freemasons (including our own Governor DeWitt Clinton), and being apprised of the principles taught by the Craft; it boggles the mind to try to understand how and why Freemasonry came under such ill repute.

This paper is to contend that there was a major factor and three elements which led to the birth of the anti-Masonic movement and the anti-Masonic political party. The major factor was jealousy mixed with greed, which grew in the hearts of those not privy to membership. Some had been denied. Others knew not how to become a member. They saw Freemasonry and Freemasons as an elite, secret society, and they were easily convinced that conspiracies and evil came from inside those secret Lodge rooms.

This common characteristic of human nature served as the fuel for igniting and inciting hatred for the unknown. But a fuel needs a mechanism to ignite it. Three groups served this purpose. Politicians saw an opportunity to gain popularity by making false accusations and insinuations. Thurlow Weed was the most successful and most damaging in his use of the incident and to claim that he was the savior, "riding in on a shiny white horse." Our own William Seward of Auburn and Millard Fillmore of Moravia made hay of the fiasco and gained political clout by using the Morgan affair as an issue.[6]

One would not have expected the clergy to lower themselves to this level of demagoguery, but such was not the case. Even former members of the Fraternity saw in this an opportunity to claim that the Freemasons were evil and that only in the church could souls be saved. And these same clergy knew full well that Freemasonry was not in the business of saving souls.

The third mechanism, which grabbed an opportunity to gain notoriety and to sell newspapers, was the press. New papers were born regularly with the one objective, to sell newsprint by leveling accusations at the Fraternity. Any dirt would do regardless of its veracity.

The anti-Masonic movement was a conspiracy to promote individual causes. The press saw a dollar in it. The clergy saw an opportunity to win new converts. The politicians grabbed the opportunity to promote themselves. The times were ripe for suspicion and distrust. Uncultivated egos led people to believe that only their church, their politics, their way of life was the correct one. Others were ignorant and in the dark.

So what is new? Can such happen again? Who will lead the attack? Will there be another Morgan affair? This writer contends that such happens every day and continues to happen.

A perfect example of a 20th century "Morgan Affair" was the Vietnam fiasco. The same elements used the same egos, distrust, and suspicions to fan the flames to force the United States Government to fight a limited engagement in Vietnam. It cost America unnecessary loss of lives and great anguish. Whether we agree with this assessment or not, the fact remains that the debate about Vietnam was a one-sided presentation by the news media, the clergy, and the politicians. A much more healthy situation would have been an honest and reasonable dialogue.

The three elements were successful in preventing an honest dialogue because the times were ripe for distrust of government. Also, egos had been honed to a new level of un-cultivation. Especially young people were prone to believe that the Government was evil and that we were sending boys over there to be slaughtered. The more difficult it became to fight a war to win, the greater became the number of Americans who were slaughtered.

Politicians used the situation to promote their political ambitions, the church switched from teaching the proper attitudes to have toward fellow human beings to preaching political diatribes from their pulpits. And of course the press, in consort with television and radio, made hay of the situation by selling more newspapers and air time. Distrust and suspicions served as the fuel to be ignited by these three forces promoting their own agendas.

These same forces– the news media, the clergy, and politicians, have not ceased in their biased and one-sided presentations of the various issues which confront us. With new technology and advances in news gathering, the power of the news media has expanded to a dangerous level. Newspapers and other news media have become political action entities instead of purveyors of news. Church membership has dwindled because so many churches have been transformed into a series of political action groups. But even with these reduced forces, the church, by virtue of its tax exempt status (constitutional or otherwise), remains a formidable influence. Politicians will always be with us and will hop onto whatever bandwagon seems to offer a ride to power.

Think of the heyday these forces would have, and do have, with a "Morgan affair" today. A recent bond issue defeat was headlined as follows: "Voters reject more jobs."[7] It could have said, "Voters reject more State debt." The latter would have been as much an opinion as the headline that did appear. An objective headline would have said, "Jobs Bond act defeated by voters." Don't hold your breath waiting for that kind of objective reporting.

Yes we have had more than one "Morgan Affair" in this country and there are more born every day. We will have more such fiascos because we don't seem to learn from history. Few have seen fit to analyze the "whys and wherefores" which made it possible for innocent forces to be caught up by the less noble characteristics of humans. The message is to be on the alert for demagogues who use any cause to further their individual programs. America must demand more objective reporting and more accurate assessments of events.

Originally printed in *Philalethes* Magazine, October 1994

References:

1 *The Morgan Affair*, Richard Eades, 1993
2 *Masonic Addresses and Writings*, Roscoe Pound, Macoy Publishing, New York, 1953
3 Address by Dr. Veranus Moore, Dean Veterinary College, Cornell University, Ithaca, NY at the cornerstone laying ceremony for Ithaca Masonic Temple, 1926
4 Congressional Record, 1938. Address by Dr. Fred P. Corson, President of Dickinson College
5 Masonic ritual
6 "The Morgan Affair and its effect on Freemasonry," R. Keith Muir, *Transactions of Quatuor Coronati Lodge No. 2076*, Volume 105, 1992
7 *The Ithaca Journal News*, Nov. 3, 1993

George Peter

Whys & Wherefores
Addendum: 09-28-94

    Dr. Kathleen Smith Kutolowski, Professor in the Dept. of History at SUNY Brockport, recently spoke to a group co-sponsored by the Philalethes Society & the Monroe County Bureau of Masonic Education. Her topic was Freemasonry on the New York Frontier: Genesee County, 1803-1826. Said topic made it obvious that she would touch upon the Morgan affair. Her research indeed led her to ask the question: "Why this furor against Freemasonry in a period when the Fraternity was held in such high regard, and when there were so many Lodges growing in size every day?" Even David Miller, the publisher who conspired with Morgan to print an expose of Freemasonry, had earlier written glowing accounts of Freemasonry.

    Prof. Kutolowski's research data refuted the commonly accepted theory that Freemasons were an elite group who were held in suspicion by the rank and file. What she found was that although the Freemasons came from all walks of life and professions, a very large majority were the leaders in their respective communities. Eighty percent of the business leaders and professionals were Freemasons. And yet they were not the economically elite. Twenty-eight percent represented the top wealthiest 20%. Twenty percent were in the bottom 20% in terms of income. Masonry was then, as it is now, a place for the "high, the low, the rich, the poor."

    But people noticed that the judges, sheriffs, juries, etc. always seemed to be Freemasons. Prof. Kutolowski also blamed the reversal in attitudes on the change in times. The Erie Canal had opened. There was a group of women anti-Masons. The evangelicals equated Freemasons with their opinion of "free-thinkers." It was a period of the second great awakening. She goes on to point out other reasons.

    But as per my theory in the paper, "Whys & Wherefores," I contend that "Morgan affairs" happen all the time and continue to happen today. The Jews were persecuted in Germany. Biases against them continue around the world. My ancestors, the Armenians, were massacred by the Turks. This happened, in small part, due to a difference in religion. But the major factor was that these were the more educated, professional people who were leaders in their respective communities.

    It is a basic, less than flattering, aspect of human nature to be jealous and resentful of what others have or are. The Morgan incident served as the justification to attack the leaders who were respected in the community. The Freemasons were a perfect target. We still have targets today. i.e.: Attacks continue against Freemasonry.

Keep an eye on the mechanisms which were used to fan the flames of hatred then. They are all necessary entities whose influence needs to be questioned.

Mormonism and Freemasonry
Examined Through the Eyes of Dr. Mervin B. Hogan – His Writings and His Influence

Part I – Introduction

This paper is to examine the voluminous and scholarly literature produced by Professor Mervin B. Hogan on the subject of "Freemasonry and Mormonism." Dr. Hogan has compiled a Masonic-Mormon bibliography. It lists 209 publications of which he has written 180. He has been published 17 times in the *Royal Arch Mason Magazine*. Brother Hogan also has written extensively for The *American Lodge of Research*, for *Philalethes*, *New Age*, and *Northern Light* magazines and for many others. His good friend, Wallace McLeod has published *A Bibliography of Works on Freemasonry Written by Mervin B. Hogan*. It contains 58 listings and is included in the appendix of this paper. As a Professor of Engineering, he has published dozens of papers on engineering and mathematics. To review that area of his interests would take another paper of at least equal length.

Dr. Bruce Widger, Past Grand Master, presented to New York College, MASONIC SOCIETAS ROSICRUCIAN IN CIVITATIBUS FOEDERATIS, Oct., 1995, a brief biography of Brother Hogan. It has been slightly condensed and modified. With his permission, it is included as part two of this paper.

This study is also to outline the role played by Brother Mervin B. Hogan in his relentless and effective drive to help break down the disharmony which developed between Freemasonry and the Mormon Church. A background for the intriguing history and interrelationship between Freemasonry and Mormonism is offered in part three. It is in the form of a condensed chronology of events. Section four is a brief presentation of quotations borrowed from the writings of Brother Hogan and from a letter to him from Brother Wallace McLeod. These quotes offer a brief outline of the status of Mormonism today and a critique of both parties involved in the

Masonic/Mormon clash. Part five, is an analysis of the events described in the chronology (part three). Part five also includes a summary. A listing of references, a bibliography and an appendix complete the sections of this treatise.

Part II - Biography of Mervin B. Hogan

This section is a review of a short paper presented by Bruce Widger on the subject of Mervin Hogan- the Man, Freemason and Mormon. Past Grand Master Widger first began corresponding with Hogan in 1982, when Dr. Widger was Grand Master in New York State. From that first contact Bruce Widger received volumes of material. Direct quotes and excerpts from Dr. Widger's paper are presented here in condensed form with minor additional information and comments:

Mervin Booth Hogan was born in Bountiful, Utah July 21, 1906, hence he is over 90 years of age and appears to be in good health. His correspondence is still very lucid and intellectual. Dr. Hogan continues to write in the same vigorous and scholarly style. He married Helen Emily Reese in 1926. Mrs. Hogan is not presently in good health and requires her husband's full attention. They have one son, Edward Reese Hogan, a graduate of Hamilton College and a Professor of Mathematics at East Stroudsburg College, Pennsylvania.

Brother Hogan has undergraduate degrees from the University of Utah and the University of Pittsburgh. His PhD degree was earned from the University of Michigan in 1936. His career has included positions as design engineer at Westinghouse, Professor of Mechanical Engineering, and department chairman at the University of Utah till 1956. In 1956 he came to Syracuse, NY as manager of product engineering for the General Electric Company. In 1965 he went with GE to Phoenix, Arizona as manager of design assurance engineering. After a two year stint as construction engineer in Waynesboro, Virginia Dr. Hogan returned to the University of Utah as Professor of Engineering until he retired as Professor Emeritus in 1976.

Dr. Hogan has received honor awards from the University of Utah, London, Yale and many others. Dr. Mervin B. Hogan is listed in *Who's Who in American Education*. He is a National Eagle Scout, and a New York DeMolay Legion of Honor awardee. Hogan is a member of Rotary, Freemasonry, Shriners, Prophets, Knights Templar, Quatuor Coronati, and eight university fraternity and/or honor societies. He belongs to several other Masonic, academic and philosophical organizations too numerous to mention.

Brother Hogan was made a Mason in Wasatch Lodge No. 1 in Salt Lake City on May 16, 1941 where he served as Master in 1947. He was Grand Lodge of Utah education committee chairman, Grand Chaplain, and Grand Orator. He was secretary of his Lodge from 1972-1977. He now is a member of three Lodges in three states– Arizona, New York, and Utah. Brother Hogan was created an Honorary 33rd At Large in 1963 Northern Masonic Jurisdiction and he was elected a fellow in The American Lodge of Research in 1948.

Brother Hogan was born and raised in the Mormon church and remains on the church roles. He has never been an active Mormon, although he was married in the Mormon church and his wife and son are active members. To the best of his knowledge he is the only Mormon taken into a Utah Masonic Lodge without demitting from the church. He says that both the Church of Latter Day Saints and the Masonic Grand Lodge of Utah now "hate my guts," but they have found it impossible to do anything about it.

Brother Hogan has been forthright and bold in his criticism of both institutions. Hogan wrote to Most Worshipful Widger and to Right Worshipful LaVerne Getman, "The Grand Lodge of Utah has got away with, since its founding, the disregarding of the Ancient Landmarks, the Constitutions of 1723, and all traditions of the Order which are not amenable to its intended modus operandi." He also wrote to them, "The Mormons have always been pro-Masonic. Any statement to the contrary is a lie originated in Illinois and viciously perpetrated by the Grand Lodge of Utah since its founding."

Hogan solicited help from the Grand Lodge of New York to put pressure on the Grand Lodge of Utah. The scheme was to threaten to withdraw recognition unless they repealed their long standing attitude toward the Mormons. The McCoy Publishing House printed a paper by Brother Hogan on the subject. According to Hogan, quiet pressure by Past Grand Master Raymond C. Ellis and Conrad Hahn of the Masonic Service Association and by his paper caused the "Masons of Utah to have a Hell of a time at their meeting in January 1984." In the end they did the honorable thing and officially removed the ban.

Brother Hogan wrote his first Mormon/Masonic paper in 1947. He tried hard to expose the hideous, so-called, Masonic malpractice in and by the Utah jurisdiction. Mervin Hogan has received many accolades about his scholarly writings on the subject of Mormonism and Freemasonry. His colleagues have said, "One cannot write objectively or factually about the subject unless that person is both a Mormon and a Mason." Brother Frank C. Olds is a practicing Mormon. He is a member of Cortlandville Lodge. He writes, "Mervin Hogan, more than anyone else, has brought Utah Masons to their knees, for Truth will cut its own way."

Mervin Hogan does not mince words about the Mormons either. He writes, "The Mormons have an ostrich view, either bury it or hide it. They have been rewriting their history." Brother Hogan's research into the restricted material of the Mormon archives was encouraged by the hierarchies of the Northern and Southern Scottish Rite jurisdictions. He has a gold card to the library archives and has even seen the Nauvoo Masonic minute book. His friendship with library manager, Earl E. Olson during the Mormon leadership of Spencer W. Kimball was his good fortune. It enabled him to write directly in opposition to Brother Sam Goodwin, the Utah Grand Secretary. Brother Hogan describes Goodwin as a professional anti-Mormon, a liar, a charlatan and a thief. After 1984 Brother Hogan's use of the Morman library archives was denied. Church President Ezra Taft Benson even refused to shake hands with Brother Hogan at a S.A.R. meeting.

Although the Grand Lodge of Utah removed the prohibition on Mormons in 1984, very few Mormons have joined. There is still the ballot box and there is also the anti-Masonic feeling in the Mormon church. For a Mormon to petition causes him trouble at home. Even so, recently a young Mormon was given the first degree in Wasatch Lodge #1. It is a very conservative Lodge and the oldest in Utah. Other Lodges in Utah have been more accepting.

Part III – Chronology of Events (Time Line)
6/1/1801: Brigham Young was born, Wittingham, VT. He was known as "the Builder." He became the first President of the Church after Joseph Smith. Hogan called it, "A 30 year, iron fisted, ungloved, totalitarian reign in Utah."
12/23/1805: Joseph Smith Jr was born at Sharon, VT.
5/17/1818: Joe Smith Sr raised in Ontario Lodge #33, Canandaigua.
Spring 1820: Joseph Smith, at age 14, received vision of God and Jesus. Told to join no church, but to prepare self for restoration of the true church.

Early 1820s: Hyrum Smith, Heber Kimball, Newell Whitney, George Miller *et al*, became Freemasons in Palmyra, Victor, Ohio, and Virginia.

9/27/1823: Joseph Smith, at age 17, received a vision from then angel Moroni.

9/12/1826: Wm. Morgan abducted from jail. He had announced plans to publish Masonic Ritual. Anti-Masonic movement started.

10/1826: Exposé of the ritual of the three Masonic degrees was published.

9/22/1827: Moroni allowed Joseph Smith to take the plates from the mountain. Note: By this time Smith was acquainted with the exposé of Freemasonry by Morgan.

6/11/1829: Joseph Smith applied for certificate to protect authorship to translation of the Book of Mormon.

3/26/1830: Book of Mormon offered for sale. Smith was 24 years old.

4/6/1830: Joseph Smith organized Church of Latter Day Saints (LDS) at the home of Peter Witmer, Fayette, Seneca County, NY.

1830: Lucinda Morgan (widow of Morgan) married George Harris (former Freemason). He & Lucinda earlier claimed they identified a body as that of Morgan. (This later proved to be false.) Harris earlier was associated with Wm. Morgan of Batavia. Later Lucinda married Joseph Smith as a plural wife while she was still married to Harris (and possibly Morgan.)

1830: William Phelps (also Masonic turn-coat) edited two anti-Masonic newspapers. He was also publisher of the first Mormon newspaper. Book of Mormon was referred to as the anti-Masonic Bible. Although some passages were anti-Masonic in nature, most early Mormon leaders did not continue anti-Masonic activities.

1833: Joseph Smith commanded to build a Temple in Kirtland, Ohio.

2/15/1835: Quorum of 12 apostles were told by Joseph Smith of his revelation to tarry in Kirtland for awaited endowment.

1839: Mormons moved to Nauvoo.

4/6/1840: Abe Jonas elected Grand Master of the new Grand Lodge of Illinois as that new Grand Lodge was born (same date). James Adams was the Deputy Grand Master. He was a Mormon who was acquainted with Joseph Smith. "Both men were ambitious, greedy, self-centered rogues."

c.a. 1840: Freemason, John Bennett, wrote to Sid Rigdon & Joseph Smith requesting to join Mormons. He arrived in Nauvoo 9/

1/1840, elected Mayor of Nauvoo, chancellor of the University, and in 1841 elected assistant president of the first presidency of the LDS church.

12/16/1840: John Bennett helped get Nauvoo charter in the State Legislature. Abe Lincoln also helped get the charter.

12/24/1841: 18 Mormon Masons went to the office of Hyrum Smith to organize Nauvoo Lodge. The next day Joseph Smith and Sid Rigdon petitioned for membership. There were 100 Masons in Illinois at this time. In the next two years four new Lodges were formed.

3/14/1842: Rigdon & Joseph Smith were made Master Masons. Rigdon was one of the early church leaders.

3/15/1842: Nauvoo Lodge was installed by Grand Master Abe Jonas.

5/3/1842: Nine men (all Freemasons) were initiated and endowed to form the Council of LDS church. They were anointed as kings and priests (similar in great detail to the Holy Royal Arch degree).

3/1842: John Bennett withdrew from LDS church, resigned as mayor and had dispute with Hyrum and Joseph Smith. He was expelled from Nauvoo and from the church. He vindictively published scathing articles about the church. He accused it of adopting Masonic ritual. According to Hogan, Bennett was another rogue.

5/1/1842: Smith preached, "There are certain signs and words by which false spirits may be detected from true..."

8/11/1842: Nauvoo was suspended. It had 286 candidates and 256 Master Masons at that time. There were only 480 Masons in 12 Lodges in all of Illinois at that time.

1842: Two more Lodges were formed– mostly of Mormons in Nauvoo.

1842: New Temple started.

1843: More irregularities (advancing too fast, not checking character, records not reported, etc.) were reported. Four Lodges, mostly of Mormons, were suspended. Some claimed fear that Mormons would control Grand Lodge. By now Joseph had introduced Temple Endowment. Lodges ignored the suspensions.

9/11/1843: Wives of men of Holy Order began to be endowed and sealed to their husbands– by Joseph Smith. All were referred to as companions. Secrecy was important to preserve the secret of plural marriages (as early as 1841).

1843: Joseph Smith introduced final ritual– the second anointing.

4/5/1844: Joseph Smith spoke at rededication of the new Temple. It was completed in less than one year. Hyrum Smith was Master.

6/7/1844: *Nauvoo Expositor* was published– a four page newspaper which blasted the leaders of Mormonism. The publishers were disenchanted members of the Church.

6/10/1844: The printing press and its associated type, which produced the *Nauvoo Expositor*, were ordered by Mayor Joseph Smith to be destroyed.

6/27/44: Joseph and Hyrum were assassinated by a mob at Carthage Prison. Some claim Joseph gave the Grand Hailing Sign of Distress and said, "Oh Lord my God...," but his plea was ignored by the Masons who were present. Joseph Smith was 39.

1844: By now there were 700 Master Masons in Nauvoo Lodge. By the end of 1845 there were over 1000. There were 1366 Masons in 5 Mormon Lodges.

1846: Mormons left Nauvoo. By now over 5669 persons endowed. Freemasonry and Mormonism sort of divorced at this time.

7/24/1847: Mormons arrived in Salt Lake City valley.

1852: Next endowment was performed.

1855: Endowment house built in Salt Lake City.

1856: President Brigham Young explained the penalties.

1/11/1872: Grand Lodge of Utah founded.

1878: Grand Master of Utah defined expulsion of Mormons.

9/28/1879: Robert Baskin, member of Mt. Moriah Lodge No. 2, published exposé of Mormon Temple Ritual, "Lifting the Vail." [sic].

1886: Mormons began to curtail use of Masonic symbols. By the turn of the century most were discarded. For most of the 20th century both bodies have prohibited membership in the other.

1964: Dr. William J. Whalen wrote an outsider's view of Mormonism.

1984: Grand Lodge of Utah repealed prohibition of Mormons from visiting and joining Utah Masonic Lodges. Success credited to efforts and writings by Professor Mervin B. Hogan.

5/5/1995: Art deHoyos, McAllen, Texas wrote to Dr. Hogan urging him to preserve his memoirs for Masonic posterity. He said: "Nobody knows the true history of Mormonism and Freemasonry like you do. Nobody else living has had an equal level of personal involvement or been more instrumental in bridging the gap. The loss of your insight would be irrecoverable."

Part IV – Quotations from the Writings of Dr. Mervin B. Hogan

Presently there are over 10 million Mormons. Their assets are over several billion dollars. They have great political influence and power. "From disregard, disdain, and ridicule society accepts the realm of Mormonism for academic and professional studies."

Comparison of Mormonism to Freemasonry:

FREEMASONRY:
Creed-less, from all religious beliefs, each man's religion is his private concern. All rests on the individual interpretation. "...Direct your steps through life by the light you there shall find and as you there shall find it." Sole aim is to instruct. This is done via symbols and ritual. Freemasonry in America grew out of the elitist form only after settlements extended West and as the Craft absorbed democratic principles. As late as 1826 it still was viewed by the public as an elitist body.

MORMONISM:
Members are advised that "they are not burdened to think for themselves." Services are provided them by the leaders. At Brigham Young University, Professors are told, "you are not hired to think; you are hired to teach. When our leaders speak, the thinking has been done." A more modern statement is: "Follow the Prophet."

Temple Endowments and Ordinances also teach by symbols. To discuss their content is to risk ex-communication. Tithing is 10% minimum. The atmosphere is "us vs. them." Convert neighbors to help keep them from harassing you. All others are shunned. In Utah, Idaho, and parts of California, political power allows Mormons to determine who gets jobs, bank loans, food stamps, etc.

Problem for Mormons grew from their unduly aggressive, ambitious and greedy for special privileges stance. Leaders lacked tact. Also their political concepts and practice of theocratic government and the introduction of polygamy were viewed as unacceptable. Yet unfair antagonism against an otherwise industrious, peaceable, and law abiding group was evident. Wallace McLeod to Hogan, 5/1893:

...I am prepared to admire faith, wheresoever it is found. But I pose as being a moderately rational person.... It is quite clear that Joseph Smith was, in a certain sense, intellectually acute, and far more literate than his scholarly background would lead one to expect. But this, in a certain way, is a miracle of God in itself; and I look for nothing more.

Part V – An Analysis of the chronological time line and a Summary

In all of his literature on the subject of Mormonism and Freemasonry Mervin Hogan demonstrates that he is objective and fair. As an engineer, a researcher, and a teacher, his purpose is to present the facts as he uncovers them. In general he presents both Freemasonry and Mormonism in a favorable light. But, at the same time, he exposes the negative aspects of the people in both institutions. It is done factually and with cautious and meticulous detail. He clearly defines the irregularities of certain Masons and Freemasonry– especially the Grand Lodge of Utah. And he pulls no punches about the early Grand Lodge of Illinois, "Two notorious, somewhat itinerant Masons– Deputy Grand Master James Adams and Grand Master Abraham Jonas– must be known and recognized as the pair of scheming, conniving, self-seeking opportunists…"

His strongest critique of Mormonism is expressed by quoting other writers. He has published the original *Nauvoo Expositor*. It is very damaging literature against the early leaders of the Church and against Joseph Smith, himself. Hogan, in many of his papers, points out that the hierarchy of the Church of Latter Day Saints down-play the less than noble characteristics or actions of some of its early leaders. And he questions the extent to which they go to be less than candid about certain aspects of the institution. He notes that they have rewritten some of the early history.

It is somewhat understandable why the leaders of the Church of LDS "hate his guts." Probably the most damaging piece by Hogan about the Church is his paper, "Freemasonry and Mormon Ritual." In it Hogan quotes Prof. William Whalen, a Roman Catholic author. Whalen makes a comparison of the three Masonic degrees to the Mormon Temple Endowments. The similarity is striking. Whalen states, "Any comparison of Masonic and Mormon ritual will reveal that the Prophet simply appropriated large chunks of the Masonic degree systems into the endowment rites."

Dr. Hogan concludes, "…little room for doubt can exist in the mind of an informed, objective analyst that the Mormon Temple Endowment and the rituals of ancient Craft Masonry are seemingly and definitely involved." Hogan would not base any of his conclusions on conjecture or heresay and yet there is a strong argument, related to timing, for a connection to Freemasonry and

Mormonism. When we study the time line of events during the formation of the Church, certain facts become obvious. The Morgan expose took place in August 1826.

In June of 1829 Joseph Smith applied for a document to protect the rights to his Book of Mormon. Hogan writes, "...both Joseph Smith and Brigham Young were impressively well informed regarding the history, tenets, principles, and practices of Universal Freemasonry." The timing factor, coupled with the reality that most of the early founders and leaders of the Church were well versed in the essence of Freemasonry, helps to fortify the conviction that there is a strong connection. The comparison of the rituals makes it hard to deny a connection.

Leaders in the Mormon hierarchy continue to deny the evidence. In a paper, "Utah Masons Among the Mormons," Hogan wrote:

> ...The Mormon church rests on the claim it was founded in an atmosphere of the supernatural and the miraculous...From its very beginning, all supposedly scholarly publications of the Church have been written under its supervision, or edited by it...nothing will be made public unless it augments the positive image of the institution...The Church cannot tolerate any tarnishing of its supernatural aura by a shadow cast by such a common, ordinary, mortal social entity of the world as Freemasonry. Hence, its goal is to esponge any trace of the Ancient Order from every page of its history.

In his paper, "Freemasonry and Academic Scholarship," Hogan includes an appendix. It is a paper, "On Being a Mormon Historian," by D. Michael Quinn, Associate Prof. of History, Brigham Young University. Quinn says, "President Brigham Young and other LDS leaders published sermons which spoke quite openly about Joseph Smith's weaknesses at the same time they testified of his prophetic calling. Why does the well-established and generally respected Mormon Church today need a protective, defensive, paranoid approach to its history that the actually embattled earlier Saints did not employ?"

We see that Dr. Hogan has always written and spoken openly and objectively about the Church and about Freemasonry. He has quoted others who have done the same. It has been a passion with him to search for the truth and to expose it in all of its luster and with all of its blemishes.

The Grand Lodge of Utah's quarrel with Hogan comes from his relentless drive to bring them to obey the Constitutions of 1723. His aim was to end the denial of membership to the Mormons. Dr. Hogan has worked through both Scottish Rite jurisdictions and others to help bring about his objective.

Whatever conclusions individuals will draw from all of the material written and conjectured about Mormonism and Freemasonry, one point is clear beyond a doubt. Dr. Mervin B. Hogan has been the most precise and prolific writer on the subject.

Further, one must conclude that he has been an effective pioneer and crusader. He has done this in a scholarly, objective, and thorough approach to the problem. He has engineered a great revolution. Through his influence and writings the Grand Lodge of Utah has finally come around to recognize one of the most basic tenets of Freemasonry.

Dr. and Brother Mervin B. Hogan is to be respected, admired and honored. It is hoped that this paper has helped to promote an appreciation for this giant of a scholar, leader, and Brother Freemason.

Bibliography

1. MBH. "Brigham Young: Yankee Colonizer." *ALR*. Vol. IX, No. 1
2. MBH. "Joseph Smith, Man and Mason." Mar. 7, 1983. University of Utah
3. MBH. "The Nauvoo Expositor and 21 Days of Hell." Aug. 13, 1995. University of Utah
4. MBH. "Freemasonry – Mormonism's Scorned Presence." University of Utah
5. MBH. "Freemasonry & Utah's Great Temple." Jan. 20, 1994. University of Utah
6. Michael W. Homer. "Similarity of Priesthood in Masonry: The Relationship between Freemasonry and Mormonism." *Dialogue*. Vol. 2, No. 3, Fall 1994
7. J. Linnwood Holloway Sr. "Mormonism and Masonry." *Miscellanea*. Vol. XI, part one, 1976
8. MBH. "Freemasonry and Mormon Ritual." May 7, 1991. University of Utah
9. MBH. "Utah Masons among the Mormons." May 26, 1992. University of Utah
10. MBH. "Death and Doom Invoked by the Nauvoo Expositor." Mar. 15, 1996. University of Utah
11. MBH. "The Involvement of John Cook Bennett with Mormonism and Freemasonry at Nauvoo." Aug. 5, 1983. University of Utah
12. MBH. "Utah Freemasonry and Mormonism." Feb. 7, 1971. University of Utah
13. MBH. "Brigham Young and Canandaigua, NY." *ALR*. Vol.XV, No. 2

14. MBH. "The Origin and Growth of Utah Masonry and Its Conflict with Mormonism. Campus Graphics, Salt Lake City, Utah. 1978
15. Edward Harter. "The Morgan Affair – The Local Tradition. *ALR*. Vol. XII, No. 3
16. Thomas C. O'Donnell. "Outline to a New Approach to the Morgan Mystery." *ALR*, Vol. III, No. 1
17. MBH. "John Cook Bennett and Pickaway Lodge No. 23." Oct. 12, 1983. University of Utah
18. MBH. "Freemasonry; The Royal Art." Jan. 27, 1992. University of Utah
19. MBH. "Masonry's Momentous Mission." *Miscellanea*.Vol.8 Part 2. 1965
20. MBH. "Temple Mormonism and Freemasonry." *Philalethes*. April 1992
21. MBH. "Battle Born Nevada's Freemasonry and its Impact on Utah." July 29, 1983. University of Utah
22. MBH. "James Adams and the Founding of the Grand Lodge of Illinois." August 2, 1983. University of Utah
23. MBH. "Freemasonry and Temple Mormonism." Sept. 12, 1991. University of Utah
24. MBH. "Brigham Young – Temple Architect." May 7, 1981. University of Utah
25. MBH. "Freemasonry and Utah's Perpetual Problem." Aug. 22, 1992. University of Utah
26. MBH. "Brigham Young – Leader and Temple Advocate." Aug. 22, 1978. University of Utah
27. MBH. "Freemasonry and Brigham Young the Speaker." Feb. 29, 1992. University of Utah
28. MBH. "Freemasonry and the Gentle Life." Nov. 3, 1991
29. Carl Carmer. "Death of the Prophet." *American Heritage*. Vol. XIV, No. 1, Dec. 1962
30. MBH. "The Ultimatum of the Nauvoo Expositor." Oct. 24, 1995. University of Utah
31. MBH. "Joseph Smith and Freemasonry." Mar. 7, 1983, University of Utah
32. MBH. "Freemasonry and the Nauvoo Ambiance." Mar. 10, 1994. University of Utah
33. MBH. "Freemasonry and Academic Scholarship." Dec. 4, 1991. University of Utah
34. John L. Brooks. *A Tangle of Strings and the Kingdom of God, The Refiner's Fire*. Cambridge University Press, NY. 1994
35. J. H. Beadle. *Mormon Difficulties and Death of the Prophet, Mysteries and Crimes of Mormonism and Polygamy*. National Publishing Company, Philadelphia. 1870
36. Jerald and Sandra Tanner, *Evolution of the Mormon Temple Ceremony: 1842-1990*. Utah Lighthouse Ministry, Salt Lake City, Utah

Donehogawa – Ely S. Parker (1826-1895)

We seldom consider the real power of Freemasonry and how it affects our lives. Collectively we don't make anywhere near the impact on Freemasonry that it makes on the life of each one of us.

This account is about how the power of Freemasonry affected one individual life. Any of us could talk about our own life and how Freemasonry made a difference. The best testimonial to Freemasonry that I know was when a young wife of one of our new members asked some of us, "What did you Masons do to my husband? He is a different person. It is great."

But this story is about the life of Ely S. Parker. His life and his contribution to society have been a profound inspiration to any who know the details. This brief sketch should lead the interested to read more about Ely S. Parker. A bibliography is enclosed.

His early Seneca name was Ha-Sa-No-An-Da, meaning "coming to the front" or "Leading Name."[1] Later, at the age of 23, when he was made Grand Sachem of the Six Nations (principal chief) he was given the name, Do-Ne-Ho-Ga-Wa, which means, "keeper of the Western Gate" or "Open Door."[2] His white man's name was, Ely S. Parker, named after the Reverend Ely Stone, a teacher at the Baptist School he attended as a young boy.

While still a very young lad, Ely was acting as interpreter for the Seneca Indian leaders who were in Albany trying to get a redress for grievances against them by land agents. The Indians of Tonawanda were being forced off their land by fraudulent claims by the white man agents. There he met an influential white man by the name of Lewis Henry Morgan.

Morgan was living in Aurora where he was born. He brought Ely Parker to Aurora and paid his tuition at the Cayuga Academy. While Parker was in Aurora, Morgan literally "picked his brain" for information about Indian culture and history. Morgan made Ely a member of a club which was called, "The Grand Order of the Iroquois". Guess where they met? Morgan's father was a member of Scipio Lodge in Aurora so it was natural that the society should meet in the famous Lodge room in Aurora, N. Y. Brothers of Scipio Lodge #110 meet in the same building where Lewis Henry Morgan and Ely S. Parker met and enjoyed their society.

It was formed for the purpose of introducing people to the true nature, history and culture of the Iroquois people. Lewis Henry Morgan became so intrigued by what he learned that he went on to write, "The

109

League of the Iroquois." It was published in 1851 and was the first "analysis of the underlying principles governing the Indian political organizations."[3] Lewis Henry Morgan is considered to be the first American anthropologist. But this story is about Parker. Suffice to say, he was influenced by Morgan and by the Masonic furniture and artifacts he witnessed in the Scipio Masonic Temple.

Ely Parker went on to study law in order to follow in the footsteps of his new good friend and benefactor, Morgan. But alas, although his grades at the bar exam were exceptional, he was not considered a citizen so failed to be accepted. Heaven help us! Disappointed, but undaunted, Ely went on to study engineering. He became a civil engineer. He advanced and by 1855 was made first assistant State engineer. In that office he engineered the locks and levees in the Pittsford and Bushnell's Basin area near Rochester. His success recommended him to the Federal Government. He built custom houses, post offices, hospitals and other structures for the inland waterways.

In Galena, Illinois he built a custom house which still stands. While there he met a young man, Capt. Hiram Ulysses Grant, who was a friendly clerk in his father's harness shop. They became good friends.[4]

In the meantime, of course, Ely Parker had other interests besides his work. His was an inquisitive and contemplative mind. He had been initiated into Indian societies which had a striking resemblance to the ritual of Freemasonry. He had been involved with Lewis Henry Morgan in the "Grand Order of the Iroquois" in Aurora where they "Indianitiated" candidates.

You guessed it. He was raised in Batavia Lodge #88 in 1847 and, on May 6, 1850, he affiliated with Valley Lodge #109 in Rochester.[5] It still exists. In 1858 he demitted to become the founding Master of Miners' Lodge #273 in Galena, Illinois.[6] In 1862 he demitted to become the first Master of Akron Lodge #527 in Akron, NY.

W Parker was named Grand Orator of the Grand Lodge of Illinois in 1861 and was grand representative of the Grand Lodge of Iowa near the Grand Lodge of Illinois. Ely Parker Lodge #1002 in Buffalo, NY is named after him.

Ely Parker was active in the Chapter, Council, and Commandery. While Master of Miners' Lodge in Galena, he raised another Civil War general– John Corson Smith. After the war, Smith became Grand Master of the Grand Lodge of Illinois. He wrote, "History of Freemasonry in Illinois." He considered Parker his "Masonic Father."[7]

When the Civil War broke out, Parker wanted to be a part of it. First he had to get permission from the Matriarchy and from his father. This was not normally granted, but his persuasive powers gained him success. He made every effort to get a commission but to no avail. He went to Washington to plead with Secretary of State Seward who told him to go home, it was a white man's war.[8]

Masonic connections do help. Through the efforts of General J.C. Smith, he was granted a commission from Illinois. Somehow he ended up in Grant's unit. He was a natural. He had education in law and in engineering, he was brave and he was a good soldier. Parker became Grant's adjutant and right hand man. Parker rose to the rank of Brig. General.

At Appomattox, he hand wrote the treaty which was signed by Lee and Grant. When Grant introduced his officers to Lee, there was an exchange between Lee and Parker that Grant didn't understand. At first he was afraid that he had offended Lee because Lee may have taken Parker for a "Negro." Parker was sufficiently swarthy to be taken as such. Lee said to Parker, "I am glad to see a real American." Parker's reply was, "we are all Americans, sir."[9] It is said that they also recognized each other as Freemasons. Grant was not.

So that is how a young Indian boy, who studied in central New York, became the person who hand wrote the treaty at Appomattox. He was truly a citizen of two worlds. He was a learned and wise man with a contemplative mind and a sense of duty. Why was he so obsessed with entering the Civil War to fight on the Union side? He obviously was influenced by the Masonic Fraternity and by the brothers he met in that order.

Ely Parker was acutely aware that we do not live in a perfect world. He saw the injustices done to his own people and he knew of the injustice meted to the Negroes in slavery. In one of his orations while still at the Academy in Aurora he said, "...it is true that religion, and learning and liberty have here their homes, but the principles of justice have governed neither the nation nor the people. If you ask me how so, let the burdened sons of Africa answer, who are calling upon God to remember their oppression."[10]

One of his most beautiful orations was delivered to a gathering of over 800 Freemasons in Chicago, Ill. He said:

> Where shall I go when the last of my race shall have gone forever? Where shall I find home and sympathy when our last council fire is extinguished? I will knock at the door of Masonry

and see if the white race will recognize me as did my ancestors, when we were strong and the white man weak. I knocked at the door of the Blue Lodge and found brotherhood around its altar. I knelt before the Great Light in the chapter and found companionship beneath the Royal Arch. I entered the commandery and found valiant Sir Knights willing to shield me without regard to race or nation. I knelt at the cross of my Savior and found Christian brotherhood, the crowning charity of the Masonic tie.....

I feel assured that when my glass has run out and I shall follow the footsteps of my departed race, Masonic sympathies will cluster round my coffin and drop in my grave the evergreen, acacia, sweet emblem of a better meeting. If my race shall disappear from this continent, I shall have the consoling hope that our memory will not perish. If the deeds of my ancestors shall not live in story, their memories remain in the names of your great lakes and rivers, your towns and cities, to call up memories otherwise forgotten.[11]

After the war, Parker campaigned for Grant for president. His oratorical skills were put to good use. Later Grant appointed him Commissioner of Indian Affairs. His final job was with the New York City Police Dept. where his desk was next to another man who would later become President of the United States– Teddy Roosevelt. Parker's health was failing from diabetes. In 1895 the New York newspapers issued "extras" declaring, "Donehogawa is Dead."[12]

Although Parker was buried (with full Masonic rites) in Fairfield, Conn., on Jan. 27, 1897 the body of the last Grand Sachem was brought to Buffalo. He was laid to rest beside his Great Uncle, Red Jacket, in Forest Lawn Cemetery. On May 30 of that year a city-wide ceremony paid tribute to this great leader.[13]

In the Fellowcraft degree charge, we are told, "Your personal contact with others may be circumscribed by the limit of the circle within which your daily life is lived; but your influence, passing through and from those whom that circle surrounds, will reach further than you can conceive."[14]

Because of its power, the influence of Freemasonry certainly passed through the life of General Ely S. Parker. Ely Parker was such a powerful man that his influence has reached thousands of people and it continues to reach all who read or hear about this great man, Seneca

Indian, Last Grand Sachem of the Six Nations, American hero and Freemason.

References
1 *Warrior in Two Camps*, William H. Armstrong, Syracuse University Press, 1978
2 "Ely S. Parker, Man and Mason," Arthur C. Parker, *American Lodge of Research*, Vol. 8 #2, 1961
3 *League of the Iroquois*, Lewis Henry Morgan, Citadel Press, Carol Communications, 1962 (written in 1851)
4 "Ely S. Parker, Man and Mason," Arthur C. Parker
5 *The Life of General Ely S. Parker*, Arthur C. Parker, Buffalo Historical Society, 1919
6 ibid
7 ibid
8 ibid
9 *Warrior In Two Camps*, William H. Armstrong
10 "Ely S. Parker, Man and Mason," Arthur C. Parker
11 *The Life of General Ely S. Parker*, Arthur C. Parker
12 "Ely S. Parker, Man and Mason," Arthur C. Parker
13 ibid
14 Masonic Ritual, Fellowcraft Degree: Charge

Bibliography
"Do-Ne-Ho-Ga-Wa," Ronald L. Brown, *Royal Arch Mason*, Winter 77-78
"American Indian Freemasonry," Arthur C. Parker, *Buffalo Consistory*, 1919
"The Mystery of Ely Parker," M. M. Knight & K. B. Brechner, *Rensselaer Alumni Magazine*, 6-91
"Indians In Masonry, Science & Philosophy," E. D. Martin, *Masonic Outlook*, Oct. - Nov. 1951
"Lewis Henry Morgan and the Grand Order of the Iroquois," Richard Carter, *American Lodge of Research*, June 15, 1991
HO-DE'-NO-SAU-NEE or People of the Long House, Stuart Sturges

The Masonic Apron of Ely S. Parker
Presented to the American Lodge of Research
Special Meeting
Aurora, New York
March 22, 1997
David A.V. Eckhardt

Do-ne-ho-ga-wa, a Seneca Indian born in 1828 on the Tonawanda Reservation of western New York, chose to live in the white man's world. He succeeded in spanning both cultures, through a variety of military and civil careers as a public servant of the United

States and as a Grand Sachem, or chief, of the Iroquois Confederacy. In addition, he was an exemplary Mason. This article briefly illuminates the contributions of this man through an examination of his Masonic apron, which has recently been brought to light as part of the Bicentennial observance of Scipio Lodge No. 110 in Aurora, New York.

At an early age, Do-ne-ho-ga-wa was sent from his reservation to learn English and obtain practical education at a nearby Baptist mission. Through the pastor of the mission, he acquired the name Ely S. Parker and became a Christian. His education continued at Yates Academy in Orleans County. In 1845, he enrolled in Cayuga Academy in Aurora, which was the hunting ground of his Seneca fore fathers. His education in Aurora was limited to less than a year, but it provided significant influences that greatly affected his subsequent public and Masonic contributions.

It was through Lewis Henry Morgan of Aurora that Parker was introduced to Freemasonry. Although Morgan was not a Mason, his father was an active member of Scipio Lodge and must have arranged for his son to use the building during the height of the William Morgan hysteria period. Morgan, who is regarded as the father of American Anthropology, had recently formed the Grand Order of the Iroquois in order to further his interest and curiosity in American Indian heritage. He met Ely on a research trip to Albany, and the two men struck upon a lasting friendship. On his return to Aurora, Morgan began correspondence with Ely and laid plans to enroll him in the Cayuga Academy. Through Parker, Morgan visited the Tonawanda Reservation to learn firsthand of the history and customs of the Seneca tribe, and he was instrumental in helping Parker with the legal defenses of the tribe. Parker became an honorary member of the Grand Order of the Iroquois, where Morgan and others in the Order learned directly of Indian culture from the native American. It was Lewis Henry Morgan who later returned the favor by introducing Parker to influential men in government, academia, and society.

While in Aurora, Ely Parker met in the Lodge room of Scipio Lodge 110 with his fellow members of the Order. He became active in the literary society of the Gordian Knot, which also met at Scipio Lodge. This was in 1845, when Scipio Lodge had briefly relinquished its Masonic charter and was not meeting. It was during these meetings that Parker was first exposed to Masonic furniture and symbols in the richly embellished Lodge room that still stands in

Aurora. It was not until completion of his formal schooling, however, that he chose to join Freemasonry.

Early in 1846, Parker was called to represent the Seneca's interest in Washington and Albany, where political deceit had moved to void treaties and sell the reservation land to the encroachment of white men. He studied law in Ellicottville but was unable to practice because he was not an American citizen. Undeterred, he went on to obtain a degree in civil engineering at Rensselaer Polytechnic Institute, and he began work in various canal projects. His first practical experience was in Rochester, where he worked on rebuilding sections of the Erie Canal. He later worked for the Federal government as Chief Engineer for the Chesapeake and Albemarle Canal and for the U.S. Customs House and Post Office, which still stands in Galena, Illinois. In Galena, he met Captain Ulysses S. Grant, and the two became close friends. When the Civil War broke out, he enlisted as an engineer in the Union Army and later became General Grant's personal secretary and Adjutant General. His role at Appomattox cemented his place in history, as he penned the formal agreement between Generals Grant and Lee that closed the war.

After the war, while Grant was President, Parker became the first Native American to take the post of Commissioner of Indian Affairs. He was a very proactive administrator, and he did much to ease the plight of the American Indians that were displaced from their land and way of life. From there, he took an engineering position with the City of New York, where he met T.R. Roosevelt. He unfortunately suffered from diabetes, and, in later years that followed his life as a public servant, he suffered a series of strokes. He died in New York City in 1895 at the age of 69. His body was interred with full Masonic rites at Forest Lawn Cemetery in Buffalo, near his birthplace and next to Red Jacket, his Great Uncle and former Seneca Sachem.

This brief synopsis of a richly varied life leads us directly to Ely Parker's involvement in Freemasonry and the main topic of this paper- his Masonic apron. He joined Freemasonry while working on rebuilding western sections of the Erie Canal in Batavia, New York. He was raised in Batavia Lodge 88 in 1847 and later joined Valley Lodge 109 in Rochester. In 1858, he demitted from his New York Lodges and became a founding member of Miners Lodge 273 in Galena, Illinois, where he had moved to direct a government building project. In 1861, he became Grand Orator of Grand Lodge of Illinois and Grand Representative to Iowa. In 1862, he demitted again when he returned to western New York, where he became the first Master of Akron Lodge 527 near Buffalo. He was active in Chapter, Council, and Commandery in the several states that he had lived. Ely Parker Lodge 1002 in Buffalo was named for him.

Here was a young native American boy from New York, who through a chance meeting with Lewis Henry Morgan rose to prominence in service to his People, to the Nation, and to Freemasonry. His success came in part through his fine penmanship, his mastery of the English language, and his education in law and engineering. His major contributions, however, came through his strong, honest character and his lifelong friendships, which were firmly rooted in his Christian faith and Masonic obligations.

His Masonic apron is representative of his foundation in the Craft. It is richly imbued with Masonic symbolism. The apron appears to be of a fine silk weave, and it is beautifully printed. The signature of M. Peabody appears in very fine print near a bottom border. The apron is frayed along its edges and ties, which show that it was worn often. In fact, it is said that Parker wore this apron to the Presidential inauguration of his friend Ulysses Grant in Washington. The apron was recently loaned to Scipio Lodge 110 in Aurora by the Cayuga Museum of History and Art of Auburn, New York, where it had been in archival storage. It is currently on display in the Lodge in Aurora. It is unknown how the museum came in possession of the apron, but it is possible that the Morgan family may have brought it back to central New York after Parker's death.

Some of the images on the apron are clearly Masonic, while others are not. The central features are clearly arranged. In the center of the top flap, the letter "G" and the Allseeing Eye of God are displayed, "under whose watchful eye even comets perform their stupendous revolutions." Directly beneath the "G" are the words "Hail Heavenly Virtue, Time's a Sacred Flame!!" The three steps that are central in the main part of the apron represent the three degrees of Masonry and the three stages of life, youth, maturity and age. The twin pillars represent the entrance to King Solomon's Temple. The earth's globe and celestial map of the heavens, and the sun, moon, stars, and comet represent the perfect harmony in the Universe. It is no small coincidence that on the night of March 22, 1997, the beautiful Hale Bopp comet was distinctly visible as Scipio Lodge celebrated its 200th year.

The three Great Lights in Masonry, as well as the three lesser lights are centrally depicted on the apron, as they symbolize the philosophical core of the Craft. The bible is open to Saint John, Chapter XV. The hour glass, scythe, and coffin show how swiftly the sands of time run in human life, and the sword and naked heart tell that sooner or later justice will overtake all of us. The pot of incense, Jacob's ladder with its foundation on the Holy Bible, the beehive, and the various working tools all are symbols that show the underpinnings of Ely Parker's faith and character. Also depicted are the Divine Ark 'that safely bears us over the tempestuous sea of troubles" and the Anchor of Faith that safely moors us "in the peaceful harbor where the wicked cease their troubling, and the weary are at rest."

Do-Ne-Ho-Ga-Wa– Ely S. Parker– had his anchor securely grounded in his faith in God. Surely, the Allseeing Eye searched the innermost recesses of Ely Parker's heart and rewarded him according to his merit. From his early life on the Seneca's reservation, through his first lessons at religious school and his formal education that followed, through civil war campaigns and official duties in Washington, and through his Masonic contributions and lifelong friendships with Grant and Morgan, Ely Parker forged an atypical life that influenced thousands of people. That we could gain a glimpse of Ely Parker through his historic apron on the day that Scipio Lodge 110 celebrated its 200th year is a reminder of how Masonry takes a good man and makes him better.

Bibliography
"Ely S. Parker, Man and Mason," Arthur C. Parker, *American Lodge of Research*, Vol. 8, No. 2, 1961.
Notes on "Ely S. Parker– Man and Mason", Temple R. Hollcroft, *American Lodge of Research*, Vol. 8, No. 2, 1961.
"Donehogawa– Ely S. Parker (1826-1895)," George Peter, *American Lodge of Research*, Vol. 14, 1995.
Warrior in Two Camps, William H. Armstrong, Syracuse University Press, 1978.
League of the Iroquois, Lewis Henry Morgan, Citadel Press, 1851.
The Life of Ely S. Parker, Arthur C. Parker, Buffalo Historical Society, 1919.

Quotations are borrowed from Masonic ritual.
Figure 1, Caption: The Masonic apron of Ely S. Parker displayed at Scipio Lodge No. 110 in Aurora, New York. (The author acknowledges the kind loan of the apron from the Cayuga Museum of History and Art, Auburn, New York, Stephanie Przybylek, Curator.)

George Peter

Powder Horn Goes Home
Press Release: To – The Empire State Mason Magazine
March 31, 2000

Brother Edgar Swart, formerly of Hobasco Lodge #716, died January 25 at the Hospicare residence in Ithaca, NY. He had a powder horn which dates to the Revolutionary War. Before his death, he asked that the horn be donated to the George Washington Masonic Historic Site at Tappan, NY. It was returned to within one mile of where it resided for many years at the home of his grandfather.

Ed's ancestors go back to a DuBois who was one of twelve original patentees who settled in New Paltz, NY in the late 1600s. They were French Huguenots who built homes of native stone. Sixteen of those homes are still standing and are open as tourists' attractions. The DuBois member of the original twelve settlers was in charge of the fortress around their settlement. There was also a Huguenot named Bevier in that group of twelve. He was an ancestor of Jackie Onasis.

Ed came by the powder horn through generations of families on his mother's side. His mother was Bessie DuBois, who inherited the horn from her father, Joseph Ennis DuBois. Ed remembers the horn displayed in a bookcase in his grandfather Joseph's home. Joseph's father (Ed's great-grandfather) inherited the horn from his father, Ephraim DuBois, who lived in Sparkhill, NY– within a mile of Tappan. Joseph DuBois is buried in the Huguenot cemetery in New Paltz, NY.

The DeWint House, built 300 years ago in 1700, is a part of the Historic Site at Tappan. It is now a Registered National Historic Landmark and is maintained as a public service by the Grand Lodge of Free and Accepted Masons of the State of New York. It is open daily from 10:00 AM until 4:00 PM. It was occupied on four different occasions by General George Washington during the Revolutionary War. Washington was a Freemason belonging to Alexandria Lodge #22 in Virginia.

Before the powder horn was sent to the museum, Dr. Sheila Edmunds, professor of Art History Emeritus at Wells College, studied the engravings on it. Her interpretations are as follows:

There is a sketch of what appears to be lower Manhattan with four churches and many other buildings. The date 1776 is engraved in bold. A windmill, several military elements, including two caissons, drums, a trumpet and piles of cannon balls are all depicted on the horn. Also There are two six pointed symbols. One is formed with a compass and the other is drawn free hand. Two English flags and what appear to be regimental flags are also engraved on the horn.

There is a ribbon with the words, "*Dieu a et mon droit*" (God and my right). There is a circle with the words "*honi soit qui mal y pense*" (Shame to you who think ill). Dr. Edmunds states that this is the motto of the "Order of the Garter," the oldest chivalric order in the world.

This leads Dr. Edmunds to conclude that the horn very well may have been the property of a British soldier. Ed Swart did not know how it came into the hands of his ancestors, as he could only trace back to four generations.

In any event the horn is a valuable piece of history. It is very fortunate that it has returned to within one mile of its early home and that it will be preserved in a recognized and well managed museum. Already it has been shown to groups of school children who learn more and better history by seeing a tangible artifact of that important period.

Originally printed in The *Empire State Mason* Magazine, Summer 2002

George Peter

Section II
The Passion of Freemasonry

Part I
Leadership

George Peter

Know Your Product

As emphasized (in the strongest manner possible) in the Leadership Development Course, the first step as a leader is to know your product. But sad to say, too few Freemasons really know the real essence, the real power of the Fraternity. There is plenty written and said about Freemasonry, and yet there is inadequate knowledge of its true nature.

Masters of Lodges are compelled to know. We mouth and hear the standard clichés of making good men better, helping the less fortunate, etc. We need to read and reread "12 Reasons For Being Loyal To Freemasonry." It's in the *24-Inch Gauge Masonic Resource Guide*. But how many of us have read it and digested that powerful list of reasons for being loyal to and being a part of the Fraternity? We need to sense the power that can be unleashed by a complete awareness of what we have in Freemasonry.

The most important reason for being loyal to Freemasonry (although they all are important) is that it is an educational institution. In a previous issue, I quoted William L. Fox, 33rd degree, Scottish Rite, Southern Masonic Jurisdiction. He says, "Freemasonry is an educational institution- a baccalaureate and graduate program in fraternalism- we must encourage fresh scholarship, as all respected educational institutions have done."

If Masters of Lodges understand this, they will not conduct communications in a boring, sloppy, painful way. They will not spend one hour or more conducting 10 minutes worth of business which should have been worked out in executive committee by the officers. Masters who know will not struggle through opening the ritual in a jerky, unprofessional, and non-inspirational way. Those who do so will find that sideliners (if there are any left) will not come back to waste their precious time.

If we do understand that Freemasonry is an educational institution, the opening ritual will be perfected and done with meaning. Each officer will know his part and deliver it with feeling. The officers and sideliners will be inspired and will be transformed from the mundane world into a sense of purpose, a sense of community, and a sense of brotherhood.

The business part of the evening will be conducted professionally and with dispatch. There will be no hesitation or looking to others for advice as to what comes next. THERE SHOULD BE A PROGRAM at each communication. The program should be of an educational nature designed to turn on the brothers about Freemasonry. As many of the officers and brothers as possible should be involved in giving programs during the year.

In a previous issue, I referred to a list of topics, prepared by Paul Bessel of the George Washington Masonic Memorial. It is available through the Masonic Service Association. A Lodge could devote one whole year or more of programs talking about just any one of the reasons for being loyal to Freemasonry. Or we can use the roster of ideas prepared by Brother Bessel.

Another most important and underemphasized reason to support Freemasonry is the role it plays to serve as a promoter of ecumenism. We need to be aware of how valuable this role has been over the ages, and we need to realize how desperately needed that role is today.

In the fall 2000 issue of this publication, I spoke of the newly formed Masonic Millennial Society and how it is addressing this issue. Dr. E. Scott Ryan's recently published book by Anchor Communications, *The Theology of Crime*, deals with the unjust crimes committed against one society by another because of differences in theology. Professor Ryan and Ken Roberts have formed a Masonic Millennial Society to help expose some of these problems. Ryan and I conducted a seminar at Cornell University where we used the Armenian genocide as the first case study of how this injustice occurs. We emphasized how Freemasonry serves to minimize this kind of disrespect for another person's religion. I quoted Rudyard Kipling who said, "Where else can I sit in a room with a Moslem, a Hindu, a Christian and a Jew and know that I am among brothers?" That's a powerful statement. Do we realize the importance of its implications? And in spite of what happened to my ancestors by members of the Ottoman Empire, I can sit in a room with a Freemason from Turkey and know that I am with a brother and a dear friend.

We have only listed two of the most important reasons for being loyal to Freemasonry– it is ecumenical and it is an educational institution. There are 10 other reasons listed. They all are important and they should make each of us more zealous in our support of this great and powerful institution.

Once we study these reasons and understand what we have here in this institution, a good leader should sit down with his officers and active members and work out a mission statement. We printed a proposed mission statement in the Summer 2002 issue of the *Empire State Mason*. Two of the most important missions were omitted. They are:

    To serve as an educational institution
    To promote ecumenism

I repeat the others:
    To teach the proper attitudes to have toward God and our fellow human beings.
    To educate us to become better citizens, parents, men, husbands and fathers.
    To promote morality, truth, honesty, integrity and respect for others.
    To help, aid and assist brothers and others- charity.

So these are the first steps to becoming an effective leader. Know your product and then prepare a mission statement and an outline of how to carry out that mission. We need to return to the conviction that Freemasonry is an educational institution. I repeat my challenge that in New York State we form a Masonic University of New York (MUNY). It has great potential.

I keep returning to the same theme: Freemasonry is an educational institution. If we forget all the other mission statements, we ought not to forget this one, or the role we play to promote ecumenism.

We have great opportunities to promote the power of Freemasonry. We ought first promote it within our own Lodges and then be better prepared to promote it to the world at large. A good start is to sponsor an in-Lodge seminar on the *Theology of Crime*. And then we can do so in the public domain.

Originally printed in The *Empire State Mason* Magazine, Spring 2003

Power Put In the Palms of the People: Five Peas in a Pod
Presented to The American Lodge of Research
New York, N.Y., October 29, 1991

What came you here to do? "Learn to subdue my passions and improve myself in Masonry!" Too many of our members are too old to worry about subduing passions, but we are never too old to learn to improve ourselves.

One of the most important missions of Freemasonry has always been to help brothers learn to improve themselves. By so doing they become leaders in the community. I contend that to be a Freemason is to be enrolled in an educational institution is to be a leader. Too few seem to understand this vital role of the Fraternity. Robert Katz writes in the *Harvard Business Review*, "..development is a continuous process; it does not end at the completion of a specified training period, but should go on throughout a man's life." That's what Freemasonry should be all about — if we understand what it is to be a Freemason.

We should all be obsessed with a search for this missing link in today's Freemasonry. We talk about the lost word. Let's get at looking for the lost mission. That mission very well can best be defined as, "to make modern day leaders". We don't need schools of management; we need schools that teach modern day concepts of leadership. We need leaders who understand that to lead is to serve.

All around us we see discord, disharmony and yes, even chaos. Recently I wrote about the events in the USSR. The title of the paper was, "Coups Happen in Different Forms."[1] Here are excerpts from that article: page 2

The hard line communist leaders who planned the failed coup were not stupid people but they were ignorant about leadership. They did not understand that, as Maitre once said, "human beings are overqualified to live under totalitarian rule." You can brow beat people only so long and then, sooner or later, they will rebel.

There was no mechanism for the coup leaders to receive feedback as to what the rank & file were thinking, nor how much they would support the leaders.

Organizations are no different. Those who rule by decree have no feedback mechanisms. No one dares tell the boss what he or she doesn't want to hear. Sooner or later there will be a coup. It may not be a takeover or a bloody revolt. Too often it is in the form of sabotage to the organization. Already experts are claiming that the average worker gives less than four hours of productive work in an eight hour day. It may as well be a real honest to goodness coup, because the organization will eventually collapse.

The message here is to get up to date in leadership skills. Involve your staff in the planning and organizing process. Use the team concept of leadership. Prevent a revolt. Better yet, help your organization and people grow.. "..Leadership can be democratic in the sense of providing the maximum opportunity for growth to each worker without creating anarchy."[2] — from *Harvard Business Review*, by W.C.H. Prentice

But we don't trust democracy in the work place and so coups happen and they are happening in industry all the time. A coup of sorts has been happening in Freemasonry. The rank and file have not been EMPOWERED to tell Masonic leaders, at all levels, what needs to be done. It doesn't get done and so people stay away from Lodges in droves.

Just maybe one of the reasons people stay away from Lodges is the hang up we have with anachronistic protocol. Back in 1986 I wrote a piece called, "Cardinals, Aprons & Titles" — (CAT)[3]. It questions the excess emphasis we place on rank, titles, and protocol. For example I state,

"While mowing the lawn the other day, I saw a beautiful, red cardinal swoop down and perch on the freshly mowed grass. The incident started my thought process:

What a beautiful bird. No wonder the Catholic Church imitates this part of the divine plan by robing its high officials in the color and name of the cardinal.

Is this a prudent thing to do? It certainly raises that office above the ordinary. Usually there are scores of swallows who swoop down for food while the lawn is being mowed. They are much more common and not nearly as strikingly beautiful as the cardinal."

The thought process continues: Is it prudent to robe any clergy in anything to set them aside, or especially above, the rank and file? What is the purpose?

As a traditionalist, I would not break a tradition lightly. But anything that symbolically, and in reality, places a leader apart or above the rank and file, should be broken. It is in direct violation of modern concepts of leadership. It is counter-productive.

The great Chinese philosopher, Lao-tsu, thousands of years ago, said, "As for the best leaders, the people do not notice their existence; the next, the people honor and praise; the next, the people fear; and the next, the people hate. When the best leaders' work is done, the people say, 'we did it ourselves'."

The most thoughtful minister I ever heard said, "Every minister should work in a coal mine, or do similar work, before serving as a minister."

We are not here to tell the churches or synagogues how to conduct their business. But, how about Freemasonry? We have our share of titles, hierarchies and regalia. The purple apron is designed to set the leader above the rest of the brethren. Masonic Protocol dictates the use of "Worshipful, Right Worshipful and Most Worshipful" as the prefix to salutations of respectively titled Masonic officers.

Is it prudent to practice these mechanisms and protocol in today's society? Can they be counter-productive? Are they perceived by those within and without the Fraternity as ancient customs which are offensive to educated people?

The most valuable and most often repeated message of Freemasonry is that we meet on the level. It packs the greatest wallop. Perhaps more people are attracted to Freemasonry because of this message than for any other reason. But we weaken, distort and corrupt that powerful message by capitulating to mechanisms which are designed mostly to promote ego.

Of greater importance, if titles and aprons were abolished, perhaps greater emphasis might be placed on leadership. It would increase the chance that a leader understands that to lead is to serve. He should be chosen or promoted on the basis of what he does and can do for Freemasonry.

Let us study modern concepts of leadership based on the principle that things are achieved best by team work. This calls for the abolition of Aprons, other than the white leather apron, and titles other than the highest title of all, "my brother."

NOTE: The author is aware that, like any essay, this one runs the risk of being considered "for the birds".

You see, the practice of Freemasonry is an enigma. We give lip service to the idea of equality, meeting on the level, a place for the high, the low, the rich the poor.[4] Then, we indulge in a protocol which is designed to segregate the leaders from the troops. It is designed to distance the leaders from the followers. Some say it is a form of honor to the office. Others consider it an insult to the intelligence of both the leaders and the followers.

Once real or artificial barriers are built between people, communication breaks down and leadership is no longer effective.

Present day workers and volunteers are not peasants. They are educated and sophisticated sufficiently to recognize and understand these barriers and they are turned off when they meet them. Freemasonry is slower to change than is industry and already the latter is in trouble. No wonder we are even more so.

Industry in America is begging for some sort of miracle cure to the mediocrity which prevails. Freemasonry is searching for a solution to dwindling membership and interest in what we preach.

A reason why neither has been successful recently is because neither has understood that you can't teach without practicing what you preach.

Freemasonry was a leader at one time. Freemasonry played a vital role in the formation of our country and our Constitution. New York State Freemasonry, under the leadership of Grand Master DeWitt Clinton, was instrumental in the establishment of the public school system.[5] We can be a leader again. The need has never been greater. We could lead industry in this country, and in the world at large. We could initiate programs to make effective leaders.

W. Bennis & B. Nanus say in their book, *Leaders: The Strategies for Taking Charge*, "If there ever was a moment in history when a strategic and comprehensive view of leadership was needed, it is now." "The new leader is the one who commits people to action, who converts followers into leaders, and who may convert leaders into agents of change."[6]

The authors of that book go on to say that, "*Leaders* have failed to instill vision, meaning and trust in their followers. They have failed to EMPOWER them." They also contend that, "leadership can be learned by anyone, taught to everyone, denied to no one."[7] Let's start with people who are here to improve themselves. Let's start with Freemasons. That's what they came here to do.

In NYS, we can do it by instituting a **Masonic University of New York (MUNY).** We can offer it to Masons and non-Masons alike. The syllabus will be so designed as to make the "Modern Concept of Leaders". Better yet, let's give credit to Freemasonry for the concept. Let's call it, "The Masonic Concept of Leadership." Even though we haven't had the good sense to practice it fully, we have been teaching it in every lesson of every degree. You see, the Masonic Concept of Leadership is called BROTHERHOOD.

Let us never forget that to **lead** is to **serve** is to **educate** is to **serve** is to **serve** is to **serve**. Let us **serve** with **love**.

References:

1. "Coups Happen in Different Forms" — George Peter
2. *Harvard Business Review* -W. C. H. Prentice
3. "Cardinals Aprons and Titles" — George Peter
4. Masonic Ritual — Middle Chamber Lecture
5. *New York Freemasonry* — Ossian Lang & Herbert Singer
6. *Leaders: Strategies for Taking Charge,* Warren Bennis & Burt Nanus, 2007
7. Ibid

Total Quality Management – Quality Improvement Program
LEADERSHIP by any other name is LEADERSHIP

Old Arab proverb:
He who knows not and knows not that he knows not is a fool–
shun him
He who knows not and knows that he knows not is an honest man– help
him
He who knows and knows that he knows is a leader –
Follow him

From the subject of **Leadership** we develop "new buzz" words every day: TQM, QIP, etc., etc.

What do they mean? To empower people. That's a new buzz word also– **to empower.**

What's Leadership by empowerment all about? I like to define it as the application of Judeo-Christian ethics in the work place.

Started with Ed Demming– concept shunned in the USA so he took it to Japan– The USA saw Japan pull ahead of us so we imported it along with Honda cars, Sony TVs, and the other stuff. The irony is that we called it: "The Japanese Concept in Leadership."

People like Tom Peters, Ken Blanchard and a host of other writers began to promote this so called new concept of leadership. Even the Military.

The Herman Miller Company has been doing it since the 1930s. Max DePree has written this fascinating book on, *Leadership is an Art* (p.21)

All progressive fortune 500 companies are getting in the act. To name a few, Corning, Proctor & Gamble, Motorola, Saturn, Cornell University Strategic planning process is ongoing. I served on one of the groups led by the Dean of the I & LR school, David Lipsky. We were discussing the Saturn operation. His comment was, "The jury is still out on the concept– they haven't had enough time to tell if the system will really work."

I thought to myself. "What the hell are you doing as dean of the I&LR school if you don't know that the system will work?" It has to work better than the old style of management because it is in harmony with human nature. The old system of **the boss is always right** is in disharmony with human nature.

Why is the concept of empowerment so difficult to accept? I contend it happens because people have egos. They tend to think that no one else can know the right answers but themselves.

How and when did I begin to see that something was wrong with the **Prussian** concept of leadership? And make no bones about it. That's exactly what the old systems are.

While serving in the Army Air Corps in 1943, I was in charge of a troubleshooting crew and took a tug to the bone yard (used plane site) to get a part. On the way back "Lt. Liverlips" stopped me and asked, "Where you been, Sgt.?" I told him that I went after this part to repair plane # so-and-so. He said, "You didn't ask me!" I replied, "You weren't around, and I thought my job was to keep these planes flying." He said, "Sgt., you're not paid to think!" I picked up my tool box, took it to the engineering officer and said, "Capt., I don't need this anymore." He said, "What's going on?" I told him that Lt. Liverlips told me that I wasn't paid to think; and I don't know how to fix these planes or use this tool box without thinking! He said, "Get your buttocks back out on the line! I'll take care of Lt. Liverlips."

My concept of what is wrong with school systems is that teachers use the easy way out. They think the students aren't competent to learn. So, the students are moved to the less difficult courses.

In my position as Trustee, it has been possible to lobby for Cornell to get involved with the Total Quality Management process. We call it Quality Improvement Program. The administration bought on to the concept once they were convinced that it was their idea.

There's a neat Chinese proverb by the great philosopher, Lao-Tse:

As for the best leaders, people do not notice their existence; the next, the people honor and praise; the next, the people fear; and the next, the people hate. When the best leaders' work is done, the people say, "We did it ourselves."

Leadership is Education is Leadership

To be a Freemason is to be a leader. To be a Freemason is to be enrolled in an educational institution. Freemasonry is an educational institution. In preparing for Cornell University's 125th anniversary, the then President Frank H. T. Rhodes talked about its mission. He said, "to accomplish our mission to serve society as a major university of the first rank, we are committed to these values: Discovery – The search for new knowledge and understanding,

Leadership through Excellence, Service – humane application of knowledge and personal commitment."

These values should be the same for all schools. Note the similarity between them and the stated values of Freemasonry. This confirms that Freemasonry is an educational institution. What came you here to do? "Learn to improve myself." In other words, each Freemason came here to seek knowledge, to learn, to grow in understanding– to discover.

Freemasonry grows leaders. We do it through an effective apprenticeship program and by many other means. "Going up the chairs" is a learning process. It develops leaders. When we use the services of our Grand Lodge and its various committees, we develop greater skills and we do it much faster.

Freemasonry provides many opportunities to give service in diverse forms. The Masonic Home, the Medical Research Lab, the Livingston Masonic Library, Drug & Alcohol Abuse program, youth programs, Child I.D. program, etc. in New York State are just some of the services provided by a Grand Lodge. Other Grand Lodges have similar programs. Lodges provide their own multitude of services. Even so, none of these are as important as the service Freemasonry provides by taking good men and helping to make each one better to serve society.

President Rhodes concluded his talk by saying that none of these values have meaning without love. Freemasonry says the same thing. Our Fraternity is based on the concept that we are all brothers. Brotherhood is another way to say, love one another. Any educational experience should help promote these same ideas. There is no doubt that Freemasonry is an educational institution. It grows seekers, leaders, and people who serve.

Some time ago, at a Leadership Seminar, I posed the following question: How many of you are presently enrolled in an educational institution? All of the Grand Line and 130 of the district leaders were in attendance. One lonely hand was raised and it turned out that he was enrolled in a community college. Hence, not a single one of the top leaders in our Craft was aware that he was enrolled in an educational institution. We are each one so enrolled by virtue of being a member of the Masonic Fraternity. I forthwith wrote the accompanying paper on the subject and requested that it be printed in a Masonic publication. It was rejected on the grounds that the rank and file brothers would be turned off. Heaven help us! The editor felt that the average brother is not interested in developing himself – in improving himself.

In 1988 the Lodge Service Committee, now Leadership Services Committee, in New York State prepared Lodge Service Letter #8801. It is called, "Back to Basics," and talks about the need to develop study groups within Lodges. The Rationale is convincing:
1. We have strayed away from the BASIC function of early Freemasonry, which was to provide a place for philosophical study and contemplation.
2. Study is the essence of Freemasonry. It is not possible to grasp the full power of Freemasonry by ritual alone. We offer study courses but without pointing and showing the way.
3. Those who stay away from Lodge miss all of the power of it. By sharing ideas and information about Freemasonry with them, we can stimulate and reactivate their enthusiasm for Freemasonry.
4. Some concordant bodies provide such study and publications, but the average Freemason does not access the material. This type of program belongs in Symbolic Freemasonry. We need to return to basics.

We were pretty smug for coming up with this new idea to promote the real essence of Freemasonry, but recently I came across an old copy of the *Square and Compass* (a Masonic publication). The April 1924 issue had this to say: "A Masonic education is indeed necessary. Study clubs within Lodges should be formed. Lodges are turning more and more to becoming facilities for education. The *Square and Compass* may be used to advantage for such education. Upon these schools depends the quality of Masonry tomorrow. Mere routine of Lodge is not enough, understanding is essential."

What great words of wisdom back in 1924! How refreshing it would be if we could have some of that in the 1990s. Is there any wonder why Freemasonry was flourishing back then and is not now? Until we Freemasons understand the REAL ESSENCE OF OUR BEING, we will be perceived as no different from any of the multitude of other fraternal organizations. And the world does not need very badly (if at all) one more fraternal organization. But the world is desperately crying out for an organization which is committed to elevating the level of human understanding. Freemasonry is, or ought to be, that organization.

Leadership is education is leadership. Leadership is education is leadership is Freemasonry. This could be the most important message of the 1990s. It was understood in 1924. Let us hope that we can understand it now.

Originally printed in *Philalethes* Magazine, June 1997

Leadership Leads

The reported title of this talk is, "Leadership Leads." I hope that you detect the various connotations contained therein. Steve Zabriskie reported in *The Word* that this is a topic dear to my heart. It may be more than that. I have become almost a zealot on the subject because we see so much lack of leadership around us in high as well as low places.

In Freemasonry we are taught to seek light, more light, and further light. Light is knowledge. We ought to be seeking knowledge. Knowledge is power. Knowledge alone is okay, but it should be put to work. Knowledge produces leaders.

Another message of Freemasonry is that we are developing from Entered Apprentices to Fellowcrafts to Master Masons. It is an apprenticeship program, and anyone going up the chairs likewise is being appreticed in the process of becoming a leader– the Master of the Lodge. Apprenticeship programs are great, but they are not enough. The program needs to have supplements. It needs to be supplemented with a leadership development program.

Way back in 1972 the Grand Lodge of Minnesota put together a leadership development program for officers of Masonic lodges. It consisted of three all-day seminars conducted by a professional team of experts. In 1974, while I was District Deputy Grand Master, we held the Aurora Conference for the Elevation of Freemasonry. It was held on three separate Saturdays in March and April at the Aurora Inn. The main message that came out of that conference was the need for leadership programs for officers of lodges.

Grand Master Cochran heard about the conference and he sent copies of the outline to all the District Deputy Grand Masters at the time. He appointed me to the Lodge Service Committee. My zeal for the subject of providing leadership material for lodge officers was not too well received by the committee system. Remember that it is made up of volunteers who don't want to get too involved. So, I suppose to shut me up, I was made chairman. It has taken a while but we do have a leadership program for lodge officers. It is about two + years old now and is very well received, except in our own district where only two or three have registered for the course. At the conclusion of this talk I will outline some details about the program.

First let's talk a bit more about leadership. Dr. Lawrence Peter wrote about the Peter Principle: in any hierarchy an individual will ultimately be promoted to his or her level of incompetence. In '78 I wrote a paper entitled, "The Root of the Peter Principle." In it I state that the Peter Principle statistic exists only in those hierarchies which refuse to admit that leaders are not born, they need to be developed.

At a recent Cornell Trustee meeting Trustee Don Berens commented that higher education was not doing a good enough job of promoting leadership concepts, especially on matters pertaining to the human relations aspect of leadership. Prof. Jim Maas, at a recent lecture at Cornell sponsored by the Graduate School of Management, stressed the need to add the human element to leadership development. He feels that such concepts need to be incorporated into the curriculum of more schools, especially the Management school. It used to be called the "B School," it now is called the "School of Management." It has one more level to reach. Perhaps it should be called "the School of Leadership."

Dr. Tom Peters, author of, *In Pursuit of Excellence* says pretty much the same thing: Manage by walking around. Get out among the staff and find out what they are thinking. Learn from them. Let them know that you care and that their work is valued.

Dr. Ken Blanchard, of *The One Minute Manager* fame, has endowed a chair at the Hotel School at Cornell. It is dedicate to providing courses in leadership, especially as it pertains to treating people as humans. It is rumored that he didn't endow the chair to the School of Management because he felt that they were not sensitive enough to this important factor. I hope that is not a fact.

In the Ground Hog day issue of *Time* magazine, the cover story deals with poor service in America. It is a several page article about the many horror stories of sloppy service by American industry. You and I could add many more to the list. One short sentence mentions the possibility that the blame may be with poor leadership at the top. There should be no doubt.

The world is crying out for better leadership. Isn't it a tragedy that very few Presidents of the USA in this century have demonstrated the kind of leadership that should be expected of them?

By contrast we have Scipio Lodge #110 and the leadership demonstrated in this room this evening. It is not by accident that Scipio Lodge is one of the most active, and it best exemplifies the essence of Freemasonry. Scipio #110 is a dynamic lodge because we have a generous lot of leaders.

But none of us are ever fully endowed with all the knowledge necessary to be an even better leader. We need to grow. To stand still is to go backward.

The Bottom Line
(Talk given to Scottish Rite Bodies)

Hurrah! Hurrah! Hurrah! "Finally, another leader at the top of the Masonic hierarchy that is aware that the bottom line is leadership." Thank you, Illustrious Francis G. Paul, Sovereign Grand Commander, Ancient Accepted Scottish Rite, Northern Masonic Jurisdiction. His message in the August issue of *The Northern Light* magazine was a ray of light in an otherwise less than illuminated emphasis on leadership. With all due respect to all our really great leaders, not for a long time has there been such a forceful statement on the need for improved leadership and what it is.

Some of us have been preaching for a long time that we need to improve leadership in Freemasonry at every level, but the message doesn't seem to be getting through. It's remindful of the story of the preacher who came to this new church. His first sermon was a humdinger. So was the second but it was the same as the first. On the third Sunday, after preaching the same sermon three Sundays in a row, the deacons cornered him and asked, "What gives? The sermon is great but why the same one every Sunday?" His reply was, *"why move on to a new topic until you begin to understand and implement the message of this one?"*

People say to me, "Oh George, you keep talking about leadership. What we really need is commitment,"

or, "what we really need is communications,"

or, "what we really need is to turn Freemasonry around,"

or, "what we really need is more members," etc., etc.

Will somebody please stand up and say that commitment and communication skills and organization skills and planning and treating people in ways to motivate them; these elements are all a part of leadership. More members and better attendance and turning

Freemasonry around and making it a more dynamic and powerful force in our society will come about when, and only when, we improve our leadership and no sooner.

The Monroe districts are to be congratulated. Right Worshipful Fritz Freidrich and Right Worshipful Paul Robertson take leadership seriously. Last year they arm-twisted over 100 officers to enroll in the 10 Lesson Leadership Development Course sponsored by the Grand Lodge Committee on Lodge Service. Congratulations to those who have completed the course. To those who have enrolled, but not completed the lessons, please persevere. Members from your districts who have completed the course will be glad to offer help and encouragement.

In the meantime we continue to select less than the best possible leaders at every level of the Masonic hierarchy. We select leaders who don't understand the elements of it or who get wrapped up in themselves or who keep stumbling over their egos. (Egos are inflated by the trappings of Freemasonry, which are contrary to the true message of the Fraternity. The trappings set the leader up above the rank and file.)

A relatively new member said it best when he observed that the Officers Training Guide/Masonic Executive Manual contained 15 pages on protocol. His comment was, "That says it all." The Committee on Lodge Service plans to rewrite that manual and to put more emphasis on leadership.

Recently I spoke to about 60 Army Reserve Officers on leadership. They probably heard what I said but I doubt that very many of them took home the message because I suggested that the Army was the least qualified to accept modern concepts of leadership. It is the least qualified because it is too hung up with titles and rank and the caste system.

I remember going to an Eastern Orthodox Church sponsored fiesta, it's called a "hafli." The Bishop sat at one level, the priests one level down, and then the parishioners at another. The Bishop was fed first, then the priests, and finally the rank and file. Now that's what I call anti-Christian and anti-leadership.

Contrast it to the statement of the great Chinese philosopher, Lao-Tse. He said, "As for the best leaders, people do not notice their existence; the next, the people honor and praise; the next, the people fear; and the next, the people hate. When the best leader's work is done, the people say, 'we did it ourselves'."

For your amusement, and hopefully to get us all to think about modern concepts of leadership, I have prepared copies of a paper I wrote some time ago entitled, "Cardinals, Aprons and Titles." Even if you can't accept the message, please read it and wonder if maybe George doesn't have a point here.

What are the elements of leadership? How can we improve on what we do now? It seems to me that the easiest first step is to insist on advancement by proven study and commitment. A leader is not a leader until he acquires knowledge of the product from A to Z. In our case, he must learn the nature and the power of Freemasonry. Learning the ritual is not enough. A leader must learn how to communicate that knowledge and to motivate and educate others to do likewise.

A leader must know how to make it fun to be involved in Freemasonry.

A leader must demonstrate true concern for the value of each individual and to teach respect for each other.

A leader must know how to plan and to organize and to understand and communicate both orally and by the written word. This means an understanding of grammar and the use of good English. A leader must know how to get results and to make Freemasonry grow in quality and quantity. A leader must be clever enough to develop feedback mechanisms to find out what is working and what is not. This may be where we, like the Army, are the greatest failures.

But this is not enough. A leader must be considerate, fair, sensitive, gentle, kind, dedicated and committed to Freemasonry. We learn from each other only to the extent that we listen. And it is imperative that we listen to the new kids on the block. We get so numb (or is it dumb?) from the mundane and routine Lodge activities that we may not grasp the perspectives that best come from new people.

I have talked now for some time and have not once alluded to the quiz which you were given at the beginning of this session. The questions are taken from the Leadership Development Course which is offered to Freemasons in the State of New York. I have asked the clerks to tabulate the scores and to report on how we did. May we have that report at this time.

Regardless of how we did on this very simple test with very definitive answers, we can do better to improve ourselves in Masonry. Sir Francis Bacon, in the early 1600s, emphasized that life is exciting, interesting, intriguing and a challenge because God has hidden knowledge from us. The quest for knowledge is the most fascinating aspect of human life. The quest to improve our effectiveness is what it is all about. Freemasonry symbolizes this quest in the legend of the lost word and how, in the concordant bodies, the word is discovered and brought to true light.

Heretofore the emphasis has been on improving ourselves in the ritual. This is important, but it is not enough. The Master of a Lodge, or the Thrice Potent Master, or the Sovereign Prince, or Most Wise Master, or the Commander in Chief is the chief executive officer and the CEO of his respective organization. He is the leader. But "leaders are not born; they need to be developed." Dr. Lawrence Peter has postulated the now famous Peter Principle. It states, "In any hierarchy a person ultimately will be promoted to his level of incompetence." We have seen that happen in Freemasonry and in practically every institution or organization we know.

I propose a new principle. I call it the George Peter Principle. It goes like this: The Peter Principle is operative only in those hierarchies which refuse to accept the reality that "leaders are not born; they need to be developed." Progressive organizations like GE, IBM, Xerox, Kodak, Cornell University, and others budget substantial monies for the purpose of developing the leadership of its supervisors, managers and executives at all levels. If we expect Freemasonry to survive, we can do no less.

At least in Symbolic Freemasonry we provide some tools. There is the Officers Training Guide/Masonic Executive Manual, the 10 lesson course, the manual for District Deputy Grand Masters and one for the Staff Officers. There is the Masonic Officers Leadership Development manual for staff officers to use in conducting district or Lodge leadership seminars. I don't know what the Scottish Rite offers. I suspect you would do well to use the material available from Grand Lodge. Why re-invent the wheel?

Now let me list some other recommendations that every Masonic body would do well to heed:

    1. Address the reality that perhaps the ritual and the amount of time required are too demanding for the best leaders to give to Freemasonry. Something may need to be modified.

    2. Develop a leadership selection process. The very best potential and only the very best should ever be considered for leadership roles.

    3. Training should be mandatory and expect a commitment.

4. Use the Officers Training Guide/Masonic Executive Manual.
5. Involve officers in leadership courses and seminars provided by Grand Lodge.
6. Conduct study groups to implement the Back to Basics program.
7. Play catch-up ball to overcome the breakdown in leadership which is prevalent in practically all organizations.
8. You have more clout than I do. Help me get a column in the *Empire State Mason* on leadership. It is more vital than the Grand Lecturer's column. But try to convince the leadership of Grand Lodge!

• "Managers are people who do things right and leaders are people who do the right thing."
• The truth is that major capacities and competencies of leadership can be learned. Furthermore, whatever natural endowments we bring to the role of leadership, they can be enhanced. Nurture is far more important than nature in determining who becomes a successful leader."
• "Learning is the essential fuel for the leader, the source of high octane energy that keeps up the momentum by continually sparking new understanding, new ideas, and new challenges. It is absolutely indispensable under today's conditions of rapid change and complexity. Very simply, those who do not learn do not long survive as leaders."

Democracy and Leadership
Hobasco Lodge #716 News

Some people think that leadership is not for everyone. I would disagree. Especially we as Freemasons should be aware that we are leaders by virtue of the fact that we are seekers of the truth. To seek light is to seek knowledge is to prepare us for leadership. "Leadership seems to be the marshaling of skills possessed by a majority but used by a minority. But it's something that can be learned by anyone, taught to everyone, denied to no one." (From *Leaders: Strategies for Taking Charge*, by Warren Bennis & Burt Nanus.)

In 1967 Pulitzer Prize writer, Ernest Becker was talking about Democracy, but what he said applies equally well to modern concepts of Leadership. He said:

"Democracy...one form of government most in accord with the promise of evolution...it has taken upon itself the task of combating the Demonic, by making each person an end in himself (sic) and a responsible, self-reliant point of authority to which power leaders and power institutions are beholden..But in recent years Power has become free-floating, precisely because there are no self-reliant men (sic); instead there are masses led by demagogues, masses who create the power that demagogues use, and who pass on the decisions over that power to those demagogues. 'The Great Leader knows best. Let the experts decide, they have the intimate knowledge. We cannot make the decisions in areas outside our competence...these words are the death groan of evolution itself. The Great Leaders MAY NOT KNOW BEST. They have made empires crumble and caused untold sufferings among their own peoples since biblical times... The fact is that EXPERTS CANNOT DECIDE SINCE THEY SEE ONLY A SMALL SEGMENT OF THE WHOLE PICTURE. Whether aware of it or not, the leader needs to be curbed, needs the broadest base of self-limiting decisions...Many of our brightest minds are watering down the ideal of Democracy to make it accord with a managerial elite philosophy and a fatalistic acceptance of the structure of things."

As in a democracy, organizations are only as successful as their ability to solicit and use input from every segment of the structure. As in a democracy, if such input is not forthcoming, everyone is to blame, and hence, everyone is to blame for the failure of the institution to reach excellence.

Freemasonry is no different than other organizations in this respect. The more broad-based the input, the more likely we will produce programs that will be attractive to the membership. With this in mind, the District Officers Assoc. of Cayuga-Tompkins (DOACT) has scheduled a Leadership Seminar which will be in the form of a workshop. Officers and interested members of Lodges are encouraged to attend to work out the details of planning a year of programs. Hobasco Lodge has prepared itself for this seminar by holding a long range planning session.

Leadership and Democracy
Talk given at Leadership Seminar, Buffalo, NY
November 11, 1989

Twenty years ago, Dr. Lawrence Peter wrote that famous book called, *The Peter Principle*. He postulated that "in any hierarchy a person ultimately is promoted to his or her level of incompetence." Even after 20 years we see the same thing happening in all kinds of organizations and businesses. Dr. Peter's message seems to have gone unheeded, or at least, the Peter Principle statistic is still well and thriving.

Let me share with you some ideas from a paper which I wrote 11 years ago, in 1978. Its title is, "The Root of the Peter Principle"; in it, I introduce the *"George Peter Principle,"* exists only in those hierarchies which refuse to admit that, "Leaders are not born; they need to be developed."

"It is imperative that organizations provide for training in basic management concepts for personnel who have been promoted to managerial positions. This is necessary for all levels of supervision from Deans, Directors and Department Heads of educational institutions to a 'straw boss' of custodians. But it is not happening.

We don't call an electrician when we need a physician. We don't call a plumber when we need someone to design a transistor. We don't call a doctor when we need someone to teach penmanship. But we tend to call experts from a variety of fields such as carpentry, medicine, astronomy, engineering, etc. and we move these people to positions of management. We do so without providing other than minimal training (if any) in management. We call the move a promotion and the person is given a salary increase and a higher position in the social pecking order. In one breath we imply, by higher rewards, that managerial positions are more responsible than other professions and in the next breath we imply that the role of the manager is so simple that no additional training is necessary. Obviously one or both of these concepts is in error." And that is why American industry is falling behind.

In Freemasonry we do even worse than industry. We say the power of Freemasonry is in that it teaches us to improve ourselves. But how many Freemasons do you know who really do so, or how many Lodges provide for programs to help improve the individual brother? So where do we get our managers, (LEADERS)? Brent Morris, in the August '89 issue of *Northern Light Magazine*, said: "We must look beyond men who have put in their time and give real leaders a chance." I say

141

we must DEMAND proof of performance. A warm body with a good attendance record is just not enough. We could learn from the military. The first thing a recruit gets is BASIC TRAINING. Our apprenticeship program of progressing up the chairs is okay, but it is breaking down from lack of quality leaders from whom to learn.

Brother Ted Honea says it best. Let me quote him: "The only thing you get when you lower the standards of what you expect is lower standards than you expected. Expect more and you will get more than you expected."

In the so called "good old days," a Sr. Deacon never advanced beyond that chair until he learned and gave the Middle Chamber Lecture (MCL). That proved some measure of intelligence and a lot of commitment. What do we expect now? Any warm body seems to be good enough. And therein lies our trouble. My message tonight is that no Lodge should allow a Sr. Deacon to move to the Jr. Warden's chair until he has completed the 10-Lesson Leadership Development Course. That should be the minimum requirement. And it is not that much commitment. It certainly is easier than learning the MCL and will do a hell-of-a-lot more good for the individual Brother, and for the Lodge, and for Freemasonry.

For too long we have allowed our egos to help us believe that leadership was not for everyone. A recent Past Grand Master told me that only a select few really can be leaders. Another Grand Lodge Official recently said, "Not everyone can be or should be trained to be a leader." Maybe that is true if we are talking about the run of the mill people (and I'm not convinced that it's true for them either) but we are talking here about Freemasons. Let me quote from two experts on the subject, Warren Bennis & Burt Nanus, in their book, *Leaders: Strategies for Taking Charge*, "Leadership seems to be the marshaling of skills possessed by a majority but used by a minority. But it's something that can be learned by anyone, taught to everyone, denied to no one."

And I contend that because Freemasonry is all about improving myself, by so doing I am making a leader. To be a Freemason is to seek light, which is to seek knowledge, which is to develop one's potential. Hence, to be a Freemason is to be a LEADER. A Freemason can be a leader without being an officer of a Lodge. He is a leader by virtue of being a Freemason (that is if he really understands what it is to be a Freemason).

So where do we miss the boat? What seems to go wrong? It is appropriate at this time, when we see a symbol built by another system of government (the communist Berlin wall) come tumbling down, that we take a closer look at what all of us take too much for granted every day. Pulitzer Prize writer Ernest Becker describes it best and tells us what goes wrong. He was talking about Democracy, but it applies equally as well to modern concepts of leadership today. In 1967 He said:

"Democracy…one form of government most in accord with the promise of evolution…it has taken upon itself the task of combating the Demonic, by making each person an end in himself and a responsible, self-reliant point of authority to which power leaders and power institutions are beholden…But in recent years Powers become free-floating, precisely because there are no self-reliant men; instead there are masses led by demagogues, masses who create the power that the demagogues use, and who pass on the decisions over that power to those demagogues. 'The Great Leader knows best. Let the experts decide, they have the intimate knowledge. We cannot make the decisions in areas outside our competence'…these words are the death groan of evolution itself. The Great Leaders MAY NOT KNOW BEST. They have made empires crumble and caused untold sufferings among their own peoples since biblical times…The fact is that EXPERTS CANNOT DECIDE SINCE THEY SEE ONLY A SMALL SEGMENT OF THE WHOLE PICTURE. Whether he knows it or not, the leader needs to be curbed, needs the broadest base of self-limiting decisions… Many of our brightest minds are today watering down the ideal of Democracy to make it accord with a managerial elite philosophy and a fatalistic acceptance of the structure of things".

I would remind you that the concepts of Democracy grew out of the concepts of Freemasonry. Freemasons were the people who championed the causes of Democracy and they helped to bring it to fruition in this country. Don't ever forget that Masonic concepts are identical to the concepts of Democracy and hence, identical to the concepts outlined by Ernest Becker.

The absolute secret to a successful organization is the ability of that organization to communicate, not just in one direction, but in multidirectional ways. An equally important secret to success is the ability to involve the "troops" in as many ways as possible and to devise mechanisms to solicit and receive feedback.

There are hundreds of ways and countless numbers of systems that can be successful but very few organizations try any. And if they do, it is done as a half-hearted effort just so that they can say (as people have said since time began), "well we tried but it just doesn't work with these people." How many times have you heard that lament?

I submit that there are alternatives to these negative, non-productive attitudes. The BACK TO BASICS program is an excellent example of positive ways to involve the troops. And there are limitless variations of this program. You will receive a copy of the outline for such a program. I think it is an exciting and challenging way to bring Freemasonry back to the basics of serving as an educational institution. That is what it is intended to be. We have gotten so wrapped up in the ritual that we have forgotten, or haven't listened to, what it says. Let's get back to basics. Let's work at developing each Freemason as a better LEADER.

In summary:

• Lodges should use the tools provided to them by the Lodge Service Committee.
• The Leadership Course is the most important.
• The Back to Basics Program is excellent.
• I leave you with copies of recent Lodge Service Letters which you should also find valuable (if you use them).
• Don't develop an elitist attitude. A part of leadership is the training of others. To be a leader is also to be a teacher and a servant.
• Don't be satisfied with unqualified leaders who are attracted to positions for the prestige instead of for the opportunity to serve and to grow.
• Involve as many Freemasons as possible in the leadership process. That is how we promote what it is to be a Freemason. That is how we make real leaders and a lot more, but NOTHING LESS.

Thanks for inviting me to share my strong convictions.

Aurora – Goddess of the Dawn
A History of Leadership Development for Freemasonry in New York State

It has been said that history is written by the victors. That's okay if we are referring to the history of leadership development for Freemasonry in New York State because everyone is a winner. Well, there may be those who refuse to get on the "band-wagon" and hence are losers. Actually there may still be some hold-outs who insist that all we need to know is ritual, rules, regulations, protocol and something about Grand Lodge. They may concede that Masonic philosophy and history are also important. They are the ones who do not understand the true essence of Freemasonry, which is to serve as an educational institution. It's been that way at least since William Preston.

First off, the above listed topics are indeed the prerequisites to any leadership training. First is to know your product. But early on it has become obvious that leadership development is an essential element in the growth of individual Freemasons and Lodges. Gone are the days when it took a brother nine or more years of going up the chairs and thus having on-the-job training. A brother can't learn from example if the examples are not qualified to be emulated.

This became apparent as early as 1973 when the then District Deputy Grand Master of the Cayuga-Tompkins District organized an "Aurora Conference for the Elevation of Freemasonry." Freemasons of the Cayuga-Tompkins District met for three Saturday sessions in early 1973. They met at the historic Aurora Inn. It was appropriate that the conference be held in Aurora, named after the Goddess of the Dawn.

From that conference ideas were born for the development of leadership training of Lodge officers. That conference led to a program in Ont-Sen-Yates district at Geneva, NY. They called their training seminar "PEP 80 (Professional Executive Program)." It was held in Geneva, NY in 1980.

Subsequent seminars were held across the state. The longest standing such program also began in 1980 and recently celebrated its 25th consecutive session. It was called "QUEST through "QUEST XXV." Its long life and continuity can be attributed to at least one "spark plug" by the name of Brother Larry Hammel. (QUEST is a play on words for "Queens United Education Seminar Today.")

Other Leadership seminars have included, but are not limited to, "SEEK – 81" in the Cayuga-Tompkins district, Masonic Education of Monroe County – 1990, others in Ont-Sen-Yates, and regular regional seminars established by Grand Lodge with the assistance of the Lodge Service Committee and the Education Committee.

For many years there was a manual provided by Grand Lodge. It was called the *Officers Training Guide* (OTG). In 1981 the Lodge Service Committee upgraded that manual and called it the *Officers Training Guide – Masonic Executive Manual*. This was to place emphasis on the need for training officers to be Lodge executives. That manual has since been replaced with the *24-Inch Gauge*, now in the process of being upgraded and re-written. The objective of the upgrading is to make the manual more a training manual than a series of reference materials.

The Grand Lodge committees involved in the development of seminars, programs, and manuals have also experienced a transition. In the late 1970's The Lodge Service Committee and the Education committee worked together, but were separate entities. Lodge Service Committee became the Leadership Services Committee. Later the Education committee was dropped, and the new title, as it is now, is the Leadership and Educational Services Committee.

In 1985 The Lodge Service Committee developed a 10-lesson Leadership Development Course which was offered in correspondence format. The course was upgraded and improved in 1993 as an eight-lesson course. It was offered both in correspondence format and in district seminars. The seminars were conducted by the District Staff Officer. The program had mixed success depending on the expertise and dedication of each District Staff Officer.

Recently the Leadership Development Course (LDC) was dropped and replaced by a course called the Masonic Development Course (MDC). This writer believes that dropping Leadership Development program is a mistake. Back in the Cayuga-Tompkins District, the Staff Officer has formed an education committee. The committee has resurrected the 8-lesson LDC and has upgraded the course. We are offering the course in the district in three separate sessions presented by a team of educators and dedicated Freemasons. We hope to persuade Grand Lodge to adopt this new program along with the others.

In the meantime, Grand Master Ed Trosin has appointed a new committee charged to provide advanced leadership training. The committee calls itself "Masonic University of New York" (MUNY). It is developing an advanced and challenging new course called the "Individual Development Course" (iDC). Co-chairman of MUNY, Brother Don Vetal, is developing the course. It will be offered in Regional areas and MUNY hopes eventually to make it available via the internet.

Note: The iDC program has now been running for three years (as of 2009) and has trained over 400 people. The program has been made available to brothers and their spouses. In late June of 2008 the Grand

Lodge of Virginia was trained in implementing the program **and has been implementing the program throughout the Grand Jurisdiction.**

Originally printed in The *Empire State Mason* Magazine, Summer 2005

We Make History

Some (including my wife, Gloria) have commented that my last article dealt with promoting good leadership instead of discussing some aspect of Masonic history. Perhaps that is because I chaired the Lodge Service Committee (now Leadership and Educational Services Committee) for twelve years and can't seem to get that chapter of history out of my system. And that is a good thing. Vanity aside, that period was good for the health of the Fraternity.

The introduction of the Leadership Development Course in 1985 was one of the most important initiatives of Grand Lodge. It started as a ten-lesson correspondence course and has evolved into an eight-lesson course offered in seminar format. Each new set of committee members offers modifications and adjustments to the program. Sometimes this is for the better and sometimes not. The important thing is that we must forge ahead and build on a vital program.

All progressive organizations know that they must train and develop their leaders. Even the best leaders need constant upgrading and updating of ideas and changes in technology and philosophy. Some time ago I wrote to a member of the Leadership Services Committee. Here are some of the comments made:

As Freemasons each of us is a leader. We are so by virtue of the purpose of the Fraternity. We came here to learn to improve ourselves. That is basic and to downplay it is to dilute and even to destruct the purpose of Freemasonry. We need to emphasize this in the "strongest manner possible" and to emphasize it often.

We don't need information about how to visit other Lodges and all that other detail that comes under the purview of the Grand Lecturer. We cannot afford to waste precious time dealing with minutia. We need to deal with the desperate need to improve the quality of leadership at **every level**. Leadership is leadership is leadership.

What goes wrong? A past Grand Master once told me that in spite of leadership training, we still are losing members each year and there are still problems with many Lodges. He is correct, but think how much worse it would be if we had not begun to address the main reason for decline. The Leadership course teaches ways to correct for malaise. There is the "Brother Bring a Friend" program which started out as a "Program to Promote Knowledge about Freemasonry." It works for those Lodges who implement it, and do so often. There are outlines for Lodge programs designed to stimulate a greater awareness of the power of Freemasonry. And there is a lot more.

"You can lead a horse to water, but you can't make him drink." The best leadership development program is for naught unless it is studied and its concepts put into action. One of the weaknesses of the program is that there is no guarantee that those who take the course are studying the concepts thoroughly. When it was in correspondence course format, the student had to read the text in order to answer all the questions. In seminar format we reach many more people, but this method relies on the presenters to innovate methods to guarantee the same diligent attention to the contents of the material. Some, but not all, do a good job at conducting the course in an effective way.

Eventually, Grand Lodge suggested that no Grand Lodge appointment would be made to anyone who had not completed the course. That works only if every district follows this mandate. And in so doing, there would be assurance that Grand Lodge elected officials would also be exposed to such training.

This is where the system breaks down. Progressive organizations know that even the top leaders need training and upgrading in their skills. We in Freemasonry must become aware that "leaders are not born; they need to be developed." All of us need to keep abreast of the basics as well as new techniques for growth and understanding. The system somewhat discourages this by assuming that titles will automatically make one knowledgeable by osmosis or some sort of miracle.

Nevertheless, changes will happen. Some changes are slower to develop than others, partly because leadership at the top must set the example. When the program first started, it took at least three Grand Masters before it was ever mentioned at Grand Lodge or at St. John's Day activities. Two Past Grand Masters took the course and were impressed enough to recommend that it be promoted.

The Leadership Services and Education Committee needs to be ever vigilant to upgrade the training of the trainers and in utilizing technology to make the system more effective. It will happen and history will continue to be made.

If any are further confused because this may not be viewed as history, be advised that history is happening every day. We are making history today. The history we make will determine whether this generation of Freemasons is up to the challenge to make an important impact on the future of Freemasonry.

Let's do it.

Originally printed in The *Empire State Mason* Magazine, Fall 2002

Discover, Lead, & Serve

Good morning brothers! The title of this opening address is Discover, Lead & Serve. The obvious reason for such title is that's what Freemasonry is all about. But first let me tell you a story of a Vermont farmer and a Professor from the University of Vermont. The Vermont farmer and the professor were riding on a train to Brattleboro. The professor struck up a conversation with the farmer and was pleasantly surprised at the knowledge the farmer possessed. You seem to be quite bright," said the Professor to the farmer. "Let us play a little game. You ask me a question and if I can't answer it I shall give you a dollar. Then I'll ask you a question and if you can't answer it, you shall give me one dollar." "Well," said the farmer, "You are a college professor and I'm just a farmer. A more fair game would be for you to ask me a question and if I can't answer it I'll give you fifty cents, but when you can't answer my question, you give me a dollar." The Professor let his ego get the best of him and he agreed to the deal. "You start with the first question," he said to the Vermont farmer. "Okay," said the farmer, "What is it that has three legs and walks?" "Darned if I know," said the professor, "here is your dollar. What is it that has three legs and walks?" "Damned if I know," said the farmer, "here is your fifty cents." What's the lesson? Let's not stumble over our own egos. Let common sense prevail.

Will Rogers had a way of describing such a situation. He said, "We are all ignorant; just on different subjects." Socrates said it in a more eloquent way, but no more succinct. He said, "I am the wisest man in Athens because I am ignorant and know it, whereas all others are ignorant but mistakenly presume to know."

That's old and good philosophy and it's as useful today as it was then. Unfortunately, by that standard, however, I must confess to being ignorant because, you see, I claim to know exactly what we need to do to give Freemasonry the prestige and influence it once had. On the other hand, I also know the ancient Arab proverb that says: "He who knows not, and knows not that he knows not is a fool- shun him. He who knows not and knows that he knows not is an honest man- help him. He who knows and knows that he knows is a LEADER- follow him."

So if I know and I know that I know, please follow me through this reasoning process: What do we need to do to provide growth and an improved image for Freemasonry? It's very simple. We need to rediscover the power of Freemasonry and we need to redefine what we came here to do. We came here to subdue our passions, but of much greater importance, we came here to improve ourselves. We are here to take part in a leadership seminar, but I contend that we must start from the beginning. What came we here to do?

The very first part of leadership is the ability to sell yourself and your product. And we know that the very first ingredient of selling is to know your product. The fact of the matter is that most Freemasons don't know their product. They don't know the real power of Freemasonry. Essentially, brothers survive the ritual and the stuff they must memorize, and that is it. No one has taken time to fill them in about the history, philosophy, and power of the Craft. They go away thinking that this is a different kind of organization- okay, but that is about the end of their thinking on the subject. What should we be doing?

We can start by redefining what Freemasonry is, or ought to be: I have contended for a long time that Freemasonry is an educational institution and we don't even know it. And if we don't know what we are, we certainly can't promote ourselves as such. Let me warn you that when I talk about Freemasonry as an educational institution people get very up-tight. "We can't say that- it will turn brothers off," they tell me. Heaven help us if such is the case. Perhaps we have gone beyond the point of no return. Or have we lowered ourselves to the level of the lowest instead of bidding men come up to us?

Frank H. T. Rhodes, President of Cornell University, defined a first rate educational institution as one which contained these three elements:

1. Discovery -- the search for knowledge

2. Leadership through excellence
3. Service – humane application of knowledge and understanding

Isn't that a description of Freemasonry also? We came here in search of light- in laymen's language, we came here to seek knowledge, to learn, to grow in understanding- to discover. Freemasonry grows leaders. Going up the chairs is one of our better apprenticeship programs to develop leaders. By use of Grand Lodge services and those of its committees, we develop even greater leadership skills. Hopefully that is what is happening here today.

Finally, be aware that we don't copy the service organizations- they copied us, albeit, sometimes they do a better job than we do. But we do a better job than any in taking good men and making them better to serve society.

President Frank Rhodes concluded his remarks with, "but none of this has meaning if we don't do all these things with love." The best definition of love is brotherhood. Hey, I tell you, the closer we examine Freemasonry, the more it looks like an educational institution.

I am the first to confess, however, that we don't do a very good job of the first element of education, which is discovery. That's why most brothers can't answer the question, "what is Freemasonry?" They can't tell you what Freemasonry is because they don't hear it anymore. Case in point, compare any issue of the *Masonic Outlook* (predecessor) to the current, *Empire State Mason* magazine. The early publication used to have articles to excite, inspire, educate, and interest its readers. It provided text material for study. Now most of the magazine deals with pomp and ceremony instead of substance. A recent issue did have an educational article- borrowed from the *Northern Light Magazine*.

We see these things so what do we do? Any good leader will tell you to start out by setting goals:

1. We should do a better job of knowing our product- helping brothers to discover, not only Freemasonry, but themselves. The first thing we ought to know about ourselves is that we are all students- students of life, and students of morality.

2. We should do a better job of developing leaders.

3. Service will take care of itself if we better promote who we are and what we came here to do. We need to put a face on Freemasonry- an improved public relations program.

Illustrious Francis G. Paul says, "We are marching backward; There is sometimes little substance to what we do; Who needs it? Why should they stay? Many of our members fumble, bumble, and stumble when they try to answer these questions." A friend of mine, RW Stephen Zabriskie, puts it this way: "When Lodges don't do anything of note, are aimless in their activities, and the members are the same, then the portrait of the Lodge is a shadow." Our goal should be to put a face on the portrait of Freemasonry– give it a recognition factor.

I haven't said anything new. People have been saying for years that this is what we have to do. The Grand Lodge of Connecticut conducted a year-long study which resulted in the MANDATE FOR CHANGE report. It was printed in *Northern Light Magazine,* May 1989. The recommendation that caught my eye was the next to the last. It called for the development of a Masonic Development Institute (MDI) to offer leadership development and other programs for Masons.

The National Survey conducted by the Masonic Renewal Task Force provided an in-depth study of pertinent factors related to Masonic membership, attitudes, interest, etc. Its important recommendations were:
- identify ways to improve communication
- determine reasons for activity and inactivity
- determine existing levels of satisfaction and dissatisfaction
- understand forces which will have significant impact upon the Fraternity in the future

There have been numerous other studies and initiatives to get Freemasonry up to becoming a force in the next century. But for all the studies, recommendations and work of so many highly concerned brothers, relatively little impact is being made. How come?

I contend that there are three major factors which prevent greater movement toward success.

1. The first and foremost is the weight of the hierarchies of Grand Lodges. Our obsession with titles, aprons, and rank are all barriers to the kind of communication necessary to make change. I wrote a paper entitled, "Cardinals, Aprons, and Titles," and I was afraid of being ostracized from the Fraternity for being so bold as to suggest that modern concepts in leadership dictate that we minimize the mechanisms which create barriers to communication. This is not to suggest that aprons and titles are wrong. There is a place for everything as long as we don't over-kill.

2. Secondly, we haven't started at the beginning. We haven't trained qualified leaders with the first ingredient– to know their product. We haven't done a good enough job of helping them discover. We've even denied that Freemasonry is an educational institution. By so doing, we have denied the essence of the Craft.

3. Another serious mistake we make is in the process of selecting leaders. Our system filters out the best leaders because the demand for memorization, and the demand of being present as a warm body at important Masonic functions, is too great for good leaders who are doing productive things elsewhere. Past leaders who may or may not understand about leadership are the ones who make the selection. That is not a modern concept of selecting leaders.

What does work?

The Connecticut plan for a Masonic Development Institute is tremendous. That is why it caught my eye. But, again, to my knowledge the program has not gotten off the ground. I had proposed a similar plan for New York State. The proposal was to call it Masonic University of NY (MUNY) or Masonic Academy of NY (MANY). This would help to develop the kind of leadership needed and the kind of study needed to help brothers realize the power of Freemasonry. This idea has received less than enthusiastic support so far.

We do have, in NYS, the Leadership Development Course, which originally began as a correspondence course. We now supplement the program by offering the course in seminar form within districts. It is a step in the right direction. I recommend something like it in every jurisdiction.

If we instituted programs such as these, we could jump start Freemasonry into the next century. These are ways to reintroduce Freemasonry to its members. Why did Freemasonry grow so rapidly in the early eighteenth century? I quote from Clyde E. Myers, Past District Deputy Grand Master Cayuga-Tompkins: "Thoughtful and concerned people saw in Masonry something they had been looking for. Its ancient ideals refined, improved, and polished by ages of trial and error, seemed to fill the gap in the aspiration of men looking for a satisfying pattern of life. It made life worth while." He continues, "Some historians believe that the sublime tenets of Freemasonry in ethics, morals and religion caught on in the early

1700's as a revulsion against the low level of morality of the times. The times were ripe for the rapid expansion of Speculative Masonry".

Hey, the times are ripe, now, in the last decade of this century. The times are ripe for the same power of Freemasonry. But it won't happen unless we start at the beginning and re-educate our current brothers and new ones as to what we are. It will happen by promoting the educational aspect of the Fraternity. Then we need to return to that education process.

We need leaders who will provide Lodge programs to educate, inspire, excite, interest, and turn on the membership about Freemasonry. We need publications that do the same thing.

Worshipful Dick Walk, in his promotion for this seminar, told you that this was my theory about every Lodge program. We need to provide quality time for our brothers or they will continue to stay away from Lodges in droves. If you want to remember those words, educate, inspire, excite, interest, and turn on the membership, they spell E, I, E, I, O. Here is a story to help jog the memory. Now any of you football players need not get offended. These two boys were from Harvard. They were a little bit less than astute. The Professor was about to flunk them, but their coach implored him to pass them one way or another. So after being cajoled by the coach and by the Dean, the professor put the kids in a room and turned on a tape player that went on for an hour playing, "Old MacDonald Had a Farm, EIEIO, over and over again. The professor then wrote on the black board: "Old MacDonald Had a _____." He told the kids to fill in the blank and they would pass. He left the room for an hour and the guys tried to solve the problem. One asked, "What do you suppose it is?" "I think that it's a farm," said the other lad. "How do you suppose it's spelled?" "I don't know, maybe it is EIEIO"

Back to what we need to do make Freemasonry grow. We need to prepare ourselves and our brothers to discover, lead, and serve with love. Then let's go out there and do it. We've talked long enough. What is needed now is action. Let's implement programs to help us be the kind of fraternity that served society in the early eighteenth century. We need to gird ourselves to tackle the challenges of the twenty-first century coming up soon.

I've come prepared with some tools to help us be the institution of learning we came here to be. You will receive a packet containing the following:

LSL 8801 Back to Basics
LSL 8802 To Increase Lodge Membership
LSL 8803 To Revitalize a Lodge
Twelve Reasons for Being Loyal to Freemasonry
Outline of Correspondence Course
Program to Promote Knowledge About Freemasonry

The literature is designed for New York State, but with a modified word here and there, it fits any Grand jurisdiction. None of it is perfect and some of it is dated, but it is better than denial that we have a problem. Let's convert that problem into a challenge, and then let's meet it!

Note: The Lodge Services Letters (LSL) mentioned above are included on pages 169-176. The LSL's have also since been incorporated into The 24-Inch Gauge Masonic Resource Guide, *available for purchase from Grand Lodge Services at 1-800-3Mason4. The Correspondence Course has been incorporated into the online Leadership Development Course (LDC-8) now offered by Masonic University of New York at www.e-muny.org.*

Keynote Address at QUEST II - March 6, 1982

Behold how good and how pleasant it is for brethren to dwell together in unity. Behold how good and how IMPORTANT it is for brethren to WORK together as we study to improve ourselves in Masonry and to improve our effectiveness as leaders of this, our beloved fraternity. And that is what we have gathered here to do today!

But first congratulations are in order to the organizers of these Queens United Education Seminar Today (QUEST). It should be obvious to most of you that the present District Grand Lodge Officers deserve a lot of credit- a) Special recognition should be given to the spark plugs behind the scenes. It should be no secret that the persons with the most enthusiasm for this and last year's QUEST are your AGL, Larry Hammel, Jr., RW Murray Silver, and W Milton Markowitz. These people acted as the catalyst to get it off the ground. I met these wonderful brothers at one of the Regional Seminars, and it became evident immediately that they shared the same excitement about the benefits of leadership training. We have corresponded regularly since, and have shared material of interest. Freemasonry has benefited by that sharing.

That said, let me continue: Freemasonry should pride itself on its excellent apprenticeship program whereby officers move up the chairs and learn the duty and ritual of each station and place. It is a special and unique system that other organizations (including governments at several levels) would do well to copy. But our system has not been perfect. It has not met all of the criteria for developing top quality leadership.

Like anything else, in order to evaluate a system accurately it needs to be compared to a reference. You've heard the story of the Vermont farmer who was asked, "How's your wife?" His answer was, "Compared to what?" If we compare our apprenticeship program to, let us say, the European apprenticeship for craftsmen or the apprenticeship of our operative brethren from whence our heritage is derived, we come out on the short end of the stick! In those systems a craftsman was and is a craftsman in the true sense of the word. No part of the trade is omitted. In Freemasonry heretofore, the emphasis has been on improving ourselves in the ritual. This is important! But it is not enough! This is not to downplay the importance of good ritual in preparing a brother to become the Master of his Lodge, but we have not placed sufficient emphasis on the main function of that office. The main function of the Master of a Lodge is to preside as a LEADER. He is the chief executive officer of a very important organization. But Leaders are not born, they need to be developed. Dr. Lawrence Peter has postulated the now famous Peter Principle. It goes like this: "In any hierarchy a person will ultimately be promoted to his level of incompetence!" You have seen that happen in Freemasonry and in many organizations and businesses. I propose a new Principle. I call it the George Peter Principle. It states that the Peter Principle is operative only in those hierarchies which refuse to accept the reality that "Leaders are not born; they need to be developed." Progressive organizations, including such as GE, IBM, Cornell U. and others, budget substantial monies each year for the purpose of developing the leadership ability of its supervisors, managers and executives at all levels. By the way, the best words I have found to define good leadership come from the Chinese philosopher, Lao-Tse. He said, "As for the best leaders, people do not notice their existence. The next best people honor and praise. The next the people fear, and the next the people hate. When the best leaders' work is done, the people say: we did it ourselves." The danger in being a leader is to adopt an elitist posture. A true leader is one who understands that to be a leader, one must be a servant. To lead is to serve. To be of service as a leader is to work, to plan, to be innovative, to motivate others, to seek ideas, to be committed, and to inspire others by setting an example.

To borrow another quotation, W.C. Fields said, "There comes a time in every man's life when he must take the bull by the tail and face the situation." (Maybe that is what happened to Mayor Ed Koch.) As Freemasons, let us take the bull by the horns: we know where to start.

So let us get on with the business of developing our executives. A true executive is more than a manager, more than an administrator; he is a leader whose role is all-encompassing. The list of duties of the Master of a Lodge is AWESOME. It ought to scare the hell out of the meek (if he is aware of the awesomeness of the duties). We tend to soften the blow by clichés like: Don't worry, anyone can be Master! Well, do the best you can. It's easy; all you have to do is open and close 20 meetings per year, etc. Herein lies the root of our problem. Just recently I was criticized for referring to officers of the Lodges as executives. "That's going to scare some people to death," I was told. My response is, "Good! It is about time!" Let us hope that those who are scared will do one of two things: either bail out and make room for the brave, or be aware of the awesomeness of the task and start to do something to prepare themselves to meet the challenge.

I have confidence that anyone can learn to be a good Master– a good executive. My critics are not so sure! But it won't happen without training. At Cornell U. for the past several years I have developed curricula and taught courses to electronics technicians. Many of the kids, and older kids (like me), get bogged down because the school systems have in the past told them that if they weren't going to college, they didn't need math. We immediately have to stop the electronics theory study and learn basic algebra and trig. The important point is that I have not run across a single student who could not learn algebra and trig. These are the same people that the school systems consider lost causes. Once the motivation to learn is there, they can and they do learn.

We Freemasons could learn. We can learn from the Vermont farmer who was approached by a city slicker from, I think, Queens, who had come up into the backwoods of Vermont expecting that people there wouldn't know the price of land. "I'd like to buy $500 worth of your land," he said to the farmer. "Ayeh," was the farmer's reply, "go fetch your wheelbarrow and I'll fill 'er up for you!" That's how we ought to feel about Freemasonry- we ought to know that we have a priceless commodity called brotherhood. Instead, too often, we tend to be like the Vermont storekeeper who was asked how come he didn't have a certain item on the shelf. His reply was, "don't stock it anymore - it moves too damn fast!

Well, the message from those two stories is that we need to be aware of the value of Freemasonry and then be willing to keep a lot of it around and share its value. More importantly, we can sell Freemasonry best when we are best motivated and prepared as leaders to do so. I would hope that we go forth from QUEST II armed with a new enthusiasm to share ideas, to promote Freemasonry, and to work to help the present and the next Grand Master to make Freemasonry a vital part of every New York State community. Let us not only place emphasis on the development of leaders, but on the reasons for providing the best trained leaders for Freemasonry. In this way we will stimulate officers to promote the Craft.

I would like to quote Illustrious George Newbury, 33° "Let us erase from the Masonic vocabulary the statement: 'You get out of Masonry what you put in.'" Illustrious George Newbury believes the phrase should be replaced by, "We are on a crusade to make a better society by improving the building blocks of that society." Let us all join that crusade, and let us always remember that the success of any endeavor is directly proportional to the caliber of the leaders.

Here is a picture of an old mill in Aurora, NY. It was built in 1823. Please note my Brothers that, like Freemasonry, the edifice is built on a solid foundation. It is not crumbling because of the foundation. But, alas, it is crumbling from the top down. What happened? The roof decayed and then moisture began to sweep into the mortar. Any organization is like an edifice. It decays from the top down. Let us not allow this to happen to Freemasonry.

What we are here for today is to share tools and information to prepare each of us to be a better roof, a better leader, a better executive, a better Master. Only as Freemasonry repairs, maintains and improves its roofs (the leaders of the Craft) can Freemasonry survive and continue to shed its beneficent influence on all mankind.

Let us learn from the three ruffians. Let us not expect to find the True Word before the Temple is completed and dedicated. Let us prepare ourselves by study. Let us become true Craftsmen. Let us complete our Temple of Preparation. *Then* we will be found worthy of being called Master builders, qualified to lead Freemasonry to greater heights and more glorious service.

The Peter Principle
Dec. 20, 1978
Revised - July 25, '89

Dr. Lawrence Peter's book, *The Peter Principle* became the talk of the town and was a best seller, when first published in 1969. The book accurately defined why things go wrong. Dr. Peter postulated that, "in a hierarchy, every employee tends to rise to his level of incompetence."

In 1972 *The Peter Prescription* was published. It told how to make things go right. This book by Dr. Peter provides 66 prescriptions to prevent a person from being promoted to his or her level of incompetence. In Part three, the author comes closest to identifying a main solution but almost hides it in his prescription #49. He suggests that administrations must provide ways to "develop the new promotee."

This essay is to suggest that a new and stronger emphasis must be placed on the need to train and develop "promotees." A new rule is needed. Let us call it, "The George Peter Principle." It states that, **"The Peter Principle exists in those hierarchies which refuse to admit that leaders are not born; they need to be developed."**

We don't call an electrician when we need a physician. We don't call a plumber when we need someone to design a transistor. But we tend to call on experts from a variety of fields such as carpentry, medicine, astronomy, engineering, etc. and we move these people to positions of management. We do so without providing other than minimal training (if any). We call the move a promotion and the person is given a salary increase and a higher position in the social pecking order. There is no doubt that the professional or specialized training is an asset in managing people within the same or related disciplines. But the point is that to expect the newly promoted manager to learn management concepts by osmosis is absurd. The paradox is that in one breath we imply, by higher rewards, that managerial positions are more responsible than other professions and in the next breath we imply that the role of the manager is so simple that no additional training is necessary. Obviously one or both of these concepts is in error.

It is imperative that organizations provide for training in basic management concepts for personnel who are "promoted" to managerial positions. This is essential for all levels of management from the lowest level of supervision to Deans, Directors, and Department Heads of educational institutions. "Leaders are not born; they need to be developed." A major element of any leadership development program should include training in human relations– how to treat people as humans.

We must examine the reasons why institutions do not put their houses in order to prevent the Peter Principle from flourishing. Managers are in a position to "manage" the Peter Principle out of existence but they don't. Why not? One of the less flattering characteristics of humans is that we tend to be provincial. We allow our uncontrolled egos to cause us to believe that our color, our race, our profession, our religion, must be the best and most important.

Managers are not immune. They allow their egos to stand in the way of adopting progressive management concepts. The first mistake is to inflate their value, their salaries, and their titles. Next they deflate the importance, salaries, and titles of everyone else in the system. As a result, many banks have more vice-presidents than tellers.

Managers are in a position to make the rules and establish the guidelines, all of which are made in their favor. An example criterion set by managers to determine salary levels is the number of dollars an individual is responsible to budget. That is convenient for them because managers are in a position to budget more monies than a chemist, an engineer, a physicist, or most any of the other professions.

The irony is that the discipline and training required to become a manager is at least an order of magnitude less than to become, for example, a chemist, a physicist, or an engineer. But the only way the latter professional can command the salary of the manager is to give up the profession, where several years of training were invested, and be "promoted" to a managerial position. Worse yet, even if training in leadership were offered, the professional will balk at being subjected to further training. This happens especially in colleges and universities where faculty members are placed in positions of leadership.

To make matters worse, the people in the professions who are discriminated against are people with sufficient intellect to be aware of the inequities generated by the system. It is a common and well known joke among them. It should be no joke to management that the inequities cause demoralization and lost productivity.

Solutions seem so simple that it is difficult to understand why the Peter Principle has not been eliminated after 20 years of exposure by Dr. Lawrence Peter. Experts for years have proven that successful management is by involving the whole group as a team. The more people involved in planning, the more people will be available to promote the program. If professionals other than managers had some say in important decisions that affect them and their organization, they would be less likely to want to give up their work, for which they are best trained, and be "promoted" to manage.

The reality is that few people in a position to manage want interference or input from any one else. It's easier "to do it myself." And besides, ego leads people to believe that no one else is qualified to help make decisions. That is why The Peter Principle is well and flourishing in most institutions.

The Peter Principle can be wiped out by adopting the George Peter Principle: The Peter Principle exists in those hierarchies which refuse to admit that "Leaders are not born; they need to be developed." Once leadership development programs are put in place to train "promotees," managers will be qualified to understand concepts which include involving others in the decision making process. Those without the energy and enthusiasm for further training will be more willing to remain in their professions of expertise.

The Sun or Black Holes

There is news in the wind that a committee may be formed to study the overall Masonic Leadership Development Program(s). It is in order to review the Leadership Development programs of The Grand Lodge of the State of New York. For years some of us have been promoting the idea of an expanded leadership development program. In 1994, while speaking to the Grand Lodge officers of the Monroe Districts in Rochester, I proposed an expanded plan and predicted that it would take several years to get the plan implemented. Previous experience had demonstrated that things move slowly. In 1985 a 10-lesson leadership development program was started and administrated from Aurora in correspondence course format. (Don't be surprised that some of us refer to Aurora and the Cayuga-Tompkins District as the seat of enlightenment. Bear in mind that Aurora is named after the Goddess of the dawn.)

For quite a few years the program was not promoted very vigorously by the Grand Lodge hierarchy, but finally enough brothers who had taken the course percolated to the top of the leadership ladder. They began to ask why the course was not being promoted.

Eventually Past Grand Masters Widger and Singer both took the course and were sufficiently impressed to help support the program.

Now the program is mostly offered in seminar format. Nothing is perfect and everything can use some upgrading and improving to keep up with new technology and the times. At least, now a Master Mason does not get a Grand Lodge appointment without first taking the course. That is good news. Where do we go from here?

Again, we return to 1994 (and even earlier). I had proposed a program called "MUNY" (Masonic University of NY), but it takes patience to get things implemented. Initial thoughts are to call it, e-MUNY or e-MANY (for Masonic Academy of NY) and to offer it via the internet. What will be the syllabus? Well, that is why really talented and visionary Brothers need to be selected to prepare the text and mechanics for running such a program on the internet.

Original thoughts are to study Masonic history, philosophy, and influence. Obviously this needs to be aimed at preparation for leadership development concepts and procedures as well. But that is not all. The course may also include the seven liberal arts and sciences, beginning with grammar.

"Grammar?!" you say! Why not? **People judge us by the words we use**. How can we expect to attract qualified leaders to the Fraternity when they hear atrocious grammar from some of us? **People judge us by the words we use**. We dress up in a coat and tie to go to Lodge because we want people to observe the respect we have for the Craft and its teachings. We hear grammar like: **"It don't matter." "Hey, you done good." "We gotta do that." "Them apples are rotten." "He don't need nothing."** And it's worse than that. Some pollute their grammar with, "you know," and, "like," in every other sentence or more. **People judge us by the words we use**. When people hear us use street talk, the coat and tie are perceived as a camouflage to hide our true ignorance or lack of respect.

We are not the only guilty ones. Recently, a radio commercial by Sears went like this, "You need no nothing." So help me, that's what the announcer said.

But, to stay in the vernacular, **"You ain't heard nothing yet."** Why not offer this program to Masons and non-Masons alike? It is needed by everyone. We can make a difference. When we talk to men and women about the philosophy, history, and influence of

Freemasonry, the women are usually twice as turned on as are the men.

To make a case for such a program, let's use an astronomy analogy. From the first formation of society, not only architecture was framed, but also, long before that, humans were aware of the power and influence of the sun. This was even before Copernicus made the point that the earth revolves around the sun and not the other way around, as earlier assumed. Freemasons even compare (symbolically) the Master of the Lodge with the Sun as he rises from the East. All energy in the form of light and heat and all the rest of the energy spectrum comes from the sun. That is good. And then there are black holes. Only recently did scientists learn of the existence of black holes. These are other forms of massive suns or stars that are so dense and so compact, and thus their gravity is so strong, that no energy escapes. That is why they have eluded scientists for so long. They offer us on earth absolutely nothing. They keep it all to themselves. It took some really sophisticated research techniques to note that they exist.

The point is that our emphasis on seeking light, which is equated with knowledge, is an important concept. Let us continue to seek light and knowledge to become more effective citizens and human beings. Let us not be dense. Let us stop acting like black holes and keeping everything to ourselves. Let's act like the sun and radiate our powerful message to others. Let's have the world know us and see us as providers of knowledge.

Some would argue that the school systems can do a better job of providing knowledge than we can. If we have any confidence and awareness of the power of the message of Freemasonry, we will not accept that assumption. Seventeenth century Freemasons shared their knowledge with the world. Why shouldn't we? That is why they were recognized and appreciated.

We can get behind this move to expand our horizons and our service to all of humankind. Let's do it!

Originally printed in The *Empire State Mason* Magazine, Winter 2003

Cardinals, Aprons, and Titles

While mowing the lawn the other day, I saw a beautiful, red cardinal swoop down and perch on the freshly mowed grass. Mine is a large lawn, hence a lot of time is available for meditation while mowing it. The cardinal started my thought process like this:

What a beautiful bird. No wonder the Catholic Church imitates this part of the divine plan by clothing its high officials in the color and name of the cardinal. Is this a prudent thing to do? It certainly raises that office above the ordinary. Usually there are scores of swallows who swoop down for food while the lawn is being mowed. They are much more common and not nearly as strikingly beautiful as the cardinal.

The thought process continues: Is it prudent to robe any clergy in anything to set them aside, or especially above, the rank and file? What is the purpose? Jesus Christ said, "Follow me." He did not vest himself even in the plain black robe, for example, of the Methodist minister. Some would argue that the purpose is to demonstrate solemnity and to cover up "earthly" garments. It is a tradition. As a traditionalist, I would not break a tradition lightly. But anything that symbolically, and in reality, places a leader apart or above the rank and file, should be broken. It is in direct violation of modern concepts of leadership. It is counter-productive.

The great Chinese philosopher, Lao-Tse, thousands of years ago, said, "As for the best leaders, the people do not notice their existence; the next, the people honor and praise; the next, the people fear; and the next, the people hate. When the best leaders' work is done, the people say, 'we did it ourselves.'"

The most thoughtful minister I ever heard said, "Every minister should work in a coal mine, or do similar work, before serving as a minister." How about Freemasonry? We have our share of titles, hierarchies and regalia. The purple apron is designed to set the leader above the rest of the brethren. Masonic Protocol dictates the use of "Worshipful, Right Worshipful, and Most Worshipful" as the prefix to salutations of respectively titled Masonic officers.

Is it prudent to practice these mechanisms and protocol in today's society? Can they be counter-productive? Are they perceived by those outside Freemasonry as ancient customs which are offensive to educated people?

My thought process continues (there is more lawn yet to mow): Is it possible that Cardinals, Aprons, and Titles, which set the leader above the rank and file, can be construed to be man-made devices designed more to promote ego than effectiveness? The most valuable and most often repeated message of Freemasonry is that we meet on the level. It packs the greatest wallop in Freemasonry. Perhaps more people are attracted to Freemasonry because of this message than for any other reason. But we weaken, distort and corrupt that powerful message by capitulating to mechanisms which can serve to promote ego.

If nothing else, think of time saved (people hours) if Lodge meetings could be conducted without the protocol of prefixing brother's names with titles! "RW and W" are used, not only during the communication, but are repeated by the Secretary during the reading of the minutes. It serves to add to the tediousness of the business part of the meeting, which is usually already too long. This alone is a reason to modify the protocol. Brothers may not stay away from meetings in quite the droves that stay away now.

Of greater importance, if titles and aprons were abolished, perhaps greater emphasis might be placed on leadership. It would increase the chance that a leader understands that to lead is to serve. He should be chosen or promoted on the basis of what he does and can do for Freemasonry.

We cannot, nor should we consider offering suggestions to the Catholic Church or to any other church. But in Freemasonry, let us get up to date on leadership. Let us study modern concepts of leadership based on the principle that things are achieved best by team work. This calls for the abolition of Aprons, other than the white leather apron, and titles other than the highest title of all, "my brother."

NOTE: The author is aware that, like any essay, this one runs the risk of being considered "for the birds"– not taken seriously and even offensive to some. The reader should remember that it is the result of a thought process which was initiated by the cardinal. Freemasons have been referred to by their enemies as being just as bad as the "free thinkers." Maybe it is time we did more free thinking.

Originally printed in *Philalethes* Magazine, October. 1996

George Peter

Part II

Education

George Peter

Freemasonry – An Educational Institution

You've heard the radio ad produced by the Mormon Church: It is cute and has an effective message. A father is answering the question, "what is a dad?" He stumbles and mumbles and says, "well, ah, a dad is a ...let's see a dad is, well you know it is ..." etc.

Well, how many Freemasons do you know who can answer the question, "what is Freemasonry?" They say, "well, let's see, it is ah, well, it is like a fraternity, ah, well it is too complex to explain."

Sad, but true, brother Freemasons have trouble explaining what the Fraternity is and why they support it. We ought to know.

Informed Freemasons are aware that the impact on the role of Freemasonry, and what it is, was established by William Preston: 1742 - 1818. Prestonian lecturer, Stephen Jones, delivered the first of these lectures in 1820. We know them in terms of our ritual, and especially the Middle Chamber Lecture. What we should not forget is that much of the ritual has been revised and reduced to the point that the basic emphasis has been diluted. It is important to review some of that emphasis in the original lectures:

- What is the Ground plan of Masonry?
  Instruction.
- Why?
  Because no man living is too wise to learn.
- What will the wise man do?
  He will diligently **seek knowledge**.
- What will the Mason do?
  He will travel to find it.
- Who are entitled to knowledge?
  All men who have a desire to gain it, and abilities to improve.
- Who are better entitled to it?
  Those who have been selected from the community at large and they rank in the character of Masons.
- Who are best entitled?
  Free and Accepted Masons.
- Why?

Because all knowledge they have acquired they will cultivate, and improve to the best advantage; and when they have

The Power and Passion of Freemasonry

so done they...they will prudently dispense it for the general good.[1]

Do you get the impression that Freemasonry is an **educational institution**? Of course it is, and was from the beginning intended to be. People have not taken us seriously enough when we keep saying this. That may be because the Craft may have deteriorated to the level of the least common denominator. It happens all the time and all over. The accepted educational institutions that we know as the public school systems have done the same thing. There was a time when a high school graduate was versed in the sciences, math, grammar, a language or two and even some astronomy and music. The graduate became learned in the seven liberal arts and sciences. Not so today! Short cuts are provided so that some graduates now are lucky if they can read and write.

William Preston's Middle Chamber lecture spells out in no uncertain terms that Freemasonry is an educational institution with the purpose of improving the minds and effectiveness of its votaries. As per that document, speculative Masonry is "to lead the contemplative to view with reverence and admiration the glorious works of creation."[2] We are taught to study the liberal arts and sciences and are exposed to the basics in architecture. We are to be speculative. We are to be contemplative. We have brothers now who deliver the Middle Chamber Lecture and can't even pronounce some of the words correctly.

But of even greater importance, we are directed in all of the lectures of Freemasonry that we came here to improve ourselves and to search for light. We mouth that term over and over and seldom equate light with its intended Masonic meaning which is KNOWLEDGE. We are supposed to be seekers of knowledge. How can we be such without being a part of an educational institution? We cannot claim to be a Freemason without a quest for knowledge. To do so is to renounce all that Freemasonry is.

And yet, we hear Freemasons make outrageous statements every day- statements that fly in the face of all that we are and statements that denigrate and insult the power of the Craft and its members. I recently heard a past high "monkey monk" in one of our concordant bodies make this statement: "Education ain't important." So help me! That is what he said. At that point the only thing to do was to go to higher ground.

If we have reduced ourselves to the least common denominator, we must rise above that level and return to the top.

169

Each of us must heed the admonition "bid men come up to you but refuse to lower yourself a single step to them."[3] That is our charge. We must continually educate ourselves and be in the business of educating our brothers.

We must stop making the mistake of thinking that Masonic education is the memorization of ritual and the learning of protocol, rules and regulations. It is more than being a warm body to sit through poorly conducted ritual and long, boring business meetings.

The first positive step to take is to understand what Freemasonry was during its heyday and when it was the most effective to influence society. Let us examine what leaders of that time were saying about Freemasonry. That will tell us what it was.

The Reverend James Anderson said: "Freemasonry is a measure of civilization and order." "Freemasons are the sons of reason, discipline and wisdom." "Freemasonry encouraged education and the Lodge is to cultivate the mind in useful branches of science and the love of literature."[4]

Prof. Steven Bullock, in his recent book, *Revolutionary Brotherhood* had this to say, "If, as Thomas Jefferson argued, the Capital represented 'the first temple dedicated to the sovereignty of the people,' then the brothers of the 1793 [cornerstone laying] ceremony served as its first high priests." Prof. Bullock goes on to say that fraternal membership and ideology helped to bring high standing to a broad range of Americans, breaking down the artificial boundaries of wealth and birth.[5]

Bullock also quotes Salem Town who said "Freemasonry is the spread of virtue." And he quotes George Washington who said, "Morality, one of the great pillars of human happiness." Oh that Freemasonry had the influence today to promote the virtue of morality. George Washington, in that same farewell address, stated, "instruction for the general diffusion of knowledge should be the object of primary importance."[6]

There is no evidence that Jefferson was a Mason; nevertheless he had great communication with Freemasons and was led to state that "schools and scholarship would provide worth and genius from every condition of life to rise above the pseudo-aristocracy who had only wealth and birth as qualifications." "It would be the keystone of the arch of government."[7] Sounds like Jefferson knew more Masonic vocabulary than do some of the members today.

Sad to say we have not matched such lofty thoughts and ideals in recent generations. But that is what Freemasonry was and that is what it did when it was viewed and acted as an educational institution to teach not only the liberal arts and sciences, but of even greater importance, to teach the virtues of morality.

So how do we return to that place from whence we came? How do we return Freemasonry to a place where "the high, the low, the rich, the poor may meet together for the one common purpose of perpetuating each other's friendship and each other's love?"[8] How do we restore Freemasonry to its highest standard instead of to the lowest common denominator? Freemasonry needs to overcome the rating of a second class non-com club.

I always like to show a picture of an old mill in Aurora, NY. The mill was built in the early 19th century but has decayed. It collapses from the top down. Every organization is like an edifice. It collapses from the top down. Keep the roof in good repair; it will last forever. The walls and foundation are solid.

For a variety of reasons, not a part of this discussion, Freemasonry began to collapse from the top down. Leadership potential is related to the number and calibre of the membership. As both declined, the quality of leadership also declined. That is how we have reached the state where a high monkey-monk in a concordant body can say, "Education ain't important."

The Grand Lodge of the State of Ohio, led and administered by Past Grand Master Royal Scofield, developed a leadership program many years ago.[9] Not to be shy about copying a good thing, I put together such a program for the State of New York. And, by the way, the idea came to me by attending one of these NE conferences on Masonic Education and Libraries. I met Scofield and he sent me a copy of his course. The difference with ours is that it deals less with ritual, rules and regulations and more with leadership skills.

There is no doubt whatsoever; the answer for improved Masonic effectiveness lies in a quality leadership development program. Ours in New York has been in use since 1981. It is not perfect, nor is the method of administering the program. Yet results have been impressive. One of the problems may occur as we attract and develop quality people to become quality leaders. It's possible that the existing hierarchy may squelch their effectiveness by dropping them from leadership roles. This is a natural phenomenon that must and can be overcome.

One of the secrets to success is to have patience. I like to show a chart of a saw tooth wave form. It is an electronically developed entity used in most electronic circuits. I show it to demonstrate that organizations follow this pattern as well. Regardless of how good the new leader may be, it takes much time to restore an organization to peak performance. But it only takes one dud of a leader to move back to the bottom of the heap.

So why do we need a leadership course for Freemasonry? There are several reasons.

First and foremost:

1. Freemasonry is an educational institution, and as such it must develop leaders with the ability, skills and perseverance to carry out the function of an educational institution.
2. We need to minimize the influence of the least common denominator. We need to move every brother up to a level of competence and understanding of his role and the role of Freemasonry in society.
3. There is no time to return to the old method when we had sufficient numbers of leaders who served as role models and mentors- as brothers moved up the chairs in nine years.
4. Every Freemason is a leader by virtue of being a Freemason. We need to train him to become an effective and dedicated one.
5. We need to prepare brothers to help return Freemasonry to its original purposes so that it can influence society in ways of virtue and morality.

What should a leadership course cover?

1. Because our system of titles, honors and aprons has the tendency to promote people with more ambition and ego than common sense and dedication, we need to begin by teaching the virtues of service and an understanding of the importance of the work in which we are engaged. This means that there must be a solid understanding of the purpose of the Fraternity. That is basic. We need to teach new and old members the product which is Freemasonry. The history, philosophy, charity and structure of the Fraternity are vital components of such a course.
2. The most important ingredient of a leadership course is a course in leadership. Leadership is leadership is leadership. We can't spell it out any differently. The elements of a leadership course are motivational skills, communication skills (oral and written) and organizational skills.

The important part of providing such a leadership course is that it serves to carry out the fundamental aspect of Freemasonry- to serve as an educational institution. For years I have tried to get my jurisdiction to develop a proper name for this program. I would like to call it: MUNY (Masonic University of New York) or it could be called MANY (Masonic Academy of New York.)[10] Other jurisdictions may want to beat us to the punch and do the same thing by fitting the term Masonic Academy or Masonic University to your (their) jurisdiction. i.e.: Mass. could be MAMA- Masonic Academy of Mass. Oh! Mama! How some people like to play with words!

I would like to see the Masonic Fraternity expand its Academy or University concept and offer courses to the public. I have written a syllabus for a course in grammar that the Freemasons should offer via the Public Access Channel on TV. It needs to be dressed up and made palatable so that it will attract people who desperately need to know how to speak English correctly. It could be a great challenge for us. But that is another subject. First, let us move forward to develop effective leadership training within the Lodges, the districts and the jurisdictions.

Talk given at North East Conference on Masonic Education and Libraries. – Portland, Maine 1998

Leadership and Communication: A Partnership

Leadership and communication- a partnership? Perhaps they are, but they are also much more than that. They are almost synonymous: "you can't have one without the other." To communicate is to inform and to be informed, to share information, to educate and to be educated, to convey and to have the skill to hear and understand what is conveyed to us. Each definition implies a two-way link: transmit and receive. Webster is less up to date: to reveal, disclose, divulge, impart, announce, publish, promulgate. But under communication Webster does say: "interchange of thoughts and opinions." We know it is even much more, e.g. it is also sharing feelings, ideas, techniques.

The first limerick I ever heard (when I was too young to know what it meant) is a good example of communication:

He was teaching her arithmetic, he said t'was his commission.

> He kissed her once, he kissed her twice and said, now that's addition.
> He kissed her and she kissed him back, he said, now that's subtraction.
> He kissed her once and many more and said, that's multiplication.
> Then her Dad appeared upon the scene. He made a quick decision.
> He kicked the lad two blocks away and said, now that's long division.

They both were more than communicators, they were also leaders. Unfortunately, Dad was a more forceful communicator and leader, though not necessarily a more sensitive leader. The true leader knows how to inform and to listen to and understand feedback. A leader is an expert at communicating, but has gone one step further. A leader has the ability to initiate new concepts and to communicate these concepts. He or she is aware that, as Will Rogers said, "We are all ignorant, it's just that some of us are ignorant about different things."

So a leader needs to be a pioneer, not just in new and innovative ways to communicate, but in new and innovative ideas: a pioneer in learning. A better title for this paper might be, "The Advancement of Knowledge." After all, that's a major message of Freemasonry. We call it, "seeking light."

Here is an example of the ultimate in communications and the ultimate in leadership: In 1974 Dr. Franke Drake, Director, NAIC was responsible for a message which went into space aimed at the globular cluster, M-13, about 25,000 light years distance from earth.[1] The signal is made up of 1679 bits of information in binary code and properly arranged to tell intelligent life something about this planet and the people who sent the message. Here is what one writer said at that time:

> The message, which was a serious scientific creation full of binary numbers and complex chemical symbols, made me cry. I cried because the sound went through me, touching the fillings in my teeth and messing up my heartbeat. And I cried because the idea of sending such a message was so wonderfully audacious. Because I felt, together with the people around me, that we were all living one of the most important moments of our lives. And because the notion of reaching across space to touch another mind made me

horribly lonely, sorry for all the failed efforts at communication in my life, desperate to hug somebody and feel whole again.[2]

Why do I share (communicate) this information with you now? None of us are going to be around 50,000 or more years from 1974. It will take that long for the signal to be heard by any civilization in M-13 and a reply received by us; even though the signal is traveling at the speed of light (186,000 miles per second). What is important is that: 1) an effort is made to communicate with other intelligent life outside our solar system; 2) by so doing a communication is sent to our own world reminding us that life beyond our solar system is very probable; 3) a communication is made to the world at large that Cornell University harbors some eccentric people, but more importantly, some people who are pioneers, innovators, thinkers, scientists; 4) by so doing the world at large is informed that Cornell University is an exciting place, things are happening. People are clamoring to be a part of such a dynamic institution.

To paraphrase the Scriptures, "Pride goeth before destruction."[4] Can it be that our pride in Masonry is blinding us to our falling membership? The record speaks volumes. Our membership is dropping at an alarming rate. We do a disservice to the Craft if we don't recognize the danger. Optimists have used statistics to demonstrate similar trends in other periods of our Craft. They seek to show that Freemasonry recovered from its greatest blow, the anti-Masonic movement of the early 1800's. They insist that the Craft can survive the drop and rise again. Can this be another example of stumbling over our own egos? Is not the present decline (steady for the past 28 years) a real, bonafide fall? Of course the Craft will survive, but not if we remain blindfolded to the real cause of the malaise. Pride alone cannot sustain us. Consider the causes for today's trend, and prepare to act on remedies.

This author wrote a paper in 1974, "The Elevation of Freemasonry."[5] In it, statistics showed the membership decline in New York State Freemasonry since 1956. The situation has worsened since. The major concern of that thesis was the desperate need for greater leadership development for all Masonic Lodge officers. That need is as acute as ever. Better leadership is the only salvation of any organization. It could be the only mechanism that will save Freemasonry.

Too long we have assumed that leadership will develop through some mysterious osmosis or simply by placing a hat on a Master's head. Not so. "Leaders are not born; they need to be developed."[6] Some jurisdictions (e.g., New York State) have a program of regional leadership seminars conducted by the Grand Lodge. This is a step in the right direction, but it is quite inadequate. The Grand Lodge of Ohio and now Connecticut[7], offer correspondence courses in Masonic leadership. We are preparing a correspondence course for Freemasons in New York State. Sample lessons were tested at the leadership seminars. We decided not to follow the Ohio and Connecticut format which seemed to deal more with protocol, rules, regulations, landmarks, etc. This is all well and good but it was our intention to deal more with leadership skills.

Most of the responses were favorable but it was disconcerting to receive a few responses like this: "the material seems too scholarly." The same person who is President of a district officers' organization wrote some sentences with dangling participles and no structure. We may not think this is important, but how do we expect to attract quality people if they are to be exposed to that kind of imperfection?

This could be a clue to Freemasonry's major problem. It is that we don't have enough members who can define leadership. Or perhaps we are all stumbling over our egos, and so blinded by pride that we haven't taken a close hard look at either the malady or the remedy. We leave it for the hierarchy of the organization to examine, diagnose, and offer remedies. If any organization's power structure had the expertise to fulfill all three responsibilities (examine, diagnose, and offer remedies), the cures would already be in place and the patient getting well. Such is not the case.

"Leaders are not born, they're made." Leadership skills do not come out of the woodwork. To expect a plumber to perform a delicate brain tumor operation is just as absurd as it is to expect the average surgeon to install a steam boiler, and to know how to set a Hartford loop. And yet we expect a professor of history, or a farmer, or a truck driver or any number of the professions represented in officers of a Masonic Lodge to know how to be effective leaders. Some of our officers may climb the ladder of success within the mystic circle and be invested with the purple of the fraternity. But this is no guarantee that, by some mysticism, they will be given the ability to lead. And to expect the same undeveloped leaders to have the expertise to train others to lead is a mere step into the absurd.

What is the answer? Simple enough: We must agree the first step is that improved leadership will be the major contributing factor to turn Freemasonry around. The second step is just as important as the first. We must wage a campaign against the Peter Principle. Dr. Lawrence Peter has postulated that in any hierarchy, every individual will be promoted to his own level of incompetence.[8] The George Peter principle insists that the Peter principle exists only in those hierarchies refusing to accept the reality that "leaders are not born; they need to be developed."

Another rule should be that it takes one to make one. We don't send young people to vocational schools to be taught electronics by an attorney. We don't expect chemists to learn their discipline from a steam fitter. Nor does a professor of physics teach business administration. Yet we expect more ridiculous juxtapositions every day. Freemasonry is not alone in this. The Peter Principle flourishes. And the number of business failures increases in proportion to the extent of the Peter Principle epidemic.

Our concern is to prevent Freemasonry from following this failure pattern. We can do so by eradicating all of the Peter Principle statistics which exist in Lodges and Grand Lodge. Leadership courses are a must. We just must not mistake courses in ritual, Masonic education, Masonic law, protocol, etc. for leadership.

Leadership is leadership is leadership. There is no substitute. It is defined as the ability to guide an organization toward successful completion of goals. Allen E. Roberts outlines the material a leadership course should cover in his book, *Shedding Light on Leadership*.[9] It includes skills such as goal setting, planning, organizing, motivating, training subordinates, programming, communicating, problem solving, etc. To communicate, one needs a variety of skills including public speaking and effective writing. To this writer, an even more ingenious skill is an ability to conduct a business meeting and not allow 10 minutes worth of business to drag on for an hour or more. There are few Masters who really do a good job of conducting a Lodge communication effectively and inspirationally. There are still more business executives who do a poor job of leading a business meeting.

Before leaving the subject of leadership, it may be appropriate to quote the great Chinese philosopher, Lao-Tse[10]: "As for the best leaders, people do not notice their existence, the next best, people honor and praise. The next, the people fear, and the next, the people hate. When the best leader's work is done the people say, 'we did it ourselves.'" If a handful of our leaders were like the best defined by

Lao-Tse, we would be well on the road to elevating Freemasonry and its image.

A major component of leadership is the skill to motivate all the members of the team to promote the product. One of the most important products of Freemasonry is Brotherhood. It takes more skill to sell brotherhood than it does to sell toothpaste or computer software or Ford cars.

Heretofore (and some have suggested that it remain that way) the policy has been to hide the glorious history, the beautiful philosophy and all of the light in Freemasonry under a "bushel." The "bushel" is called a Lodge room. That policy may have worked in days gone by. We are living now in the twentieth century, and fast approaching the twenty-first. Change and competition surround us. People have gone to the moon. We have landed a vehicle on Mars. There is speculation that the planet Venus can be nudged into a closer orbit to the Sun. This would cause the planet eventually to be inhabitable by human life when and if the need rises to evacuate the planet earth. These are exciting times.

Freemasonry must keep up with these times or be left behind. We live in the past. New and innovative approaches are needed to keep up with the competition for the loyalty of individual members and potential members. Instead, we in Freemasonry have tended to be like the Vermont storekeeper who was asked how come he didn't have a certain item on the shelf. "Don't stock it anymore," was his reply. "How come?" "Moves too damned fast."

That's how we are dealing with Freemasonry. We have not made an effort to stock or promote the product. Yet every competitor imaginable has been promoting everything from baseball, to television, to bowling, to traveling.

This seeming reluctance to expose Freemasonry to the mundane world is all the more disconcerting when we consider that an important message of our brotherhood is to promote the advancement of knowledge. Knowledge is power. Little can be accomplished without it. Along with being taught to seek light (the advancement of knowledge) we are taught to be charitable to a brother, all brothers under the Fatherhood of God. To hide the light of Freemasonry to ourselves is to deny charity to society. If we really believe that Freemasonry has a role to play in the restoration of stability and civility to society, then we are compelled to tell the world at large who we are, what we are, and what is our mission.

Only in this way can we promote the advancement of knowledge, and the cause of brotherhood.

What prevents Freemasonry from promoting its cause? Apparently a serious obstacle has been a confusion between the concept of promoting knowledge about Freemasonry and the term, "solicitation." There is a great distinction between promotion and solicitation. Promotion of knowledge about a cause has a positive connotation. Solicitation is negative in nature. What prevents us from spreading our message over the globe? We need not send it to the cluster of stars called M-13, but at least we could spread the message in our own neighborhood.

Perhaps it starts with the Entered Apprentice. He comes home and his wife asks him what Freemasonry is all about. "Oh honey, I can't tell you a thing." He has visions of his tongue buried out on some lonely beach where the tide comes in and goes out twice every 24 hours. "It's all secret," he tells her, whereas he could tell her the gist of the message of Freemasonry. He could tell her that it will help him be a better man, a better husband, and a better citizen of this great republic. He could tell her all this and more, but Freemasons are so hung up about secrecy and secret codes– we don't make them to be easily broken here on earth or elsewhere. Perhaps that is why the advocates of 19th century modes of operation would have us believe that to promote Freemasonry is to be involved in solicitation. Solicitation in some form has always taken place, and it continues. Too often it works like this: a brother, who may not be well versed in Masonic education but supportive of the precepts, will say to a friend, "You ought to consider joining the Masons." He may be even more subtle with, "Have you ever considered joining the Masonic Fraternity?" If the friend takes the "hook," he is brought into the fraternity with little or no education as to its philosophy or history. He comes in the first night literally and figuratively blindfolded to Freemasonry.

The important point here is that, to some extent, the new brother has been solicited. Even if the approach was, "You know I can't ask you to but if you are interested, I would be honored to bring in your petition," this example is a mild form of solicitation. What is so evil about it? Should we wait until the aspirant learns by some accident that he must ask for a petition? How else may we inform quality people that Freemasonry needs them as much as they need Freemasonry? Shall we be concerned if our product "moves too damned fast?" The answer is simple: Prepare a list of people of good report. Sponsor a program to promote knowledge about Freemasonry. Invite guests from the list. Tell the public about the program. Such meetings have been conducted in a highly professional and dignified manner. It can be planned to assure that it is designed to promote knowledge about Freemasonry rather than to solicit. An ill-informed brother can go out on his own to "nudge" or drop hints to a friend with the hope that he will join. Such is usually done in an awkward and clumsy way that can be a turn-off to the potential candidate. But such methods have been common in the past, and we have the results to demonstrate how unsuccessfully the system has worked (or, rather, not worked).

What proof is there that the system proposed here can work any better? The first obvious evidence is common sense: Train officers of Lodges to be more effective leaders. A part of leadership is the skill to communicate. This skill will result in a more professionally organized program to disseminate knowledge about Freemasonry. Some Lodges in New York State have conducted such programs. The results are exciting and impressive. Where the Master and officers have been innovative and thorough in planning and conducting such events, the results have been successful. One Lodge increased its rolls from 31 members to 54 in three years. Before such a program began, the situation was similar to that of too many Lodges. The Past Masters used to draw straws each year to see who was to get stuck with being Master for the ensuing year. Now several new brothers are waiting in the wings hoping that they can demonstrate adequate leadership potential to be asked to start through the chairs. Most of the new members are the same young people who had branded as "not interested in Freemasonry." When they learned about the heritage and philosophy of Freemasonry they liked what they heard and since have shown fantastic enthusiasm and interest in the Craft.

Exposed to Freemasonry at a public meeting, only those genuinely turned on asked for a petition. Yet there are those who argue against this method of informing the public. They continue to argue that such a program "is the most flagrant kind of improper solicitation."[11] Their contention is that such programs cannot be controlled. Our experience is that such programs have been much more controlled and dignified than the methods used by those opposed to this system of education.

We would argue further that the only way a person can come into Freemasonry under the concept perceived to be non-solicitation is, in fact, by solicitation. How else would a potential candidate know about Freemasonry except by some form of communication on the subject? In the strict sense of the word, any form of communication is solicitation. When the issue is really addressed, it boils down to this: The true landmark of the Craft is that a person must join of "his own free will and accord." Over the years, Freemasons have misinterpreted this landmark to mean that we cannot lift the light of Freemasonry out from under the bushel. It is about time we corrected this serious mistake. Furthermore, many misguided Freemasons have been violating their own interpretation of the landmark; hence it is time that they were allowed to clear their guilty consciences by correcting their understanding of the real landmark on this subject. It is time we all started communicating the power of Freemasonry to others.

The image of Freemasonry can be elevated. The Craft can be the power in society that it deserves to be, and which is so desperately needed. All of this can happen when we meet head-on the issue of developing competent leadership. Lodges taking in enough new members to provide a base from which to choose leaders show this. But if we continue to believe the myth that we can have quality without quantity, we will continue to follow the trends of the Oddfellows and the Grange and many others.

We will get the necessary quantity when we offer knowledge of Freemasonry to the uninformed. Those of quality will want to join. If we don't believe that Freemasonry will attract only people of quality, we don't have a true understanding of the nature and the power of the fraternity. We seem to be overly obsessed with the one black-ball rule. We would do better to rid Freemasonry of this atrocity. To do so will attract people of intellect who tend to be offended by it.[12] Those not in agreement with our principles won't be interested in joining us.

In summary: The foundation of Freemasonry is solid and strong. We must develop and maintain the caliber of leadership necessary to perpetuate progress. This can be done by professional leadership development programs geared to improve leadership skills of Lodge Officers. Such must be designed and implemented by people with expertise in leadership education. If need be, we must look outside our fraternity for such skills.

Finally, providing knowledge about Freemasonry to the world at large is a must. In other words, we must communicate our message. It will expose the precepts and history of Freemasonry to non-Masons, bring in new members to provide a base of potential leaders, promote the value of our fraternity and the advancement of knowledge. All of these will help the fraternity shed its beneficent influence on more of mankind. THAT IS OUR CHARGE!

REFERENCES
1. Carl Sagan, *Cosmos*.
2. Dava Sobel, *Ithaca Journal*, November 27, 1974.
3. Foley, "What the Old Timer Said to the City Slicker."
4. *The Holy Bible*, Proverbs 16:10.
5. George Peter, "The Elevation of Freemasonry," 1974.
6. "The Minnesota Plan"
7. Grand Lodge of Connecticut Officer Leadership Course
8. Lawrence Peter, *The Peter Principle*
9. Allen E. Roberts, *Shedding Light on Leadership*.
10. "The Writings of Lao-Te"
11. Brent Morris, *The Siren Song of Solicitation*, 1983.
12. George Peter, "An Editorial," *SEEK* Publication for Cayuga/Tompkins, 1981.

Why Communicate?

Why communicate? Why do organizations advertise? The reasons are so obvious we ought not even raise the question. First of all we should note that we, as Freemasons, have done a miserable job of communicating amongst ourselves and to those in the profane world. If we were to be graded by the old fashioned method of 0 to 100%, perhaps it would be generous to give ourselves a grade of something from about 12 to 17%. If we were to be graded by the A+ through F method, we would be lucky to get a grade of F-. Then we wonder why the detractors of Freemasonry are so successful in their vicious attacks on us.

The first thing we must do is to communicate with our own members. Each brother needs a better understanding of what it is to be a Freemason. He needs to grasp the POWER, the influence, and the potential of the Craft. Unless we do a better job of communicating to our members, the brothers will develop no loyalty, will give little support, and will have no idea of the POWER of the Fraternity. How many members really have gotten the message about the influence of and the potential of Freemasonry? How many understand the service to freedom of thought and the liberty of faith which are promoted by Freemasonry? The great author Rev. Joseph

Fort Newton put it this way: "Down through the centuries– often in times when the highest crime was not murder, but thinking, and the human conscience was a captive dragged at the wheel of the ecclesiastical chariot– always and everywhere, Masonry has stood for the right of the soul to know the truth…"

By contrast, the news media and various other groups tend to say inaccurate and, sometimes, offensive things about Freemasonry. To a great extent it is our fault. We keep the truth from them. Most Grand Lodges do a less than mediocre job of preserving and promoting our heritage. At the district and Lodge levels we do an even worse job of it. We need to do a better job at every level.

What is the public saying about us? The natural tendency is for the news media to refer to Freemasonry as a secret society. For example, the *New York Times*, in an otherwise favorable report about the Grand Lodge dedication of its building, in its Dec. 14, 1997 issue, referred to the Fraternity as a secret society. Why does this happen? Inaccurate and nasty things are said about Freemasonry because we are so quiet, and yes, so secretive, about who and what we are. The reality is that we are quiet and secretive because the average brother knows so little about Freemasonry.

But why worry about what they say? P.T. Barnum said, "It doesn't matter what they say about us as long as they are talking about us." That may have been okay for the circus industry but it is not good advice for Freemasonry. Freemasonry seems to be under attack more and more these days. On the internet reports claim that Freemasonry is the organized conspiracy which assassinated John F. Kennedy. The report goes on to say that Masons then covered up the deed in the form of another conspiracy. Another internet message states that Jack Kemp is a 33rd degree Mason and therefore is privy to the highest secrets of Satan and Satan-worshippers.

That's just the tip of the iceberg. A main agenda item of the Southern Baptist Convention (Houston, Texas, 1993) was the question: Should all Freemasons be expelled from the Church unless they renounce membership in the Fraternity? That proposal failed, but a resolution did pass which made it clear, in no uncertain terms, that the Church held Freemasonry in ill repute. John Ankerberg makes a small fortune selling a video tape which exposes all the secrets of Freemasonry– and it's only $29.95. Pat Robertson's new book, *New World Order*, offers more alleged proof that Freemasonry is evil. Louis Farrakhan has done Freemasonry a favor by telling his followers how bad we are. And the list goes on.

Interestingly enough, at the same time, academic scholars are beginning to write about Freemasonry. And they are presenting the Fraternity in a favorable light. Dr. Kathleen Smith Kutolowski, Professor in the Department of History at SUNY Brockport, has researched the effects of Freemasonry on American history. Her favorable assessment of the role played by Freemasonry is a breath of fresh air. She spoke on the subject in Rochester at a program sponsored by the Finger Lakes Chapter of the Philalethes Society.

The fall 1996 issue of the *Empire State Mason* magazine featured a book review by the editor, Scott D. Harris. The book by Steven C. Bullock, *Revolutionary Brotherhood: Freemasonry and the Transformation of the American Social Order, 1730-1840*, was published in 1994. It is complimentary to Freemasonry and to the role played by the Fraternity in the making of America. Bullock says, ". . .The fraternalism expressed in Masonry offered a set of resources that could be used for a wide range of purposes. Although the order cannot be seen as a master key to all early American history, it opens up that mysterious ground where pragmatic action... intersects with attempts to create moral and intellectual coherence out of experience."

Scipio Lodge #110 was fortunate enough to have Prof. Bullock speak at our Bicentennial Celebration. What he said deserves to be heard by more Freemasons across the State and Nation. As a non-Mason, Bullock's assessment of the role of Freemasonry in the making of America deserves special attention because it comes from an unbiased position. I liked especially what he said about the importance to learn from the past. Freemasonry and Freemasons were there and they made their indelible mark on the transformation of America into a more civil society than it otherwise would have been.

In the August/September 1996 issue of *Civilization* magazine an article by Richard Brookhiser is entitled, "Ancient, Earnest, Secret, and Fraternal." Brookhiser writes, "Since the founding of the first American Lodges in the 1730s, Freemasons have attracted prominent members, done good deeds– and sometimes sparked open hostility." (Brookhiser got three out of the four correct in his title. We are not a secret society.) He does present Freemasonry in an approving light, as have other recent scholarly writers. He nevertheless, still leaves out two important elements of a complete discussion on the subject of Freemasonry and its detractors. To that end I submitted to the publication a letter in which I suggested that a more complete discussion of the nature of Freemasonry would have been useful. Also submitted to the publication was a paper by me, "Whys and Wherefores." It was published in the October 1994 issue of *Philalethes Magazine*.

We must be aware that it behooves each of us to be alert as to what the public can learn about Freemasonry. That means that we should be vigilant to preserve our history, to know our history, and to share our history with the rest of the world. Let us tell the world the truth about Freemasonry. We must do so for the following reasons:

1. To deflect the false image which our detractors spread
2. To give accurate accounts of the real power of Freemasonry
3. To discover that the more we know about our history and philosophy, the more excited we become about the Craft
4. To realize that the more we know about the Craft, the greater our potential will be to spread its beneficent influence on all mankind

How shall we proceed?

1. Provide programs at the district level which are designed to educate the officers of Masonic Lodges.
2. Provide a Lodge or district newspaper to disseminate Masonic news and information.
3. Provide material in the publications and education programs which are designed to educate, inspire, excite, interest, and turn on the membership- and any one else who is exposed to
the material.
4. Don't stop there. Submit articles of historical and philosophical nature to the local press, radio and TV networks.
5. Offer to provide a regular column in local newspapers. Most everyone is interested in history. Such a column could prove to be a real plus for the Craft. But it must be done very professionally and with tact. Use material already available. Create new material and ideas.
6. In all endeavors, emphasize the role played by Freemasonry in the shaping of America and the role it plays in making a civilized society.

7. Encourage Grand Lodges to provide educational, interesting, exciting, and inspiring material in their memos and publications. Most material should be designed to turn on the brotherhood. We need more substance and less pomp and circumstance.

8. Each Lodge should establish Masonic study groups from within itself. We are an educational institution and should carry out that role more effectively.

9. Be proud. Be humble. Be aggressive. Be innovative. Be industrious and active.

10. Be a Brother Freemason.

That is our charge. Let's do it! The alternative is defined by Dr. Sidney Kase, Past Grand Master of Masons in the State of Washington. He wrote:

"We have a product of great value. Each of us represents Freemasonry to someone. We must become so educated and so dedicated that we can explain Masonry to others, be an example for others, and thus, sell OTHERS, MOTIVATE THEM TO BECOME MEMBERS OF THE CRAFT. We are a people business. As such we need to learn how to attract desirable customers and to keep them interested and dedicated to the product. The basic requirement is education."

"We must first educate our own members and then utilize every ethical and effective means of selling. That means public relations. Most of the public knows little or nothing about Freemasonry. Worse yet, as we have seen, they have often heard untruths and misconceptions about us." Grand Master Kase went on to quote something he read in a business-oriented publication. It was nine ways to kill your business. He says substitute the word Masonry for business and there you have it:

1. Just pretend everyone knows what you have to sell. Don't advertise.

2. Convince yourself you have been in business so long customers will automatically come to you. Don't advertise.

3. Forget there are new potential customers who would do business with you if they were invited to do so. Don't advertise.

4. Tell yourself you just don't have time to spend thinking about promoting your business. Don't advertise.

5. Forget you have competition trying to attract customers away from you. Don't advertise.
6. Tell yourself it costs too much to advertise and that you don't get enough out of it. Don't advertise.
7. Overlook the fact that advertising is an investment in selling, not an expense. Don't advertise.
8. Don't keep reminding your established customers that you appreciate their business. Don't advertise.
9. Be sure you don't provide an adequate advertising budget. Don't advertise.

So to sum up why to communicate: The answer is: communication is advertising our product, first to our own brothers and then to the public. If we don't do both effectively, we will be in the business of killing our business. We will be in the business of killing brotherhood. Finally, we can't communicate, we cannot advertise to ourselves and to others, unless we know our product. I started a ten-lesson leadership course in 1985 or thereabouts. The first lesson was labeled "Know Your Product." That's the first step in leadership. That is the first step in the first step to leadership, which is the ability to communicate. We cannot communicate the power of Freemasonry until we know our product.

Let's prepare Lodge, district, and state-wide programs designed to educate our brothers. It can be done by designing each Lodge, district, and state program and communication tool to educate, inspire, excite, interest, and turn on the membership and others about the power of Freemasonry.

How Long?
Grand Lodge Committee on Lodge Service

Nearly everyone, at one time or another, is called upon to give a talk, chair a meeting, or preside over a discussion. There are very few who cannot use some help to be more effective in these roles. Even if a talk is scheduled for only a few minutes, it needs to be planned. *"Have something to say, say it, then stop."*[1] Most speeches are too long. A keynote address, an after dinner speech, or a summation address at a seminar, all should be terse and to the point. An after dinner speech should be kept to a MAXIMUM of 20 minutes. Fifteen minutes is even better. A keynote or summation address should be no more than 15 minutes. Ten or eight minutes is much better. Reports should be much shorter with plenty of time left for questions. Few seem to understand that it is much more effective to leave the audience with a whetted appetite rather than to overstuff them with excess verbiage and too many main points.

Woodrow Wilson was asked how long it took him to prepare a speech. His answer was, "It depends on how long you want me to talk. If you want a ten minute speech, it takes me about two weeks to prepare, if you want a half hour speech, it takes me a few days to prepare, but if you want me to talk for two hours, I am prepared right now."

There is the story of the itinerant preacher who came up to Vermont to give a sermon. When only one farmer showed up, the preacher asked if he should give the sermon. The farmer's reply was, "If I go to feed the cows and only one shows up I feed her anyhow." So the preacher got the message and delivered one of his best and long winded sermons. It went on and on. When he had completed the sermon, he asked the farmer what he thought of it. This time the reply was, "If I go to feed the cows and only one shows up, I don't give her the whole load."

We can learn from these two stories. The most valuable asset any of us has is TIME. When there is an audience of 25 people, every wasted moment is multiplied by 25. It is discourteous and crude to waste the time of any person. When we are not properly prepared and end up repeating and rambling, we are robbing the time of all those present.

An equally serious crime is to select a speaker who you can't control and who wastes the time of the audience. Likewise wasted time caused by poor control of a meeting is equally harmful and devastating to an organization. It causes people to stay away from the next meeting and the next.

Someone put it this way: "To attend that organization's meeting a second time is like why a woman has a second child. She forgets how much pain she went through with the first." People come back to a meeting because they forget how painful it is to listen to dragged out business agendas and poorly prepared programs. Most won't forget more than once. The challenge is to make it so that people look forward to the next meeting with anticipation. We can be prepared and we can select speakers who understand about TIME. We can tell them how much time they are allotted and insist that they stick to it. TIME is precious. The most effective speeches are those that are limited in length. The most effective meetings are those that are conducted with dispatch.

[1] From "Oral Communication," prepared by Prof. R. D. Martin, Cornell Univ. It is used in lesson #5 of the 10-lesson leadership course conducted by The Grand Lodge Committee on Lodge Service.

Grammar

Whenever I am asked to speak, people usually give me the prerogative to choose my topic. They perhaps expect that I will limit my subject to Masonic history. That doesn't always happen. We need to know that we are in the business of making history every day and so what we do as Freemasons today is a part of the process of making Masonic history for tomorrow.

With that justification, I will instead discuss grammar. In the Middle Chamber Lecture we are reminded of the seven liberal arts and sciences, the first listed being grammar. "It teaches us how to express our ideas in correct language." But who seems to give a hoot about correct grammar anymore?

As individuals, and especially as Freemasons, we need to remember that people judge us by the words we use. Our potential advancement, in whatever our career may be, is limited by our ability to communicate in an effective and accurate way. The mundane world judges Freemasonry and Freemasons by the words we use and how professionally we behave. The words we use as leaders and members are used as factors for making judgments just as much as are our actions. Double negatives, improper conjugation of verbs, inaccurate use of adjectives and adverbs– all of these common practices stick out like sore thumbs to people who know correct grammar.

The English language has been replaced with common street talk. Too many educators seem to be saying that it doesn't matter. Worse yet, some of them say, "It don't matter." Heaven help us! The problem is aggravated by the trend of TV and radio announcers who substitute street talk for English. They seem to think that it makes them "cool" and that they are "with it."

Worse yet, they have added all the irritating crutches which make for very tedious listening. Every sentence is defiled with phrases such as, "you know," and, "the fact of the matter is," and, "like," and, "basically," and, "in any event," and the list goes on.

We Freemasons need not lower our standards to the level of the least common denominator. We must bid others to come up to our level and refuse to lower ourselves a single step to them. By the very nature of Freemasonry we should be ever striving for an improved standard of excellence in all that we do and say.

To be shoddy in one's grammar leaves the impression that one is shabby in other aspects of his life. It may only be symbolic, but who knows better than Freemasons that we learn by symbolism? By proper use of grammar we symbolically make a statement that proclaims, "I am a person who promotes excellence in all that I do." As Freemasons we proclaim, "We promote excellence in all that we do."

Some time ago I proposed that a challenging project for a Masonic Lodge or District might be to sponsor a mini-course on grammar. It could be done on public access television channels, in senior centers, or in a multitude of venues. A part of such a course could be incorporated in the "Road to the East" program. I prepared a curriculum for such a course and offered it for consideration. Perhaps someone, with more energy and time than I, would like to pursue this as an exciting and desperately needed project.

Remember that grammar is the first and most important of the seven liberal arts and sciences. Once we have mastered grammar, we can move on to rhetoric, logic, arithmetic, geometry, astronomy, and music. Freemasonry is, or ought to be, an educational institution. The first phase of education is to learn to speak.

Originally printed in The *Empire State Mason* Magazine, Spring 2001

"You Know" and Poor Grammar

Let's take a look into the future (50 or 100 years from now) and note what historians of that time will conclude. Freemasonry will have doubled its membership and its influence. Historians will look back to see that our period was one of the low points in Masonic history.

The year 2050 historian will read the written word by Freemasons and by every one else. He or she will be shocked at the grammatical abomination (street talk) used by our generation. That historian will conclude that you and I lived during a period of illiteracy.

Educators of today seem to have taken the position that it is not politically correct to criticize street talk. They, instead, copy the same so as to appear to be "with it." Heaven help us! This is not to be an elitist and to look down at others. I am reminded of what Will Rogers once said, "We are all ignorant, just on different subjects." On the other hand, "people do judge us by the words we use" and the language we practice.

In my last report I referred to a proposal made at the Northeast Conference on Masonic Education and Libraries by Dr. Walter McDougal, PhD, of Maine. He suggested the formation of a Masonic College. He has been promoting the idea of having a weekend or more once per year to study Masonic material. I have been toying with a different, or additional, concept. Freemasonry needs to make an impact on society by providing schooling in basic grammar. That school would be geared to correcting the **grammatical abominations** which we hear not only on the street, but on television and radio and everywhere we go.

I have counted the use of "you know" phrases 55 times in 55 minutes by a person being interviewed for the presidency of a prestigious university. Newscasters, politicians, educators, and especially sports people use "you know" in every other sentence. Everyone says "you got" when they mean you have. Well, these are just a few examples of the garbage we hear.

The most obnoxious term is "it don't matter." People just don't understand about the conjugation of verbs. They don't know what you are talking about when you point out that a subject must agree with its antecedent.

The opportunity is there for Freemasonry to take up the challenge and to encourage or shame school systems into teaching grammar. Our Masonic University of New York (MUNY) could make a difference. The historian of 2050 will have seen the effects of correcting an illiterate society. And, in the process, there would be a reversal in the trend toward a decline in Masonic numbers and influence.

Originally printed in The *Empire State Mason* Magazine, Winter 1999

Back to Basics
Talk to be given at QUEST X
March 10, 1990

We've all been taught never to start a talk by apologizing about our inadequacies. There is nothing written, however, that says it is wrong to start out with immodesty. So here goes. This humble servant absolutely KNOWS, and he KNOWS that he KNOWS what we need to do to get Freemasonry off dead center. So please heed this message.

Let me tell you a true story. We could call it, "A funny thing happened on the way to the cosmos": I came back from Puerto Rico in 1962, after spending 2 years helping with the installation of the radio telescope there. I was put in charge of a small radio astronomy & Research and Development lab near the Cornell Campus. The lab was immaculate– not a thing out of place, and yet there had not been any conception (conception of new ideas, that is) since it was built. Every bench had a tool box with a pad lock almost the size of the box. My first direction to the team that I had inherited was, "let's get rid of these damned padlocks and set the tools out where we can use them."

I tell you this story because it is the most important point that can be made here today. The Grand Lodge Committee on Lodge Service has been providing you with some very valuable tools. They won't do you an ounce of good unless you unlock them and put them to use. If you want to **conceive** new ideas and gain some success, you are going to have to use these tools. I cannot stress this enough.

Obviously, the most valuable tool we have provided is the Leadership Development course, but I am not to talk about that today, except to sneak in this one commercial for it.

It's the BACK TO BASICS program that we are going to talk about. BACK TO BASICS can have many meanings and connotations. For example: two bunnies were watching a magician pull a rabbit out of a hat. One bunny says to the other, "I liked the old way much better." Everyone wants to get back to basics. Our BACK TO BASICS program is more fun too. It is to promote INVOLVEMENT of the brothers, and that is how it becomes a useful tool to revitalize Freemasonry and your Lodge.

Learn what it is and what it can do. Don't be like the 4-year-old boy who was talking to his 5-year-old brother. The 5-year-old said that he had found a condom on the veranda. The 4-year-old asks, "What's a veranda?" You know what a veranda is and you probably know what a condom is. How about the BACK to BASICS program?

Copies of Lodge Service Letter #8801 are included in the packet you received this morning. It defines the program in detail and gives suggested ways to get started. There are no more excuses for poor attendance, poor participation or poor programs– not if you initiate this BACK TO BASICS program in your Lodge.

What are the greatest complaints by Masters of Lodges? Poor attendance is numero uno– number one. Lack of new candidates is a close second. Dull meetings and uninteresting programs combine to make for more problems. If we take care of the number one problem all the rest go away.

The KEY ingredient to all success is INVOLVEMENT. We need to involve the Brothers in the programs and in the plans for the Lodge. You heard about the very proper Englishman who attended a football game for the first time. He said that it looked like a good sport but there were just too many committee meetings. Those committee meetings are vital to the success of every play. The hell with what the Englishman said. We could learn from those huddles.

Joachim Maitre, a Dean at Boston University fled East Germany in 1953. Speaking of recent events in that part of the world, he said, "People forfeited everything and embraced the uncertain status of refugees because HUMAN BEINGS ARE OVERQUALIFIED TO LIVE IN A COMMUNIST STATE." Wow, what a powerful statement. I contend that industry and all organizations need to learn that PEOPLE ARE OVERQUALIFIED TO WORK IN AN ENVIRONMENT THAT DOES NOT CALL THEM TO THEIR FULL POTENTIAL.

A Pulitzer Prize-winning writer said something about Democracy that is equally true about any organization, and especially about volunteer organizations like Freemasonry. In 1967 Ernest Becker said, "Democracy is one form of government most in accord with the promise of evolution…it has taken upon itself the task of combating the Demonic, by making each person an end in himself and a responsible, self-reliant point of authority…" This in contrast to the concept that the great leaders know best. "The fact is that the great leaders may not know best. They have made empires crumble and caused untold sufferings among their own peoples since biblical times…[and by the way, they continue to do so today]. Experts cannot decide since they see only a small segment of the whole picture."

Here are recent statistics released by a National Fund Raiser group of The United Methodist Church: In any volunteer organization only 5% of the members understand the purpose and meaning of the organization. They respond to be workers. 20% will be responsible if asked to do a specific thing. 25% will be responsive to a special plea if they are in the right mood and if they are approached properly. 50% (one half) of the members are inert. This means inactive, lifeless, listless, static. Some of us contend that things don't have to be this way. Good leadership will figure out how to INVOLVE more people in the programs and to improve those percentages and thus revitalize the organization.

Now let us review what Freemasonry is supposed to be all about. We seem to have forgotten that the essence of Freemasonry is to learn to IMPROVE ourselves. Freemasonry is an educational institution. We cannot improve ourselves without education.

The good son decided to send his mother a special gift. He selected a parrot that was proficient in eight languages. He called home later and asked his mother how she liked the gift. She said that the parrot was very tasty. "You mean you ate that well educated parrot?" said the son. "He could speak eight languages!" "Well, why didn't he say something?" was the mother's reply.

We can learn from that story too. Let us not only involve our brothers in a self-education program, let us give them a chance to say something to us about what they have learned.

Attendance problems will go away if the programs are of the right stuff- programs that can only be found in Freemasonry. This means that the programs need to be about Freemasonry or about Freemasons. This is how interest is developed and commitment is gained.

The important thing is that the kinds of programs to come out of the BACK to BASICS concept are those that develop loyalty to the Craft. The more we learn about Freemasonry, the more respect we gain for it.

It bears repeating: what we need to do is to improve attendance. We will never compete against the 2001 other interests that are promoted by professional advertising techniques on radio, television, and newspapers, unless we have something to offer that is better and better promoted. We don't have to be dumb like the guy who opened up a tuxedo shop in a hippie neighborhood. We have options.

There is something better and it can be better promoted. It is INDIVIDUAL INVOLVEMENT. Absolutely nothing else can compete. It is that simple. The fact that we don't involve enough members is the reason why attendance is down, and that is why people are embarrassed to recommend a friend to Freemasonry. We don't have anything to compete with the professional extravaganzas like we saw at half-time at the Super Bowl. We shouldn't try to compete with that by doing something more extravagant. We can't do it, and even if we could, we couldn't afford it. We must compete by involving the brothers in the programs. By so doing we will gain their support, their loyalty, their interest and their enthusiasm for the Craft. Once we get them attending Lodge, we have them hooked into bringing in new members. But they will very seldom bring in a new member unless they are excited about what goes on in the Lodge room.

None of this is to say that degree work is not attractive, and especially to those who are involved in doing the work. But therein lies the clue. It does attract those who do the work. They are involved. Let's do the same for the rest of the trestleboard.

I suggest that we open up the tool box provided to us by the Lodge Service Committee and we try the BACK to BASICS program. Maybe it needs sharpening, maybe it needs honing, but we can use the general concept. We must INVOLVE the brothers and reverse the trend of people staying away from Lodges in droves.

Once we get them to attend, soon the degree work will have to be assigned for special nights because there will be too many good programs involving the Brothers to have time for degree work on regularly scheduled dates. It can happen to you and your Lodge. Get on the BACK TO BASICS bandwagon. Enjoy.

GRAND LODGE
FREE AND ACCEPTED MASONS
OF THE
STATE OF NEW YORK

Service Letter COMMITTEE ON LODGE SERVICE
Number 8801

This is to propose that Masonic Lodges re-establish study groups. These could be formal or very informal structures. The Master would request and encourage those interested in doing so to write short papers. A sampling of topics are:

- Masonic History
- Masonic Charity
- Individual Freemasons, famous or otherwise
- Masonic Philosophy
- Masonic Events
- Other?

As a start it might be good to request short papers of a page or two in length, but if there is interest in writing a more lengthy paper, it should be encouraged also.

The program committee of the lodge should review these papers and arrange to have the best ones read in lodge as evening programs. The best ones should be submitted for publication in a local newsletter and in the *Empire State Mason*. All papers should be distributed to the membership via mail.

A second part of such a program could be to solicit talks from the members. These should be 3 to 5 minutes in length. Four or five such talks could be selected to make up an evening program. It could be left to the individual brother to select a topic of his choice. This make a good ladies night program with ladies encouraged to be prepared to speak also. The best of these could be submitted for publication also.

Some lodges may want to set up a contest. Others may prefer to keep it very informal and uncompetitive. The possibilities and variations to these kinds of programs are unlimited.

RATIONALE:
1. Freemasonry teaches that we are to seek light. Light is knowledge. A reason that Freemasonry may not be attracting as many thinking people is that we have strayed away from the BASIC function of early Freemasonry, which was to provide a place for philosophical study and contemplation.
2. Over the years more emphasis has been placed on ritual than on contemplation. Study is the essence of Freemasonry. It is not possible to grasp the full power of Freemasonry by ritual alone. We offer study courses but without pointing and showing the way.
3. Those who stay away from lodge miss all the power of it. By sharing ideas and information about Freemasonry with them, we can stimulate and reactivate their enthusiasm for the power of freemasonry.
4. Some concordant bodies provide such study and publications but the average freemason does not have access to the material. This type of program belongs in Symbolic Freemasonry. We need to return to the basics.

Sample Back to Basics Letter:

Date
Dear Brother:

_____ Lodge #_____ is initiating a BACK to BASICS program. Its purpose is to involve every brother in lodge programming and to help each of us "improve ourselves in Masonry". In early spring a lodge program will consist of the first of a series of talks given by YOU and other interested brothers.

Please consider preparing such a talk of a topic and length of your choosing. Write about anything which you would like to express and share with us. (Remember that religion and politics are not topics for discussion in a Masonic meeting.)

Not everyone will be inclined to write a prepared talk. But don't be shy. You are encouraged to talk for 15 to 20 minutes or just a few. You set the time. It can be a very informal statement of your opinion or concern on a subject of interest to you.

If you need more time than by early March to complete your talk, let us know and we can schedule your presentation for a later date. Please inform me or the Lodge Secretary of your participation as soon as possible.

Thank you for being involved in this exciting program. We look forward to hearing from you soon.

Fraternally Yours,

_____, Master

BACK to BASICS
Report Form

Date: _____

Brother: _____

Address: _____

_____

_____

Telephone: _____ Home

_____ Cell

Email:

_____

Title of Talk:

_____

Brief outline of the talk (Points to be covered):

Date to be completed:

_____

Approximate length of the talk:
_____
Other members of family or friends who may be interested presenting a talk to the lodge (please include address and phone number):

Comments:
GRAND LODGE
FREE AND ACCEPTED MASONS
OF THE
STATE OF NEW YORK

Service Letter COMMITTEE ON LODGE SERVICE Number 8802

TO INCREASE LODGE MEMBERSHIP

PREMISE: WHY INCREASE MEMBERSHIP?

· The most valid reason for wanting to increase the number of members is because the quantity of members determines the extent to which Freemasonry can shed its beneficent influence. Quality is obviously important, but to believe that quality can be gained without also reaching for quantity is to delude ourselves.
• Unless new "blood" is being infused into an organization regularly, the organization with die a natural death.
• New members are the raw material for future leadership development.

ANALYSIS: WHY WILL PEOPLE WANT TO JOIN FREEMASONRY TODAY?
• Most potential members are attracted by the charitable works of Freemasonry. Men of the 1980's and 90's are poised and ready to attach their loyalty to an organization involved in volunteer work where they can feel a sense of doing good.
• Others are attracted to the social aspect of Freemasonry.

- Some would be attracted to the Craft by the opportunity to study the philosophical and historical aspect of the Fraternity. This area of interest needs to be promoted.

CONVICTION: WHY BE A FREEMASON?

Be convinced of the POWER and value of the Fraternity. Study the twelve reasons for being loyal to Freemasonry. Know the charities of Grand Lodge, local Masonic volunteer activities and the charities of the various Concordant Masonic Bodies. Be convinced that it is important to promote the principles and precepts of the Fraternity. Be aware that they are needed in today's society more than ever before. If we don't believe these things, it will be very difficult to convince others that they should be Freemasons.

DIRECTION: PURPOSE FOR EXISTENCE

Establish long-term goals and direction for the Lodge. Involve the members in this process to help develop commitment from them. Focus energies; put the POWER to work. Determine the Lodge's identity, and work to enhance its image in the community.

PROCESS/MECHANICS: HOW TO INCREASE MEMBERSHIP?

We are fast approaching the 21st century. Demand for a man's time has increased a hundredfold since the days when people flocked to Freemasonry, literally of their own free will and accord. The competition uses professional salesmanship to enlist a person's time and loyalty. The least we must do for the Fraternity is to promote who we are, what we are and what we do.

Implement a program to promote knowledge about Freemasonry (see page 202). The program works to the extent that it is followed step by step. It fails miserably when not followed in every detail. There are numerous variations on this program, but the mechanics and details cannot be omitted. Testimonials of success come from those leaders who know how to conduct a program. Reports of failure come from the rest.

A Lodge must get involved in worthwhile volunteer community program. If the local lodge is not doing anything worthwhile, it will not attract the kind of people who will be turned on by Freemasonry. The number and variety of volunteer activities that a lodge can promote are vast, and unique to each community. Two of the nation's greatest embarrassments are the drug abuse problem and the plight of the homeless. If a lodge cannot think of any other programs to initiate, either of these would be a good place to start. Any, any program to promote the well-being of our youth would be a welcome endeavor.

Lodge programs that are Masonic or Mason oriented and designed to be exciting, interesting, educational and inspiring will turn on the membership. It will motivate them to talk about Freemasonry to their friends. The alternative is long, dull business meetings. They bore the members to the point they simply stay home, and are too embarrassed to invite their friends to join. Lodge programs must have substance to compete with the thousand and one slick appeals for a man's allegiance.

So how do we compete without the talents of sophisticated professionals? The answer is simple: Involvement of the brothers in the planning and implementation of the Lodge goals, direction and programs. Get them involved in community work. Help them develop Masonic Programs. Use the "Back to Basics" plan for Masonic study groups and programming as a blueprint for involving members in the promotion of knowledge about the craft.

Summary:
- Know why you want to increase membership
- Know why people join Freemasonry
- Know what Freemasonry is and its power
- Know Lodge focus, goals, direction and member commitment
- Outline mechanics to effect increased membership

1. Community projects with a purpose
2. Programs to promote knowledge about Freemasonry (see page 202).
3. Lodge programs that are Mason or Masonic oriented through member involvement – Back to Basics Program.

GRAND LODGE
FREE AND ACCEPTED MASONS
OF THE
STATE OF NEW YORK

Service Letter COMMITTEE ON LODGE SERVICE Number 8803

TO REVITALIZE A LODGE

1. Call Past Masters, Line Officers and interested brothers to a Rededication Meeting.

2. Prepare and distribute the agenda (preferably in advance).

Sample Agenda

Assess Options:
A - - Restore your Lodge
    a) Leadership potential is in place or can be restored.
    b) Commitment from a core group can be expected
B - Consolidate with another Lodge
    a) If other Lodge has sufficient leadership
    b) If your Lodge is completely devoid of leadership potential
Note: Consolidation should not be considered unless there is absolutely no hope for developing potential leadership from within. A small number of members is not a reason to merge. It is a potential for growth.

Option A - To Restore Your Lodge
- Establish Goals
  - Increase membership by at least 5% per year.
  - Educate members as to the power of Freemasonry.
  - Promote community involvement by the lodge.
- Initiate Programs
  - Use outline of program to promote knowledge about Freemasonry
  - Start Back to Basics program
  - Enroll all members (especially new brothers) in the Leadership Development Course.
  - Outline a schedule for the year of Masonic Education. (can be incorporated into the Back to Basics program)
  - Participate in district educational programs such as the Road to the East or the Masonic Development Course. Contact the District Staff Officer for additional details about when the program will be offered.

Option B - Consolidate with another Lodge
- To consolidate contact the Grand Lodge Committee on Charters and your District Deputy Grand Master for procedures.

George Peter

An Outline for a Public Program
To Promote Knowledge about Freemasonry

Purpose of the Program:

o To inform the uninitiated about the history, precepts, landmarks, traditions and mission of Freemasonry.

o To minimize the chances of someone asking to become a member out of curiosity – not knowing the essence of Freemasonry.

o To rekindle enthusiasm and loyalty to the Craft by the present members.

Steps:
1. Prepare a news release in the local paper(s). Through it, invite the public to visit the Masonic Temple and to attend a meeting at which the program will feature a brief history and philosophy of Freemasonry. Plans should include both men and women.
2. In order to insure a minimum attendance, ask each brother, at several communications of the Lodge, to submit names and addresses of friends and acquaintances who he believes might be interested in learning about Freemasonry.
3. From the various lists submitted, duplications should be eliminated and a master list compiled of those who should be invited.
4. Prepare a letter signed by the Master to be mailed to each of those who are to receive a personal invitation.
5. Assign to each of the officers and active members the names and addresses of two or three of the proposed guests. Ask each caller to invite his list of guests and to offer transportation to and from the meeting.
6. Appoint a telephone committee and assign members to be called who live within reasonable distance of the Temple. Urge each member to support the program by his attendance. Unless a good turnout of the brothers is assured, the effect on the guests may be more negative than positive.
7. Use the best talent in your Lodge to deliver talks on:

>   a. A brief history of Freemasonry.
>   b. History of the local Masonic Lodge.
>   c. The philosophy of Freemasonry.

Note: It is strongly recommended that each of the talks be limited to 8 to 10 minutes. More than that will kill the effect of the program.

8. If the Master is uncomfortable as Master of Ceremonies, he should welcome the guests and brothers and then turn the meeting over to a qualified M.C.

9. The M.C., at the conclusion of the talks, should make certain that the guests understand the landmarks of the Craft. No Masonic Lodge or member ever asks anyone to join the Fraternity. Those interested in becoming members must be sufficiently impressed with Freemasonry to ask for an application (petition) from the Mason he knows best.

10. Distribute copies of the Grand Lodge publication, "Q & A Answers to Questions about the Masonic Fraternity."

11. Serve refreshments at the conclusion of the program.

12. Many variations of the program can be effective. The set of slides with narration, available from Grand Lodge, is a good program. The important thing is, do not use the slides and then have speakers repeat the same information. Keep the program to a maximum of 45 minutes. **Do not omit any steps 1 through 6.** If the program does not work for your Lodge it is only because the outline was not followed in detail.

Masonic University of New York (MUNY)

This report begins with excerpts from a talk given to the newly designated DDGM's and Staff Officers at the training session on March 31, 2006. I always begin by asking how many present are enrolled in an educational institution. Not enough raise their hands. They are reminded that each of them is enrolled in an educational institution. It is called Freemasonry. Every Freemason is a student. We've been repeating this mantra for many years, now.

Perhaps with the establishment of MUNY Brothers will begin to understand the essence of Freemasonry and that it is an educational institution. It is and has been such, at least since the reformation of the Ritual by William Preston. And long before that. We come here to improve ourselves (but to memorize ritual and to learn rules, regulations, and protocol is not enough).

This is perhaps heresy, but just maybe we have placed so much emphasis on the above that it has been to the detriment of what we really came here to do – to promote Freemasonry as the educational institution that it is.

MUNY is formed and, although it is in the early stage of life, programs have been initiated and action is begun. The important thing is that it will attract people of intellect and interest. New and revitalized Brothers will bring new and refreshing enlightenment and new enthusiasm to our work. Freemasonry will become once again respected and admired for what it does.

To some extent, that is what happened with the original Leadership Development Course – LDC. Graduates of that program are the leaders of the Craft now and many are the leaders of MUNY. Don't underestimate the power of education.

It is worth repeating the mission statement of MUNY because every Lodge should have a similar or equivalent mission.

MISSION OF MUNY:

In recognition of our mandate and responsibility as Freemasons to provide service to our Brothers and to the public at large, the mission of MUNY is to improve the caliber of leadership education at all levels of Freemasonry and beyond. We must do so by developing, implementing and maintaining programs of basic and advanced instructional resources, forums, seminars and mentoring.

These formal and informal developmental opportunities will serve first to strengthen the individual Freemason's understanding of the foundations and relevance of Freemasonry. It will provide him with the ever dynamic leadership skill-sets necessary to insure the future success and growth of our Craft, and will develop within him the ability to identify and implement the strategies necessary to capitalize on the internal and external potential of Freemasonry.

An equally important mission is to reach beyond Masonic circles to offer Masonic understanding, knowledge and insights to the general public. It should come as no surprise that we recommend to every Masonic Lodge that a Lodge mission statement be put in place.

And the above mission is appropriate for a Lodge mission as well as for MUNY – because we are, or ought to be, all on the same mission.

Now for a listing of established programs to date:
• A Masonic speaker's bureau is in place and is growing.
• The Individual Development Course (iDC) has just given diplomas to its first round of graduates. This is an extensive seven-month program (one all-day lesson, one Saturday per month).

• An improved and updated Leadership Development Course (LDC-8) has been tested in the Cayuga-Tompkins District for the last two years. It will be made available to be presented in seminar format within Lodges or Districts or via the Internet.

    This is the beginning. We ask that you submit ideas for future and added course material. The future is unlimited. The challenge is to improve leadership skills of the individual, the Lodge, the District and state leaders. Of equal importance is to improve leadership skills for your career, family, community and to be a more effective human being.

Originally printed in The *Empire State Mason* Magazine, Summer 2006

Note: Visit www.e-muny.org to find out more information about the current MUNY educational programs.

George Peter

Section III

Post Script

George Peter

Swan Song— Adios

Your Grand Historian (since 1993) has decided to resign the office at the young age of 86. In the Proceedings of Grand Lodge for 1994 I quoted Right Worshipful Emerson: "The use of history is to give value to the present hour and its duty." I also quoted James Russell Lowell who said, "History is clarified experience." These two quotations tell us of the value and importance of history. We can never do an adequate job of recording the same – the task is too formidable.

One of the first programs that I initiated was to select eighteen Area Historians, who have each made a valuable contribution to the recording of Masonic history in the State of New York. We helped with the Bicentennial issue of The *Empire State Mason* Magazine and the assembly of histories of every Lodge in the State for the important book, *A Masonic Portrait of the Empire State*, published in 2002. Many Area Historians have assembled histories of their Lodges and of their areas. All have been dedicated workers. Nevertheless, we have only scratched the surface of things that can and should be done. The challenge is daunting.

The historians have tried to adhere to the admonition of RW Emerson – "The use of history is to give value to the present hour and its duty." We have perceived our duty to be an important part of the role of Freemasonry: To make good men better. But clichés are not enough. We make men better via an education process.

To that end we have been making history by being a part of the newly created Masonic University of New York (MUNY). Not only has MUNY set to work to upgrade the leadership skills of Brothers and officers, but also it has attracted the brightest and most dedicated Brothers to be a part of the training process. The potential is unlimited. I am very excited about the future history of the work and of the Craft.

It is not for me to suggest to a successor the path to follow. Suffice to say that I feel inadequate to continue. Some have suggested that the role of the Grand Historian is as important as that of the Grand Lecturer and that said person should make official visits to every area as does the Lecturer. One person suggested that it should be a paid position as is the Grand Lecturer. But I am cognizant of the fact that funding would be impractical in these times of declining membership. I am not trying to promote a grandiose role for the work that we do. I am relaying suggestions that have come to me.

For my "swan song" it is best for me to stick to acknowledging important people. First is to thank each Brother in the State of New York for your support and encouragement. Next is to thank the Area Historians who have helped to make the work possible. I thank the Past Grand Masters under whose leadership I have served.

To each of you, Go with God. —
Adios.

Summer 2008
The *Empire State Mason* Magazine

In Memoriam
Obituary for George Peter
Educator, Author, Leader, Historian

On August 10th 2008, George Peter, 86, was reunited with his beloved wife Gloria Barnell (1924-2005). George's life and work was a reflection of his passion for learning, for his community, and for those he held dear. He will be remembered for his dedication to the multiple roles he fulfilled within the communities he loved: Cornell University, the Village of Aurora, NY and the Brotherhood of the Masonic Order. George was a beloved brother, husband, father, grandfather and great-grandfather, role model, mentor, and friend.

Born on October 21, 1921 in Ithaca NY to an Armenian father, Joseph Peter (nee Hovsep Bedros Karamardian) and Syrian mother, Helen Mike, George grew up with his eight siblings on a farm in the hills of South Danby. He graduated from Ithaca High School in 1940 and shortly after enlisted in the Army Air Corps. While in service to his country from 1942-1946, he met the love of his life Gloria Barnell in Lincoln, Nebraska. They were married on June 11, 1945 and remained devoted to each other until her death on June 22nd 2005 just 11 days after their 60th wedding anniversary.

George spent his early career operating his own TV repair business, as well as working full time at Cornell University from 1947. George remained at Cornell until his retirement in 1988. He began his tenure at the University as an electronics technician and went on to teach courses in electronics, and eventually to serve as one of the four professionals appointed to undertake the installation of the world's first fixed-base radio telescope at Arecibo Puerto Rico, where he moved with his family in 1960. After two years in Puerto Rico, George returned to Ithaca to direct the Research and Development Lab of the National Astronomy & Ionosphere Center (NAIC) that continued to design, build and install the radio astronomy receivers used at the Arecibo Telescope. Arecibo remains the largest radio astronomy telescope in the world.

A lover of "life, love, liberty, and the pursuit of happiness," George worked tirelessly in his "spare time" as an advocate for his colleagues—the more than 5,000 Cornell University employees. Greatly inspired by the founding principals, and principles, of his country, George created employee representation on the University governance body called the Cornell Senate (which previously included only faculty and students). In 1975, he became the first employee representative to the Cornell Board of Trustees and served 4 terms in that role, serving on the executive committee of the board for most of that time, and on the search committees for two of Cornell's presidents. He was appointed Trustee Emeritus in 1988. He was one of the founders of the Cornell Recreation Club and an active member of Cornell Retirees Association.

In recognition of George's service to Cornell, the George Peter Dedicated Service Award was established – and George personally attended those awards ceremonies up until his death. In support of his fellow employees, George wrote a weekly column entitled "Leadership Leads" in the Cornell employee newspaper he helped to found, *The Paw Print*, for which he was broadly recognized and appreciated.

But perhaps nowhere were George's personal values better exemplified than in his volunteer work as a member of the Masonic Order. He is Past Master of both Hobasco Lodge #716 and Scipio Lodge #110, and past District Deputy Grand Master for the Cayuga-Tompkins District. He also served as Grand Historian for the Grand Lodge of the State of New York from 1993 until 2008, when he was appointed Grand Historian Emeritus. He was also a member of the York Rite and Scottish Rite Bodies, AMD, Chief Adept NY College SRICF, Past Master of the American Lodge of Research, member Philalethes Society, member Quatuor Coronati, member Kalurah, A.A.O.N.M.S., Past Dad Advisor and Chairman of Advisory Board Order of DeMolay for Boys in Ithaca.

George's passion for leadership development and education was expressed in Masonic circles through his 12 years as chairman of the Lodge Services Committee (later renamed the Leadership and Educational Services Committee). The son of hard-working immigrant parents, George himself had limited educational opportunities but yet committed himself to furthering the educational opportunities of others by co-founding leadership development courses for Freemasons across NY State. This initiative evolved into what is now known as the Masonic University of New York, or MUNY. For many years he participated in the North East Conference of Masonic Education and Libraries, which involved Masonic educators from Maine to Virginia in planning for the betterment of their membership.

For these contributions, George has been honored by the Grand Lodges of New York and Connecticut. The Masonic Lodge of Research in New Haven presented the 2006 James Royal Case Fellowship in May of 2007. There have been 15 Case Fellows, named in honor of the late Grand Historian of Connecticut, and George was the third New York Mason in the group of "internationally famed Masonic writers and educators." In 2007 the Grand Lodge of the State of New York developed the George Peter Award to recognize a Mason who has devoted himself to the education of his Brothers, struck a medal bearing George's likeness, and made him the first recipient of the honor.

Upon his death, George was completing three books which represent his areas of passion: *The Power and Passion of Freemasonry, Leadership Leads,* and twelve chapters of his family life growing up on the South Danby farm during the Depression Era. Each of these are soon to be published.

Of enormous importance to George and Gloria was their beloved community of Aurora, NY which they adopted upon their move from Ithaca in 1971. They quickly became pillars of community spirit in Aurora, and for many years hosted the community's annual ice cream social. In 1974 George rallied his neighbors to create what became the yearly Aurorafest celebration, which continues to this day. The Village of Aurora and its inhabitants have been an inspiration and comfort to George and Gloria over the years and, collectively, they supported George through Gloria's illness and eventual death. They have been an invaluable support to George and his family.

Finally, George's life was underscored by his large and loving family. In addition to his beloved wife and his parents, he was pre-deceased by his brothers Jacob and Moses Peter, sister-in-law Hazel Peter, brothers-in-law Horen Bakerjian and Bill Smith, nephew Samuel, nieces Judy Peter Fallon and Lorraine Peter Droste, and a grandnephew, Brian Walpole. He is survived by his children: Michael J. Peter and his wife Wilnive, known as TC (Ft. Lauderdale, FL), Patrice DiLorenzo and her husband Scottie Morris (Key West, FL), Denice Peter Karamardian (Ithaca, NY), Paula J. Peter and her partner Michael Ward (Ithaca, NY). He is also survived by his grandchildren Aubryn Allyn Sidle, Lauren Skye DiLorenzo, C. Connor Sidle, Savan Karamardian DeSouza, and great-granddaughter Aurora Gale Atkins. George's surviving siblings and spouses are John and Charlotte Peter (Syracuse, NY) Susie Bakerjian (Los Palos Verdes, CA.), Mitchell and Pat Peter (Naples, FL), Samuel and Ruth Peter (Ithaca, NY and Bonita Springs, FL), Laura Smith

(Trumansburg, NY) and Lois Peter (Bradenton, FL). Numerous nieces and nephews, Masonic Brothers, surrogate family, and friends from around the world loved and will miss their Uncle/Brother George.

Provided by the Family – August 2008

The George Peter Medal
For Education Achievement
Established 2007

Freemasonry, at its heart, is an educational institution. Upon his Raising, every Freemason begins a search for light that takes his entire lifetime and beyond to find. Searching for light means a quest to become more knowledgeable about the Craft, our world and our inner self. The search means we must be involved in education. The George Peter Medal is given to those Brothers who have attained a high degree of Masonic Education and have dedicated their Masonic lives to educating others.

In every generation, there appear among us giants who shape and alter the world around them in a highly positive way. George Peter is one of those giants in the Grand Lodge of Free and Accepted Masons of the State of New York. He has helped spawn a generation of Masons who firmly believe in the value of Masonic Education and the effect that Masonic Education has on leadership. Brother Peter has always taught that "leadership is education and education is leadership." George Peter's Masonic life has been centered on the precepts so eloquently put forth in our Ritual. Brother Peter believes in performing excellent ritual work and living out the meaning of the Ritual in his daily life.

George Peter has lived out this creed with the utmost distinction. He has brought to light the essence of Freemasonry and has led many of the Craft's leaders to be involved in "higher thoughts and greater achievements." Brother Peter has stood as a beacon of light for Masonic Education his entire life. It is a good thing we do to pay homage to this outstanding man and Mason.

NOTE: The George Peter Medal may be given to only one Brother statewide each year. It is not to be awarded annually if there is no qualified candidate. George was the first recipient of the award.

George Peter

Personal Mini-biography

• Born October 21, 1921 near Ithaca, NY and grew up in the farming hills of South Danby, New York.
• 1942 to 1946 Army Air Corps.
• 1947 Cornell University as electronics technician while auditing courses leading to the equivalent of a BS in electrical engineering.
• 1963 Ithaca, New York - established and directed a research and development laboratory for the specialized, low-noise radio astronomy receiver and antenna systems. Also developed and taught courses in advanced electronics while authoring technical articles and training materials. Also a guest lectured a course on Astronomy receiver systems.
• 1970 to1974 Served on Cornell Senate executive committee.
• 1975 Elected first staff member to the Board of Trustees of Cornell University. Reelected four more three-year terms and finally elected as Trustee Emeritus.
• 1980 Founded and served on the editorial board of Cornell's newspaper, "The Paw Print," for and by the Cornell staff. Provided a by-lined column called "Leadership Leads."
• 1988 Retired from Cornell University as Director of Laboratory Operations for the National Astronomy and Ionosphere Center in the Department of Astronomy. Major work effort was the on-site participation in the development and construction of the world's largest radio/radar telescope at Arecibo, Puerto Rico.
• 1998 Published his first book, *Leadership Leads,* consisting of a compilation of his columns of the same name.

Masonic Mini-biography

• 1949 March - Joined Freemasonry.
• 1979-1993 Chairman of the Grand Lodge Service Committee/ Leadership Services Committee.
• 1985 Designed and administered a 10-lesson Leadership Development Course in Freemasonry. The course used a correspondence course format with a mentor.
• 2004 Founded "The Masonic University of New York" (MUNY).
• 1993 – 2008 Grand Historian of The Grand Lodge Free and Accepted Masons of the State of New York.

- 2004 – 2008 Served as Chairman and Co-chairman of MUNY committee.
- 2007 – Recipient of the First George Peter Medal for Education Achievement, presented by the Grand Lodge of Free and Accepted Masons of the State of New York.